1991 FASA CORPORATION

TABLE OF CONTENTS

LONDON/UNITED KINGDOM SOURCEBOOK

Writing
Carl Sargent
Marc Gascoigne

Development
Tom Dowd

Editorial Staff
Senior Editor
Donna Ippolito
Assistant Editor
Sharon Turner Mulvihill

Production Staff
Art Director
Dana Knutson
Cover Art
Jim Nelson
Cover Design
Jeff Laubenstein
Color Ad Design
Jeff Laubenstein
Joel Biske
Mike Nielsen
Color Photography
Yates Photography
Color Plates
Jim Nelson
Jeff Laubenstein
Joel Biske
Black and White Ad Designs
Jeff Laubenstein
Joel Biske
Tara Gallagher
Mike "Leslie" Nielsen
Dana Knutson
Illustrations
Joel Biske
Mike Nielsen
Layout
Tara Gallagher

Published by
FASA Corporation
P.O. Box 6930
Chicago, IL 60680

The London/United Kingdom Sourcebook is a supplement for the **Shadowrun** game system. A comprehensive guide to life in the shadows of the British establishment in the 2050s, it includes detailed notes on the country's history, politics, economics, and crime situation. Another major feature is a section on Inner London, with a guide to the key neighbourhoods and locations likely to be of use or interest to shadowrunners. For quick reference, there is also a **Timeline** (p. 146) of the important events related to this part of the world.

The British are a secretive lot, but the local deckers have managed to discover and access numerous hidden files for information to be included in this guidebook. The gamemaster may decide whether to treat these comments, observations, and information as valid. Only he knows whether every astonishing bit of "shadow information" from Britain's deckers is true.

Following the guidebook material is a **Gamemaster's Section**, several chapters of rules or background information specific to the U.K. for paranormal animals, weapons and equipment, druids, and British slang.

Gamemasters may also wish to refer to **Sprawl Sites**, **The Grimoire**, and **The Neo-Anarchist's Guide to North America**, all of them good supplements to information or rules in this book.

Greetings. As Minister for Tourism in His Majesty's Government, I have been asked by the British Tourist Board to extend my heartiest welcome to you. It gives me the greatest pleasure to wish you an enjoyable stay in our country, and I hope you will return many times. As this fine guidebook reveals, Great Britain is a land of many facets. The combination of its vast heritage of tradition and glory with the most futuristic developments makes it a land unlike any other.

One has only to stroll the streets of our great capital city to step back in time to a glorious age. History comes alive in London, where all the pageantry and pomp of our royal traditions are on parade every day of the week. The hallowed halls of London's many fine museums present visitors with much of Britain's heritage, but there is no substitute for wandering the streets. While ambling in the shadows of the Bank of England or atop the keep of the Tower of London, one can reach out and touch the past as if it were alive.

That is not to say that Britain is a land that lives solely in its memories. The City of London is the financial centre of Europe, and its futuristic new developments will ensure that it remains so for many lifetimes to come. Nor can anyone say that Britain lacks ambition. The astonishing West End Underplex was constructed in record time at the heart of our largest city, creating an entire new business community that is one of the new wonders of the world! In this way, and in so many others, Britain continues to prove itself a world leader in creativity and innovation.

Of course, as in any great country, some aspects of life might need improvement, but rest assured that His Majesty's Government has everything well under control. With the strength of heritage and tradition at our backs, we go forward with our eyes trained steadily on the future.

Readers of this guide and visitors to our country will discover all this and more.

—Nigel Bentinck, Minister for Tourism

>>>>>[Stuff that for a lark; this is where it's at. If you can read this, welcome to the shadows of the U.K. sprawl. What the British establishment has never realized, not in all these years of "glorious heritage and tradition," is that an entire underclass lives in the shadows of their safe little world of petty intrigue and ridiculous ritual. Within the framework of this guidebook is a second guide, one that reveals the truth about life in Britain's shadowlands. These entries cover everything a certain kind of visitor needs to know, from the locations of seedy pubs to the backstreet suppliers for many officially forbidden items (and, believe me, in the U.K., it's all forbidden).

We hope that by using these datafiles, you will come to appreciate the true face of Britain. This is a land where secrets rule, yet the establishment is so engrossed in the past that it cannot come to grips with the most basic computer security procedures—which explains our presence in this guide. A wide range of deckers have tapped in to contribute their own recommendations, warnings, and advice. Some were specially invited, others certainly were not, but all have something useful to say.

One word of warning: the pace of change moves faster than a speeding bullet. By the time some readers find this guide, some of the entries may be in need of update. Others, I have to admit, may not provide the entire truth about a situation. But those experienced at living in the shadows will find that the old methods of protection are still the best. Be aware, and all will go well. And hey, if anyone finds that an entry is incomplete or that the facts have changed, be my guest, hack in and adjust the relevant section.

This guide, BTW, is a composite document, pieced together from at least three sources, some buttoned-down and others raving neo-anarchist, so as to provide you, gentle reader, with a full range of facts and opinions.

That's enough of my yakking. Jack in at the file called "History," and don't stop till you reach exactly where it is you want to be. If you get my meaning. Be lucky!]<<<<<
—Egon Rowan, Shadow Entries Editor (07:16:31/ 1-NOV-51)

>>>>>[Received this day this datapack of information on jolly old England, long may she reign blah blah blah. Read and enjoy. Be warned. It's written in BritSpeak, which might get a bit wicked and warped for some of youse. Oh, and check out the Brits' use of archaic measurements—miles, feet, inches—instead of good old metric. Like I said, we just let it stand. You have been warned.]<<<<<
—Control (08:12:06/7-AUG-52)

FACTS AT YOUR FINGER TIPS

WHEN TO GO

In southern England, the hottest month is July, with an average temperature of 22° Celsius, while the coldest month is January, with an average temperature of 7°. The annual average temperature is 16°. Humidity is moderately high (70%+), but not oppressively so. British weather is variable, depending on latitude; in northern Scotland the average January temperature is 1°, and the northernmost roads are snow-blocked for many weeks on end. Extreme weather phenomena are rare in the U.K.; severe storms, blizzards and the like are truly exceptional. The best times to visit Britain are between late August and late September, or during May, when the weather is best.

TRAVELLING TO THE U.K.

Because the U.K. is an island, it is usual to travel there by air, save for European visitors using the Chunnel. Sea travel is less common as an alternative.

BY PLANE

London Heathrow International is the third-busiest airport in the world (and would be the busiest save that Gatwick and Stevenage airports just outside the central London sprawl have taken over its overspill). There are also major airports with significant international flight loads at Edinburgh in Scotsprawl, Manchester, Birmingham in the central U.K. sprawl, and at Newcastle in the northern Tynesprawl. Some typical international flight prices are as given below (one-way into Heathrow; add up to £75/30¥ for flights to other U.K. airports). Prices are shown below in £, pounds sterling, and in nuyen. The statistical average exchange rate for the last two years, which is heavily stabilized by international banking networks, is £2.50 = 1¥.

AIRFARES TO THE U.K.

City of Origin	Cost¥	Cost £
Paris	125	312
Rome	200	500
Stockholm	200	500
Frankfurt	180	450
Lisbon	175	438
Jerusalem	520	1,300
Riyadh	700	1,750
New York	750	1,875
Washington	800	2,000
Seattle	1,400	3,500
Tokyo	2,000	5,000
Tokyo (transorbital)	3,500	8,750

>>>>>[Catch me, terms. The baggies have the ports wrapped so tight, you gotta say "May I please?" just to snatch a breather.]<<<<<
—Alex (05:32:19/02-FEB-52)

BY ROAD

European access to the U.K. is mainly through the Channel Tunnel, known popularly as "The Chunnel," which exits at both Dover and Calais (informational accuracy is subject to no terrorist action intervening since the date of going to press). This is a road and rail link, which is subject to extreme security at both ends because of Anglo-French political hostilities. Bullet trains convey most passengers on the Paris (Le Gard du Nord)-Calais-Dover-London (Victoria Station) route, with French and British customs/security checks during each leg of the journey. Paris-London travel time averages 53 minutes. Breakdowns are rare on this service, unlike the rest of the BritRail network, probably because the trains are 50 percent British and 50 percent French from the SRNF network. Cost for the Paris-London rail ticket (one-way) is 100¥/£250 first class (which includes no privileges, only a slightly less uncomfortable seat) and 60¥/£150 second class (there are only two classes of ticket).

BY SEA

Ferry travel to the U.K. from Europe is now rare since the construction of the Chunnel. The only remaining regular ferry service is from Portsmouth on the south coast to Santander in Spain (cost: 85¥/£212 for single-class accommodation overnight, or 250¥/£625 for one automobile with up to five passengers, one-way trip). Transatlantic liner from New York to Southampton is a true luxury; the journey averages seven days, and the cost per person (for a cabin shared by two, one-way only) is 2,500¥/£6,250 ordinary class and 3,500¥/£8,750 first class. Only the White Star Company, with their liners *King George* and *King Charles*, currently run this route.

ON ARRIVAL

DOCUMENTS

The U.K. is a highly bureaucratic country. Visitors from other countries will need the following documents on arrival: a current passport, a current visa issued by His Majesty's Government (available through a British embassy or consulate), any necessary medical documentation (evidence of innoculations for visitors from countries where communicable diseases are endemic), and licenses and permits for all forms of controlled equipment.

It is necessary to have licenses from the Lord Protector's Administrative Bureau (issued through British embassies and consulates) for all forms of personal cyberware, weaponry of any kind, Matrix software, and other personal-enhancement technology. A full list of prohibited possessions is available on request from the sources noted. Licenses and permits usually take four to six weeks to be issued (or a notification of refusal delivered), so it is essential for visitors to apply well in advance of travel.

All practitioners of magical and adept callings must register with the Lord Protector's offices (at The Temple,

Chancellery Lane, Inner London) before being legally licensed for indulgence in any magical activity whatsoever. Likewise, any and all enchanted items must be licensed by the same authority. British embassies and consulates can process such applications, but registration must be attended in person at the Administrative Bureau of the Lord Protector's Department.

>>>>>[And we all know what being licensed means, don't we? File away those corpuscles, Lord Protector sir. Fry my flesh from afar when it suits you fine, thank you please.]<<<<<
—Magister (19:52:06/25-JAN-52)

MONEY

The British pound sterling (£) is the national currency. Visitors may exchange dollars, nuyen, or other currencies into pounds at any bank (Bureau de Change). Several banks have offices at all major airports, rail stations, and so on. British shops and restaurants will not accept currencies other than pounds or, in some cases, nuyen (enquire first). Major chain stores, prestige establishments, and the like will accept nuyen, typically converting pound prices into nuyen, with a 3 to 5 percent surcharge above the fixed bank rate.

One pound is composed of 100 pennies (100p), and the following British currency units are in general circulation: the copper 5p and 10p pieces, the "silver" (actually a white alloy) 20p (small) and 50p (large) pieces, the red copper £1, £2, and £5 coins, the blue £5 note, the brown £10 note, the brown-green £20 note, the blue-yellow £50 note, the blue-silver £100 and £200 notes, and the (highest denomination) blue-black £500 note.

TIME

Britain has Greenwich Mean Time (GMT) from late October to early April, and British Summer Time (BST, one hour advanced) at other times. GMT is five hours ahead of Eastern, six hours ahead of Central, and seven to eight hours ahead of Pacific Time Zones within the American states.

Two oddities of British timekeeping require noting by the American visitor. First, dates are recorded with the day before the month. So, January 15, 2050 would be written by the British as 15-1-50 (and not 1/15/50, as in American notation). Second, 24-hour clocks and timekeeping are used only in travel timetables in Britain. Otherwise, hours are referred to almost universally as A.M. (morning) and P.M. (evening). 7 A.M. is 07:00, 7 P.M. is 19:00, and so on.

>>>>>[To keep you from scratching your hair out, I've gone through the file and dropped in a three-letter month code in place of the numeric month code. You can thank me later.]<<<<<
—Egon (07:23:51/1-NOV-51)

INFORMATION

All major U.K. cities have signposted Tourist Information Centres where mundane information on the local area (street maps, lists of public amenities, places to see, restaurants, hotels, sights) is readily available. Britain's C-net Matrix system (details follow) is the standard public amenity for accessing national data.

GETTING AROUND

Travel within the U.K. is not as agreeable a matter as in many foreign countries. The standard of public provision, in particular, is relatively poor.

AIR TRAVEL

Air travel within the U.K. is notably expensive by foreign standards. The major domestic airports are at Gatwick, Stanstead, East Midlands (outside Nottingham), Manchester, Cardiff, Liverpool, Edinburgh, Newcastle, and Glasgow. As a rule of thumb, expect to pay some 60¥/£150 for up to the first 50 kilometers and 40¥/£100 for every 50 kilometers after that. The major internal U.K. airlines are: British Midair, Geordie Airlines, British Comet, and the infamous C5 planes of Sinclair Skies.

FAST, SAFE, AND INEXPENSIVE
WHY USE ANYONE ELSE?

ROAD TRAVEL

The motorway network of the U.K. sprawl is generally considered of poor quality. Average travel speed between major cities within the central developed area (Manchester, Liverpool, Leeds, Nottingham, Birmingham, Bristol, London, and others) has been computed at 60.9 kph during daylight hours and 64.6 kph in the hours of darkness. Delays are frequent due to road resurfacing, which is conducted both slowly and with little attention to quality or durability of the completed work. However, traffic violence is low by American standards, and wrecking gangs and the like are virtually unknown.

Road systems within major cities feature roads much narrower than American drivers are used to, and particular attention must be paid to British road signs, which are frequently too small, badly maintained, and barely legible. Road quality is poor outside areas that receive significant private funding (corporate-owned and -maintained areas).

British coach and bus services are operated by regional companies that integrate their services. In southern England, Blue Line Buses is the major operator; in the central areas, Whippet Buses; in Tynesprawl, Metroplex; in Scotland, the quaintly named Dr. Knox's Coach Company. Bus fares typically cost 25 percent of air fares between cities, while intra-city fares vary from 30 to 40p to £5 or so for long journeys.

Finally, American automobile drivers should note that in Britain, people drive on the left-hand side of the road.

>>>>>[Though I'd suppose that all depends on what you're driving.]<<<<<
—Needles (12-25-35/06-JUN-52)

RAIL TRAVEL

A single national operator, BritRail, controls a national monopoly, the only exceptions being some minor scenic lines in Wales, Scotland, and more peripheral areas of the U.K. BritRail Intercity fares are 40 percent (second class) to 70 percent (first class) of air fares noted. The service is notoriously unpunctual, even for the fastest services (the bullet trains through the Northern Zone from Edinburgh and Glasgow to London, and the London-Birmingham-Manchester-Liverpool service). Trains are frequently overcrowded, and violence among passengers in second-class accommodation is not unknown. Visitors are warned especially to avoid any British trains conveying significant numbers of persons to any major sporting events. British rail stations are often plagued by beggars and vagrants; in some cases, permanent communities of such people live right alongside the tracks.

>>>>>[Up Man Utd!]<<<<<
—Footman (05:49:03/3-MAR-52)

BRITISH LAW AND LAW ENFORCEMENT

The British legal system differs from the systems of justice in America, France, Japan, and other countries. One crucial difference is that contingency arrangements with lawyers are not legal in the U.K. Nor is legal aid available, except for U.K. nationals. For non-British nationals, dealing with the law becomes either dangerous, expensive, or both. The following London numbers are important contacts for aliens having trouble with British law:

British Council for Civil Liberties: 711-446-4444
American Allied Legal Defense Inc: 711-285-2233
Legal Network: 711-333-3888

The BCCL can provide help with simple questions pertaining to personal rights in custody, legal procedures, and the like. They also maintain hotlines for metahumans with special legal requirements or concerns. The AALD is an American government-funded and subsidized group of American-trained British lawyers who can represent American nationals in British courts. In many cases, these lawyers can provide services at a reduced rate because of governmental subsidy. The Legal Network is a non-profit-making group of young British barristers and solicitors who accept cases for reduced fees in the case of foreign nationals handicapped by reason of language barrier, provable penury, theft of their personal effects, and the like.

A national British police force enforces British law. There is no equivalent of federal, state, and other law in Britain, only national law and national law enforcement. Private security organizations and law enforcement are highly restricted in Britain. Let the visitor beware that the British police do not take lightly any suggestion that their ethics are soluble in pounds (or nuyen).

Note also the difference between barristers and solicitors. Those in need deal exclusively with the solicitor, who handles the paperwork and extra effort needed to prepare the defense. At trial time, the solicitor then hires the barrister, who handles all actual in-court work.

ILLEGAL AND ADDICTIVE SUBSTANCES

British law is tolerant concerning alcohol, except for harsh punishments for drinking and driving (there is no safe legal level of alcohol in the blood of anyone at the wheel of an automobile). Alcohol is readily available throughout the U.K. 24 hours a day (in theory) in British shops. Nicotine products are not illegal, as in many other European countries, but the distribution is strictly controlled through a small number of licensed retail outlets.

Any form of dealing or possession of other addictive and controlled substances is subject to harsh penalties. Again, be warned.

EMERGENCIES

Call 999 in the event of an urgent need for police, fire services, or emergency medical assistance (for those without private medical cover). This number connects to an operator who will then link the caller to the appropriate emergency service. This number is national, and requires no area code.

MEDICAL ASSISTANCE

The British National Health Service (government-funded) is universally free so far as emergency attention is concerned. That is, NHS ambulances are despatched to attend emergencies and bring wounded or severely ill people to NHS hospitals. Emergency care in hospital is free for the first 24 hours. After that, only basic maintenance care is provided for non-U.K. nationals. Intensive care, pharmacological treatment, laser treatments, surgery, and so on are charged to the appropriate embassy. Arrangements for payments have been made with all American states, and the visitor will have to repay his government should he require further NHS service.

There are also two major private medical organizations that provide their own hospitals, doctors, and emergency services in return for suitable premiums. These are Care and BUCM. They can provide insurance for fixed-term visits or foreign residents of variable standard (fixed- or no-limit insurance, and so on). Within the U.K., central contact numbers are:

Careline: 818-808-2222
BUCM: 715-715-0715

Careline and BUCM offer services similar to those obtainable via Doc Wagon™ in North America.

WHAT DOES IT COST?

Prices in Britain are generally higher than American visitors are used to in their own country. This applies especially to certain categories of commodity: fresh foods, cyberware, and electronic goods. London prices are at least 10 percent higher than those in the rest of the U.K.; prices quoted below are U.K. averages, except where otherwise noted. Some services, notably sightseeing and tourist, can be cheaper in the U.K., however.

Accommodations span the full range of prices. Spartan accommodation at YMCAs, YWCAs, and metahuman hostels are available from as little as £8 per night (shared dormitories). Out-of-term university or college bedroom accommodation is sometimes available for as little as £35–£40 per night, but their availability is low and often only advertised by word of mouth or through corporate contacts.

A modest hotel room in a major U.K. city costs £55–£85 per night (not including any meals). On the other hand, the Winston Churchill Suite at the Savoy in London costs £6,500 per night. Those who want luxury can find it in the famous London hotels known for their extravagant elegance and discretion.

Restaurants in most U.K. cities reflect the ethnic diversity of the British population, but they do not feature the hybrids of Pacific Northwest cuisine. Chinese, Malaysian, Persian, Lebanese, Polish, Hungarian, Indian, Pakistani, Corsican, Zairean, French, and a half-dozen other cuisines are often available within an area of a square mile or so. Traditional British cuisine is either exceptionally good (about 5 percent of the time) or stodgy and rather bland (the rest of the time). Wine lists are superior to those found in America, primarily because of the readier availability and cheaper prices for French wines.

MODEST EXPENSES FOR ONE PERSON

Moderate hotel room	£70
Hotel breakfast, including tip	£14
Lunch at moderate restaurant, including tip	
(including half-bottle of wine)	£30
Dinner at moderate restaurant, including tip	
(including bottle of wine)	£70
Sightseeing tour (whole morning or afternoon)	£12
Nightclub membership, 7 days	£75
Admission to museum or historical site	£3–£8
Ticket to major sporting event (other than	
Test Match cricket; moderate seats)	£35–£50
Car rental, per day (including insurance)	£150
Car rental, per week (including insurance)	£450
Taxi ride, per kilometer	
(add tip of 10–15% for total journey)	£3
Pair of jeans	£45–£60
Pair of shoes (moderate quality)	£65
Pair of shoes (bespoke)	£400
1 week Medical Insurance, full cover	£600

>>>>>[Bribe for simple info (where to get what) £50
Bribe for more sensitive info
(who's doing what to whom and why) £400+
Simple sexual pleasures £100
The English Vice £250
BTL chip £175
And, by the way, the all-in medical insurance won't get you picked up from any area the police won't set foot in. Watch the small print.]<<<<<
—MesoStim (22:13:22/11-JAN-52)

THE BRITISH MATRIX

The British Telecommunications Grid (BTG) is a national system. There are no Regional Telecommunications Grids within the U.K. The Matrix is subdivided into Local Telecommunications Grids, or LTGs, only. The security code for the BTG is Orange-5. The BTG is owned and operated by BriTelecom, a national monopoly that is a byword for inefficient service, inaccurate bills, and profiteering. But the lines do work, and the static is not too bad.

Britain has a public service network within the Matrix, C-net, which stores data on public events, update news, transport, weather, public service announcements, group meetings in indexed local areas, and a great deal else in the public domain.

>>>>>[If you want to discover more interesting things, get into EyeNet, operated on a non-profit-making basis from a base somewhere in—well, who needs to know? No corporate backing. No government backing or interference. No crazy right-wing fundamentalist media-mogul paying us. Just information and views. Major subdivisions within EyeNet are:
•EcoNet. Provides updates on major ecological issues and events around the world. Specialists in data analysis and logistics provide excellent summaries of environmental implications of corporate and other activities.
•IdenNet. A bulletin board and database for all aspects of race relations in our troubled world. Workshops, seminars, and arranged meets are posted here. Please, sysops keep watch for any fascists among you. Don't waste our time.
•InfoNet-A. Be careful! This is a free and easy BBS for rumours, harder facts, suggestions, and whatever else people want to feed the system. Use your judgement about what you hear, and if inputting data or comments, please specify whether you have first-hand knowledge, whether supporting evidence exists, and if so, where it can be found. If you require a real-time interactive converse system, please use:
•Talk Talk. Sysops don't deal with this, it's hands off. Whether you want to alert everyone to a major hazard or you're looking for that very special elven person with highly unusual preferences in personal-enhancement technology, try your luck here. We're not listening. Honest.]<<<<<
— Paul K (00:03:25/7-FEB-52)

QUICK BRIT-THINK

—Excerpt from *Think Globally*, the in-flight magazine of TransGlobal Airlines

Visiting from the UCAS? Jetting in from the Confederated American States, or taking the suborbital from Seattle? Your employer will have briefed YOU on the way to successful business dealing with the British. But TransGlobe brings you a fun insight into Brit-think with this helpful little brochure. A few minutes of amusing reading will help YOU deal with Brits of all classes and understand some quaint British habits and lifestyle quirks.

Quick Brit-Think is provided for your reading enjoyment by TransGlobe, IAAF-certified low-band terrorist-risk air travel experts! Fly secure with TransGlobe!

MONEY

Americans know that Money is Good. Money gives you possibilities, opens doors, and your nuyen and dollars always talk. Brit-think is: unless you were born with it, you got it by exploiting someone else. Making money is bad, and having lots of it is worse unless it wasn't your fault (like, you won a lottery). Brits point out that the pursuit of money is dumb because you can't take it with you when you go; Americans never understand that. Brits also know that you can't have it all; where would you put it?

DEATH

Americans think death is optional. If you die, it's your fault. After all, you could have stayed beautiful and young if you (1) had the right surgeons, (2) got the right cyberware, and (3) got enough exercise and never smoked. Brits know that life has to be lived with some detachment; death can come any second, and events must be allowed to run their own course. Interfering with nature is always bad (see **New and Improved**). Brit-think is: it's arrogant to try to interfere with one's destiny.

FOOD

Americans eat whole piles of stuff, preferably forms of goo in which it's possible to be smothered (wet burgers, ice cream, fudge sundaes, Pastrami Coronary Columns). They also share food socially, eat like slobs, and eat out as often as possible. Brits are food fascists. They prefer food that is impossible to enjoy, and mumble "eat to live, not live to eat." They always avoid food they don't know. They are very polite eaters, though. Some of them even eat burgers with forks (and knives, too).

POLITICS

Official politics and personal politics are weirdly different. Official American politics is dull as hell; all the parties are the same. Bubbling under, though, are some

ugly policlub folks who like burning people of different somatypes and skin colours. Brit politics is different. The political parties hate each other, they scream and yell abuse, and some even preach nailing the other party to doors with industrial bolters. This letting-off of steam is a Brit national pastime. But there's less truly ugly, life-hating racism among the Brits. Ask an ork.

CLASS

Brits know you can't buy class. What matters is what your father did for a living, which school you went to, and how noble a profession you have. How much you earn has nothing to do with it. New money is usually vulgar. Actually, this one is impossibly complicated. The subtle nuances of British class definitions are too complex even for the Brits to fathom fully.

NEW AND IMPROVED

Americans love new things. They like new toys, credsticks, cyberware, games, food processors, autos, lovers, and therapists. Basically, they're just large, hyper-active children with a concentration span of about 15 minutes (on a good day) with a regular need to be diverted by the appeal of the New. New is Good. Brits think New is Bad, or at least it'll never be any better than the old. Brits wave away the New with the traditional refrain, This Is How We've Always Done Things. Personal-enhancement body shops are frowned upon because they're New and they cheat biological destiny (see **Death**).

Brits know the best homes were built 150 years ago, sport was more fun before skillsoft cheats ruined it, and a half-century of progress has polluted and ravaged the once green and pleasant land.

SEX

The main difference here is oral. That is, Americans talk about sex a lot more than Brits, before it, during it (especially females), and in-between-times. Americans can't experience true erotic bliss unless they've talked about Sharing The Experience first. Brits just get on with it and don't have the same penchant for (1) introspection, (2) modifying nature through training and skillsofts, and (3) reading endless books and magazines on the subject.

BEING CUTE

It's imperative to understand that Brits have no notion of this concept and are likely to be offended at being considered cute, especially if male. Brit-think dimly senses that small furry animals and babies are Cute, and maybe the dumber members of the Royal Family, but that's as far as it goes. American visitors to Britain must be very careful with this word.

SWIFT TRANSLATION GUIDE

Following is a quick checklist of the most important word differences between British and American English, which regularly confuse the unwary.

British	American
Pavement	Sidewalk
Van	Pickup
Pickup	Hooker
Car	Automobile
Motorway	Expressway, freeway
Number plate	License plate
Windscreen	Windshield
Petrol	Gas(oline)
Trousers	Pants
Knickerbockers	Knickers
Knickers	Underpants
Vest	Undershirt
Waistcoat	Vest
Marrow	Squash
Squash	Fruit Drink (v. unpleasant)
Potato chips	French fries
Crisps	Potato chips
Ground floor	First floor
First floor, and so on	Second floor, and so on
Behind	In back of
Biscuits	Cookies
Bonnet	Car hood
Boot	Car trunk
Braces	Suspenders
Suspender belt	Garter belt
Chemist	Drug store, pharmacy
Tap	Faucet
Underground/Tube	Subway

GREAT BRITAIN

HISTORY

BRITAIN'S NEW MILLENNIUM

Watch these guys, chummer. Britain's a small place, but did you ever see a map of the British Empire?
—Chuck Odom, UCAS Cultural Attaché (retired)

In the world of 2051, Britain is still a country with power and influence beyond its small size, a global player worth keeping an eye on. It is also a country of many contradictions. Although untouched by the catastrophic Euro Wars, the land has been ravaged and polluted by greedy exploiters past and present. Stylish aristocrats and royalty rule a country where pockets of appalling poverty and mindless brutality are common. British research brains are coveted by almost all megacorps, and British research teams hover at the cutting edge of technological innovations; yet one of the land's major powers is the druidic cult, and the Parliament is dominated by the conservationist Green Party. (There is a Conservationist Party, too, who pretend to be Green, but they are neo-fascists. This is confusing for visitors, but is fairly typical of British life.) Britain has repressive laws and is a secretive society; yet it has elven aristocrats, punk culture, wild Celtic shamans, gritty Northern dwarfs, brilliant computer scientists, Tongs unrivalled in power outside China itself, and myriad other subcultures in a mix that somehow manages to get along, even throwing in a dash of tolerance for the other bloke here and there.

>>>>>[The PR boys certainly toot a good tune about U.K. techno-industrial might, but you can be sure the new-tech development boys pop more antacid pills per day here than anywhere else. Got to stay on top, don't ya know.]<<<<<
—Luda (21:05:44/21-JAN-52)

A QUIET LIFE?

In the last decade of the 20th century, British political life seemed dull enough to make even TV political pundits despair. More than 20 years of Conservative Party rule, featuring uninspiring men in grey suits in the major offices of state, lulled the British electorate into settling for the status quo whenever a new election came around. Corporate interests insinuated themselves into power in ways subtler than elsewhere, or at least not so brutishly obvi-

ous. Usually, government hotshots angled policy formation toward corporate interests, in return for which a whole slew of fat company directorships landed in their steadily spreading laps upon retirement from politics. Britain's unique institution of public schools (funded entirely privately; Brits specialize in confusing nomenclature) ensured that the sons and daughters of the high and mighty were raised and schooled together and knew how to feather each other's nests in later life. Brits don't take bribes; they come to understandings. Smart corporate interests from Japan and America learned how to deal with this inward-looking, incestuous world: find some impoverished old money, some aristo fallen on hard times, and pump nuyen into him. Then he can get you into where you need to be, talking to the people who have power, lunching and taking cocktails at the discreet places and gentleman's clubs foreigners never even hear about, let alone enter.

Another paradox: as foreign corporates increasingly infiltrated Britain, Britain increasingly distanced itself from the rest of the European Economic Community. Differences over economic policy, loss of sovereignty to a Brussels-based central EEC bureaucracy, and anxiety about the overweeningly strong Franco-German axis made Brits apprehensive about the EEC. Though Britain remained part of the EEC, it defied EEC decision-making in some areas, used its veto powers to frustrate moves to European unity, and became increasingly isolated within Europe. Instead, successive Conservative prime ministers cultivated the "special relationship" with the U.S.A. The effects of this policy decision resonate to this day in the form of Britain's strong links with the UCAS and Tir Tairngire, but that is a longer story for another time.

QUIET BEFORE THE STORM

The first decade of the new millenium seemed to maintain this peacefulness, yet ecological events foreshadowed some of the anarchy and chaos of the years to come. Just as the Conservative Party hung on to power until January 2011 when the socialist Labour Party finally won an election and formed the new government, Queen Elizabeth II stayed in the throne for a staggering 57 years until the accession of Charles III in 2009. Charles' coronation awakened the yearning for change in the British public, and brought the new government in its wake. The well-known sympathies of the new king for "green" thinking and awareness and for spiritual and mystical reflections were an important spur to the growth and development of groups ridiculed as tired, old, "New-Age" relics. There was one powerful exception. The New Druidic Movement (NDM) was born of diverse origins. The Welsh Nationalists, Plaid Cymru, acquired the vestments of radical deep-green movements, and the NDM attracted many of these passionate Celts. The symbology of the NDM drew on, and appealed to, many other sources: Freemasonry, Qhabbalistic mysticism, arcane religious cults, and others. The origins of the new druids may have been a mish-mash, and the later schisms between the Celtic-shamanic and English-hermetic druids were surely born in these days, but a force was beginning to re-awaken in the British collective psyche.

The threat of a fragmented Britain seemed to have been well-averted in this new decade. The Conservatives were no fools. They threw a sop to the increasingly restive Welsh and Scottish nationalist movements by installing a new level of local government in Cardiff and Edinburgh. These local assemblies, modelled on state legislatures in the U.S.A., seemed to devolve power downward to Wales and Scotland, but this devolution was largely discretionary. In truth, power remained in the hands of the English at Westminster. In the same way, Ulster remained intact and Ireland stayed divided. Terrorist outrages seemed to diminish in frequency, but the British government's clever manipulation of the media ensured that the public never did get to hear the truth. It would not be until 2014, with the sensational Anglo-Irish Peace Conference in Galway, that the British public would realize anything of what had really been happening in the Emerald Isle.

British technological innovation was a constant source of pride to the British people during this false dawn of the new century; just as the Anglo-French *Concorde* had smashed Mach-2 in trans-Atlantic flights, the unveiling of the Anglo-Japanese suborbital *Ghost* in 2003 was a powerful symbol of British design and manufacturing know-how. London Heathrow International to Boston in 76 minutes, London to Tokyo in a few hours; the pencil-thin, grey-alloyed *Ghost* made even the military *Stealth* planes of the U.S.A. look cumbersome.

An influx of foreign money stabilized British high-tech industry. Japanese-based megacorps, in particular, realized the value of keeping their best brains happy—and if Brits liked to live in Britain, well, pay them Japanese wages and keep them sweet. The British economy was not too sick, though not as healthy as the government statistics (doctored by legions of "public servants" long used to grovelling sycophancy to the government of the day) would have a gullible public believe. New oil-field finds in the North Sea and in the Wyche Farm oil-fields of southern Britain swelled the GNP and tax coffers. A massive natural gas field discovered off the coast of Cornwall fed cheap natural energy into the economy. With the political, ecological, and economic costs of nuclear energy mounting, Britain's huge coal reserves

again became an asset. Britain looked secure, attracted foreign money, and the British people could look at the rest of the world's troubles with something of their traditional mix of sympathy and disdain. It took the pandemic of VITAS (Virally Induced Toxic Allergy Syndrome) and UGE (Unexplained Genetic Expression) to change that. British complacency would never be the same.

CHAOS AND AFTERMATH

The main force of the VITAS epidemic struck Britain in the winter of 2010-2011, killing 26 percent of the population. This loss synchronized with a series of ecological disasters for which the emergency services could barely manage even a damage-limitation strategy. Heavy spring floods in western England, landslides in Wales and along the length of the Pennines in central England, and even an earthquake in central Scotland came together with a string of toxic waste leaks from landfill sites, chemical spills into rivers, and the Sizewell meltdown that killed 7,800 people within a month and ten times the number from cancers in the next 30 years. The meltdown at Dounreay in Scotland was less costly in terms of loss of life but created an irradiated zone that grew to massive proportions.

By way of paradox, amidst all this death and destruction came an astonishing baby boom among the aristocracy. In Britain, this coincided (if it was coincidence) with powerful UGE. Research shows that 31 percent of the children registered born to titled parents in 2011 were elves; only 1 percent were dwarfs. Paradoxically, working-class, blue-collar parents—especially in the more deprived and polluted north of England—bore proportionately more dwarf babies. To account for this, research scientists at Adams-Hoffmann's Human-Metahuman Genetics Research Unit produced a string of theories about genetic predispositions interacting with environmental pollution. The truth is, no one knows why UGE took the form it did in Britain. All that is certain is that suddenly there were an awful lot of young elven aristocrats. And that would powerfully shape Britain's future in later decades.

>>>>>[Hell, we know what happened, don't we? Elven babies are cute and perfect; dwarf squealers twisted and grotesque. A quick pillow is all it takes, my friends.]<<<<<
—Stitch (02:24:49/16-JUL-52)

>>>>>[How do you know that? You can't, so stop bandering it about like you do. I'll bet you work for one of those trashfaxes, don't you?]<<<<<
—Miss Mary (16:22:08/22-JUL-52)

>>>>>[Mary, my love, just check out the number of "miscarriages" among the aristos that year. Then you tell me why.]<<<<<
—Stitch (23:16:55/05-AUG-52)

The earth really did move for us that night. We were driving back from friends in the valleys. It was Boxing Day, so we'd had a drink or two, but no more. The police really watch the roads at Christmas, so it's stupid to take risks. Anyway, you'd need a whole lot of medicine to hallucinate what we saw.

We were just heading down the hill, past the old rail line to Cardiff, when it glided over us and into the field. It was huge—must have been 30 meters nose to tail—and it glistened red and gold in the sodium light. Then, he—it just seemed to be a he, I guess—was, well, undulating on the ground. Just like a cat rubbing its back on the garden path. And he seemed just to melt into the ground, to sink into it, and this huge furrow of ground just moved like a wave down to the old Roman bull ring, getting a little shallower as it moved along. Like a ripple spreading out through the water. One heck of a sight; enough for a few stiff brandies when we made it home.

Didn't really see the details of him, we were so startled, and I had to try not to crash as I pulled up. But he was pretty close to the dragon on the Welsh flag. I remember his head in particular; the eyes were further forward and more elongated than the traditional Welsh dragon. Of course, at the time everyone thought we were crazy. But that was before the habitat started to spring up over the bull ring and the electric fences went up.

—Eye-witness account by one who preferred to remain anonymous, Radio Wales, 15 February, 2012

Two days after the first dragon was sighted in Japan, the first unquestioned heraldings of the Sixth World brought the tumultuous year toward its close. In the ancient Roman fortress town of Caerleon, the Great Welsh Dragon Celedyr was sighted, and no less than 14 mediums and clairvoyants reported astral sensings of the energizing of the Stalker ley. In various British sites, most spectacularly in the centre of the Welsh town of Brecon—where the town centre was simply flattened—stone circles and standing stones erupted through the earth, forming patterns of sacred sites extending along these great ley lines.

>>>>>[You know, the institutes are full of poor souls who went mad that day. Catatonics all.]<<<<<
—Ward VII (09:02:33/15-JUL-52)

With hindsight, both these events had more significance than they were deemed to have at the time. After all, Brits regard flying dragons and magical energizings as far less important than a good Royal story. The first day of 2012 brought one of those from the top drawer. Charles III abdicated in favour of his third son, George VII, his first two sons having been killed in a tragic plane crash. The king's New Year Message announced his intention of joining an unspecified esoteric order; to this day, no one knows where he took himself off to. If British gutter-press journalists couldn't find out (and they never got a sniff of his whereabouts after he left the throne), no one else had much chance. The young King George, barely of age, relied increasingly for advice on a "Palace Cabinet" drawn mostly from the hereditary peers of the House of Lords. Among these was the young and charismatic Lord Marchment, and his friendship with the king would prepare the young noble for his pivotal role in British politics for decades to come.

A series of weak governments, coalitions of centrist Democrats with either the unstable or indecisive Conservative or left-wing Labour parties, did not help Britain's struggle to recover from ecological disasters and VITAS. To be sure, shock greeted the assassination of Prime Minister Lena Rodale in 2016, but with no culprit immediately available, life went on much as usual the next day. The Brits became apathetic about which collection of has-beens was ruling the country month to month and just got on with their lives.

The major political upheavals were outside Britain. In 2014, after three years of escalating and brilliantly targeted terrorist attacks, mainland British public opinion forced the Democrat/Labour government to hold a referendum on Northern Ireland. By a large majority, the people voted to exclude the province from the United Kingdom. Left to fend for itself, the leaders of Northern Ireland carried on some frantic diplomacy with Eire, which created the United Free Republic of Ireland later in the year.

Within five years, Britain was again stung overseas. As Hong Kong seceded from mainland China, Britain was duped into trying to move in to protect and give aid to the new enclave, only to find that corporate interests had wholly taken over Hong Kong and played Britain for a sucker. These two reverses made Brits resentful of international snubs, and began a drift to nationalism and isolationism.

These dangerous currents, along with the growing New Druidic Movement, would dominate the tides of political life for the next two decades.

THE ROYAL SCHISM

The wave of goblinization of 2021 had one spectacular exemplar in Britain: in this year, the king was announced dead. Rumours have persisted ever since that he was transformed into a troll. Appalled at the idea of a troll-king, senior figures in the aristocracy and military are said to have ordered the king slain as he lay in the agony of his metamorphosis.

The king died without issue, and for three years two rival bloodlines competed for the throne of Britain. Eventually, George Edward Richard Windsor-Hanover, the

the **natural** way to get fried!

Britain was not an active participant in the Euro Wars to begin with, but there are persistent rumours regarding its tactical and covert involvement, culminating in the alleged *Nightwraith* bomber strike of 2033, which ended the European arena for the Euro Wars.

>>>>>[And none too soon. Word had leaked out that the nasty toys were about to be rolled out by one side or the other, and we know where that would have led. Better to shut them both down.]<<<<<
—Dog Soldier (04:43:10/02-AUG-52)

>>>>>[Yeah, you would believe that story. Let's admit it; the Brits, the Americans, the French, the Germans, and everybody else all have their own version of that event (and history). Not likely we're going to find out soon.]<<<<<
—Vostok Vamp (05:31:00/12-AUG-52)

>>>>>[A shaker of mine flew *Nightwraith*s back then. He says they didn't fly that night. You figure it out.]<<<<<
—Dooger (17:45:08/21-AUG-52)

The war was good for Britain's economy; its arms industry burgeoned. The IWS corporation found that bombing and sabotage had ravaged its continental competition, and that it had a firm grip on supplying those Third World dictators to whom the various North American states were not shipping out arms. Given British isolationism, the U.K.'s political relations with the fractionating North American states were fairly cool but not hostile. In some cases, "unofficial" channels between powerful British political interests and American states were of dominant importance. A good example of this were the links between the elven Sinsearach tribe, soon to form Tir Tairngire, and the youthful elven aristocrats of Britain.

GOVERNMENT IN DISGRACE

The Euro Wars were a godsend to the Conservationists. With growing inner-city violence and some racial riots in localized British areas (copycat versions of the Alamos 20,000 actions in America) thrown in, the country seemed ready to accept an authoritarian, repressive government. The Lord Protector used this national mood to extend his powers still further through passage of a series of Acts, slowly taking over a whole range of administrative and regulatory functions from other government departments. His proposals always claimed plausible reasons such as organizational efficiency and/or national security, and his charisma was enough to guarantee support from the Conservationist Party. Even though Lord Marchment was fairly well-known as a druidic sympathizer, and the Green Party was beginning to become the most important opposition party, a whole string of cumulating small-scale ecological hazards and minor disasters began to get publicity.

candidate of corporate interests, won out over the candidate of the growing druidic interests, but the druids gained much for acquiescing in the complicated genealogical pavanne that spun around the throne for so long.

The United Kingdom Constitution Act of 2025 created the office of Lord Protector, a post with many powers relating to administration of internal and national security. The first, and so far only, Lord Protector was the powerful young druid Lord Marchment. Originally, the Lord Protector headed the Ministry of the Interior, but this name (whilst still technically correct) has been omitted from official nomenclature in recent years, with reference made simply to the Lord Protector's Department. In the long term, the druids got by far the best of the deal, because the backers of King George VIII (as he became) were swimming against the tide of British nationalism.

That nationalism was reflected in the election of a Conservationist Party government in 2025, which stayed in power for nearly 16 years. Anti-European, it took Britain out of the European Economic Community and resorted to increasingly repressive measures to deal with internal dissent. Though the government grew increasingly unpopular, the Euro Wars reversed that trend in later years; there's nothing as good for a right-wing government as a good war to rally the electorate behind it.

In Wales and Scotland, the Wild Lands were growing. The first truly dramatic evidence came in the year 2036 when it became apparent to what extent Scottish druidic magics had transformed acres of the pine forests—grown for paper and mostly as a tax dodge, being wholly unsuited to Scottish ecology—into deciduous forest.

When the absentee landowners went out to check on their lands, they discovered bears and wolves had returned to Britain. In Wales, the elves of Gwynedd, with financial backing from several hidden sources, began to establish a racial enclave in the north of the Celtic land. They worked with Welsh-speaking locals to regenerate a ruined and spent land, and to develop sustainable alternative technologies for land use and energy sources. A green pulse of life was beginning to grow even as whole sections of Britain had to be abandoned to toxic, chemical, and radioactive decay.

The year 2039 proved the downfall and end of the Conservationist Party. A massive chemical spill on Teeside (also known as Teesprawl locally) killed more than 70,000 people from nerve-gas poisoning. An outcry over the ecological (and secret military) implications of this event put great pressure on the government. Later the same year the Pan-Europa strike on London resulted in terrorists releasing a paraviral agent that had immensely destructive effects on biofabrics of the sort used to construct the London Dome, whose construction was then in progress to regulate the environment of the capital. Normally, this would have led to support for a strong right-wing government, but not now. Rather, the government was blamed for not having dealt with the ecological problems that made necessary the construction of a dome in the first place. Then came the denouement.

Late in 2038, ork journalists reported the existence, in London, of a top-secret study on gene pool-manipulation by scientists of the Adams-Hoffmann Corporation. Shortly afterward they unearthed evidence of government complicity to the very highest levels. Put simply, the British government had sanctioned, even approved, the use of malign genetic manipulation on its own people, human and metahuman alike. The resulting eruption of violence had two effects. It forced the government to powerful repressive measures, of which the existence of the Lambeth Containment Zone is the most enduring legacy. But when an election was forced in early 2041, the Conservationists were driven from power, routed, and destroyed as a political force by a bitter and betrayed electorate who turned to the Green Party as a radical alternative.

THE LAST DECADE

The Green government has been able to maintain popular support with its claim that it will take decades to mop up the mess left by more than 200 years of abuse of Britain's lands and resources. Toxic spills and their sequels, such as the explosive poison-gas plume north of Merseysprawl in 2048, are almost everyday occurrences. Large areas of Britain have been evacuated, leaving behind only a few hardy settlers or those so desperate that they will live in the new toxic zones; the Victorian sewers of Liverpool have collapsed, leaving an inheritance of vicious and swarming devil rats and epidemics of cholera and typhoid. In the lands beyond, paranormal forces, wild druids, Awakened creatures, or more benign agencies have almost established an alternative Britain where the government still rules—but only after a fashion. From the spires of Castle Harlech, it is not the Chief Constable of police but the enigmatic Countess of Snowdon who holds the reins of power through her Cyberknights of Glendower. The police do not venture into many areas of the central sprawls. Law is in the hands of those strong enough to use it.

Strangely enough, a counterpointed Britain also exists. There are research laboratories where the new advances in organic chipping, wetware, is as far advanced as anywhere in the world. Research in Edinburgh, Cambridge, Nottingham, and London is producing medical and cybertech advances the equal of any in America, Japan, or Korea. And there are still nobles, fox hunting, and stately homes; there is still a theatre among green grass lawns at Stratford-upon-Avon, where foreigners can see productions of William Shakespeare's timeless comedies, tragedies, and history plays; and above all, there is still cricket played at Lord's Cricket Ground. Britain has not yet sunk into the sunset. Not quite...

GOVERNMENT AND POWER

POLITICAL ORGANIZATION

In theory, Britain is a parliamentary democracy, but it is also a monarchy. The national government, Parliament, is a two-chamber affair. The House of Nobles has an unfixed number of members, mixing hereditary peers with lifetime peers (who do not pass on the titles to their children). Lifetime peers are there because a king or prime minister, grateful for political toadying, puts them there. The second chamber of Parliament is the House of Commons (Common[er]s being non-aristocrats), whose members are elected from the 540 parliamentary constituencies that cover the whole of Britain. Elections to the House of Commons involve all members being up for re-election every five years maximum (sooner if the government thinks it can do better with a snap election). The system of election is first-past-the-post. The government is the political party (or parties in a coalition) holding the most seats in the House of Commons. The Houses of Parliament, a favourite tourist trap, are in the Westminster District of Inner London. Both Houses have formal sessions when all members of Parliament (MPs for the House of Commons) are present to debate, discuss, and vote on bills. Precise dates are variable, but are usually:

End of second week of January until Easter,

One month after Easter until the end of June, and

First week of September until the end of the third week of December.

Outside of these times, the functions of government are administered by civil servants and the Lord Protector's office. Major new legislation is not enacted outside session time. If a desperate need arises, say, in response to a major national crisis, the prime minister can recall Parliament at any time.

The balance of power between the Commons and Nobles is a subtle thing, almost unique to the British system. The Nobles never actually challenge the Commons. Their role is to consult, persuade, cajole, insinuate, suggest. They rarely initiate any new laws, and they cannot block a law passed by the Commons. They can return a draft bill for reconsideration, with amendments, or just delay matters if they wish (but not major matters such as a budget). The Nobles can, however, send draft bills to the Lord Protector's office, which then sends them to the Commons after making suitable amendments, a tortuous path into policy formation.

The prime minister, leader of the governing party, selects the ministers of state from the government. These comprise both senior and junior ministers. The seniors, primarily selected from the House of Commons by convention, are the ones who count. The others are their toadies and lackeys, who receive some recognition for their hard work and general groveling. The major U.K. ministers of state at the current time are:

Prime Minister: James Winstanley
Deputy Prime Minister: Earl of Southampton
Speaker of the House: Philip Russell
Chancellor of the Exchequer: Henry Rochester
Foreign Secretary: Simon Farquhuar
Home Secretary: Caroline Carradine
Minister of State for Trade and Industry: Peter Marshall
Minister of State for Health and Social Security: Richard Hume
Minister of State for Transport and Communications: George Carmichael
Minister of State for the Environment: Michael Hazeldean
Minister of State for Defence: Basil de Villiers
Lord Protector: Lord Marchment

>>>>>[Actually, gentlemen, there isn't a prime minister and there never has been one. The correct nomenclature is First Lord of the Treasury.]<<<<<
—Hampstead Hi-Jack (15:13:54/4-FEB-52)

>>>>>[Well, what d'ya know? Is this guy for real?]<<<<<
—MesoStim (16:43:21/4-FEB-52)

>>>>>[For all our visitors, who may have a Congress or a Knesset or a Praesidium at home, a quick lowdown: the Deputy PM means nothing, it's a token job. Same for the Speaker of the House—he's actually nonpolitical and gets elected unopposed. He's just there to keep order when it's feeding time at the zoo they call the House of Commons. Have you seen those freaks on the trideo? Home Secretary deals with lots of domestic stuff—education, law reform, judicial system—and what he doesn't deal with the Lord Protector swallows up. Hell, you know about HIM. Environment is BIG—it means planning permission for buildings, corporate developments, as well as giving permits to screw up the earth. There's a lot of power there. Watch Hazeldean; he's ambitious and he's got a fix on Winstanley's back.]<<<<<
—Mole Man (22:11:16/4-FEB-52)

>>>>>[If you wanna see 'em for real, visiting time is two 'til five weekday afternoons in the Strangers Gallery at the Commons. Best day is Fridays, two-fifteen sharp. That's when they have Prime Minister's Question Time, which is utter mayhem. The security for admission is PHENOMENAL.]<<<<<
—MesoStim (15:12:12/5-FEB-52)

At national level, two other forces are important: the Crown (King), and the Lord Protector. Technically, both are subservient to Parliament. In practice, both have an influence, in different ways. King George VIII has an influence on Parliament through his extensive contacts with the (human) aristocracy and the House of Nobles. The king does not often choose to exercise this power to any extent, however. It is a power best used sparingly. Given the existence of a rival bloodline, the king's supporters don't want the king stepping out of line too much.

The Lord Protector's office is a different matter. Increasingly, this complex organization has taken over many of the duties that used to fall to the Home Office: drafting bills on public order issues, policing and prison services, registration laws (for magicians, foreigners resident in the U.K., cyberware, and much else) and even higher education. If one needs a form or a license or a permit to do it in the U.K., this is where to apply for it. The Lord Protector's office also has a role in supplying and training the civil servants who actually draft bills and laws, which lets the Lord Protector know what is going on almost anywhere in Parliament very, very fast. The Lord Protector is a leading druid, and the smiling gents of this office are dealt with later.

Local government is really a sham in the U.K. Wales and Scotland have regional assemblies, which, technically, have powers to raise taxes and spend on education, health and welfare, street cleansing, and similar humdrum matters. These assemblies are elected as the House of Commons is, one-sentient, one-vote. In actual fact, the hands of these assemblies are tied. They cannot levy total taxation of more than 2 percent of total per-capita income of those who live in their domains, they cannot levy indirect taxes, and they are 82 percent funded by hand-outs from Parliament. They really only get the money the government feels like giving them. When it comes to spending, they are hemmed in by a huge wedge of statutory duties that leave them minimal discretionary spending power. So, this sop to the Celtic fringe is largely powerless, and the ordinary people are not fooled by it.

Major British cities have local metropolitan councils (again, with little real power) and Lord Mayors. Lord Mayors exist to be wheeled out a few times a year to host banquets for important corporate patrons and visitors and to dress in their fake-medieval dress and chains of office to act as camera fodder for the tourist trade. Some spirited Brit will occasionally indulge in the traditional pastime of throwing eggs or tomatoes at a posing Lord Mayor to remind everyone of the degrading nature of this spectacle.

POLITICAL PARTIES

Britain is almost a one-party state today. The Greens have taken the entire mid-spectrum of U.K. politics, and were elected on a landslide in the last general election. Following are descriptions of the major political parties, with their share of the popular vote at that election and the number of seats they have in the House of Commons.

CONSERVATIONIST (9%, 32 seats)

The Conservationist Party is the neo-fascist rump of the old Conservative Party. They are ugly nationalists who are currently flirting with Deep Green propaganda as a cynical ploy to curry favour with the electorate. They are allegedly funded by a tiny number of megacorporate billionaires of rabidly right-wing persuasions. Despite its British nationalism, the Conservationist Party has definite links with neo-fascist, anti-metahuman, and eco-terrorist groups in Europe. Its leader is John Andersen, a 44-year old ex-SAS member.

DEMOCRATS (17%, 99 seats)

The Democrats are a rather gutless and uninspired remnant of a party that spent many earlier years acting as a power broker and the junior partner in a series of dreary coalitions. It has managed to hold on to a fair wedge of support from liberals who are suspicious of the various Green bandwagons and the spectrum of intellectuals, media-aware souls, poseurs, and muesli-eaters who populate the nicer areas of the London sprawl. Its leader is Janet Richards, a charismatic 41-year-old lady without whom this party's vote would probably be halved.

GREEN PARTY (70%, 387 seats)

The Green Party is a broad coalition, ranging from devolutionist-socialists to libertarian anarchists to some simpler souls who just get very upset at seeing the land of Britain being turned into a bigger toxic hazard than it already is. The more anarchic and left-wing elements periodically drop out and then join up again, making life in the Green Party somewhat tricky. Party leader James Winstanley, at 52, is a master of diplomacy and he needs to be. He's oilier than a North Sea rig, and eight years as PM have taught him a lot about politics. He's terrific in front of a trideo, able to evade the bluntest of questions with real panache, and his good looks are debonair enough to appeal to women, but bland enough not to alienate men. The Lord Protector and the druids are the true force behind the Green Party; most of its ordinary, honourable MPs and followers in the House of Nobles are unknowingly along for the ride.

SOCIALIST WORKER'S PARTY (2%, 22 seats)

This is the only residual sign of the old Labour Party. An ultra-hard-left party, the SWP has localized support in severely polluted and/or deprived areas such as Tynesprawl. Its members are neo-Trotskyists who are alleged to have links with terrorists, but this is just smear stuff put about by the Conservationists and their megacorp masters. The party is actually a passionately anti-racist, anti-elitist organization with some decent (if probably misguided) souls in its midst. Unfortunately, its leader Martha Michelson combines goodness of heart with a real lack of any visible sense of humour, so trideo coverage does not get these folk any extra votes.

>>>>>[A factoid for you gentlemen: 62 percent of Conservationist MPs elected in the last decade have a background in the military. Fifty-five percent have freelanced for corporate muscle overseas in various, ah, theatres of action, if that's the correct expression. Thirty percent currently work in areas related to insurance. Some inquisitive people out there might find it interesting to check out exactly how.]<<<<<
　　—Hampstead Hi-Jack (13:55:04/7-JAN-52)

LAW AND ORDER

Britain does not have a Bill of Rights, Freedom of Information Act, or anything similar. It does have its Constitution Act of 2025, but this merely defined the powers of local and national government, the Lord Protector's Office and the Crown, and does not address the rights of the average citizen or visitor. It is a very secretive society, but one where centralized record-keeping on its population is the full-time occupation of almost 200,000 people. The major datanets for this information, which are packed with IC of fearsome complexity and lethality, are the Central Criminal Register, the Public Health and Welfare Datanet, and the Chancellery Net.

CENTRAL CRIMINAL REGISTER

Located at Hendon in the London Sprawl, this is the police computer.

>>>>>[A tough little nut, but not impossible, despite what you may hear. Call it a Red-5, I'd say.]<<<<<
　　—Ringer (05:13:52/3-JAN-52)

PUBLIC HEALTH AND WELFARE DATANET

Located in Oxford, this system contains all data on DNA typing, health and welfare benefits and payments, social data, and economic data allegedly used for government planning. It is widely rumoured that PHW data is routinely sold cheap to corporate interests that are supportive of government policies.

>>>>>[Chiploads of data to be had, here. Tag this one as Red-4.]<<<<<
　　—Ringer (05:14:20/3-JAN-52)

CHANCELLERY NET

This is the system of the Lord Protector's office and contains information on DNA typing (together with samples of DNA from licensed practitioners of magic), plus an awful lot else.

>>>>>[Oh, this one's as black as my own heart. Don't know anyone who's lived to tell the tale of its hallowed paths.]<<<<<
—Ringer (05:15:51/3-JAN-52)

The government can also routinely access megacorporate datanets if it so wishes. A small group of expert deckers is permanently on call in the Lord Protector's offices to perform such access if needed.

The repressive nature of the British systems of law and law enforcement must be seen against this backdrop of secrecy and data-collection. It is also vital to realize that the British legal system has nothing to do with justice. It is a system of law. By precedent, laws that have stood on the statute books for 800 years or more are still part of the system of jurisprudence. It is a nightmare system, made worse by the very closed nature of legal practice. Only British-qualified (or licensed) legal practitioners can operate in British courts; these are barristers and they protect their monopoly zealously. They are all licensed by the Lord Protector's office, which also oversees the appointments of all major judges. If someone's got nuyen to burn, this system will work for him. If not, forget it.

LAW ENFORCEMENT AGENCIES

The police in Britain are an armed, national force. The country is technically divided into a number of local sprawl areas over which chief constables have jurisdiction, but co-operation is so extensive and instantaneous that the system is really a national one. The British police are hard to bribe, hard to bluff, and generally do not overlook minor misdemeanours. They are corrupt in more fundamental ways. Racism is endemic (both anti-metahuman and anti-ethnic) and so is a genuine dislike for people at the bottom of the social ladder. The British police are not nice people, but they don't express their prejudices too overtly most of the time. They're good at their job, too, as evidenced by the number of A/AA/AAA-rated neighbourhoods and districts around the sprawl.

A major difference from many foreign countries is that Britain is fiercely restrictive of corporate security forces. These are usually allowed to operate only in small numbers, within highly defined areas, and in pursuit of narrowly defined objectives (maintaining security, protecting data, and so on). Or so goes the theory. In practice, at least at major arms-manufacturing sites, quite sizeable forces may exist, shrouded in secrecy. It is also rumoured that the Conservationist government made use of corpo-

rate security personnel in police uniforms during the troubles of the 2030s. Because many corporate security men come from the police or the military, cooperation is highly likely. In Britain, it's just a lot harder to nail this kind of thing.

>>>>>[Corporate sec-forces tend to be elite pro-bastards in Britain. The baggers keep them locked down so that when they do go they have to make sure they go *right*.]<<<<<
—Dog Soldier (17:12:32/5-APR-52)

Large condo complexes, elite residential areas, and the like use private security firms in addition to regular policing. Private security men are not usually licensed to carry any form of firearms, except in areas where many government employees live and in a handful of ultra-high-class locations. Several competing security firms exist, rather than any one major corporation, although it is rumoured that the HBK megacorporation owns a controlling influence in several of these minor agencies. London Security, Risk Minimizers PLC, ScotSecure, and Midland Guard are examples of such small organizations.

Lastly, Britain has a particularly sinister secret police, the SAS (Special Air Services is their full title). Their original anti-terrorist brief was merged with that of the more traditional MI5 anti-subversion role to form a security force whose accountability is almost impossible to pin down (to the Home Office, the Lord Protector, to the Chiefs of Staff at the War Office, to the prime minister direct). The SAS eschew any form of magical firepower or detection, but are equipped with technofixes of amazing ingenuity. The SAS are, simply, state terrorists, but they're an organization anyone in his right mind keeps well away from. The trouble is that it's very hard to be sure exactly who they are after, and if it's you, you won't know until you get a bullet through the back of your skull.

>>>>>[Those SAS boys, phew! My daddy told me how they played it in Ireland in the old days. They didn't go out killing the terrorists themselves…well, not so often after Gibraltar in '87, when they got caught. What they'd do, they'd infiltrate the Protestant paramilitaries and ship 'em info on alleged IRA sympathizers and get the Prods to kill the IRA for them! Except when the names got a bit muddled up, of course, and a couple of ordinary Joes got boxed. Well, that's war for you.]<<<<<
—MesoStim (19:44:46/4-FEB-52)

>>>>>[Quite a cynic, aren't you?]<<<<<
—Slammer (19:55:12/4-FEB-52)

>>>>>[Just a realist, matey.]<<<<<
—MesoStim (19:55:27/4-FEB-52)

CRIMES AND PUNISHMENT

There is no system of local laws in Britain, only national laws. Punishments are generally more draconian than in North American states and, indeed, in Europe generally. Britain has a higher percentage of its population in penal institutions than any major European nation (in excess of 0.2 percent of the total population).

CONTROLLED WEAPONS AND EQUIPMENT

The Weapon Fines and Punishment table below corresponds to that of other nations, with the addition of four new categories of controlled items:

•**Class M1**: either controlled substances of addictive nature or biotechnical devices.

•**Class M2:** controlled substances of nonaddictive nature other than alcohol and nicotine (which are frequently legal, at least for purposes of possession, abroad).

•**Class CD**: Unregistered cyberdecks and Matrix program software.

•**Class N**: Unregistered magical items of any nature (fetishes, grimoires, spell focuses, and so on).

In all cases, dealing in or trading in these restricted items brings a fine of up to 10 times the figure shown for possession, depending on the scale of the offence, and/ or a jail term of between 6 months and 20 years (trading in addictives).

The category of "Transport" does not exist as a separate offence in Britain. Possession of a restricted or illegal item, threatening or dangerous behaviour with it, and actual use of the item are recognized as categories of offence. There is no division between "use" and "intent" as in North American law; if someone used the thing, it's assumed he was not doing it for the hell of it (if a lenient court decides he was, then this is dangerous behaviour with the item). That is, to the Brits, any actual usage implies intent. It makes for a simpler system of justice that way, albeit a more punitive one.

The figures in the table below are only averages. Judges (including the magistrates who preside at smaller courts dealing with minor offences) usually have the discretion to increase fines and terms of imprisonment by up to 50 percent above the figures shown. Special circumstances may always increase sentences quite sharply. For example, evidence suggesting that a suspect is a member of a terrorist group would greatly increase the sentence for possessing explosives.

>>>>>[Yeah, it just depends on whether the old swine got juiced up on port wine the night before.]<<<<<
—MesoStim (22:16:34/27-DEC-52)

WEAPON FINES AND PUNISHMENT TABLE

Weapon Type	Offence and Fine/Imprisonment		
	1 Possession	**2** Threat/Danger	**3** Use
(A) Small Bladed Weapon	—	£5,000	£15K/6 mo
(B) Large Bladed Weapon	—	£10K	£25K/9 mo
(C) Blunt Weapon	—	£5,000	£20K/6 mo
(D) Projectile Weapon	—	£5,000	£20K/6 mo
(E) Pistol	£7,000/9 mo	£15K/9 mo	3 yrs
(F) Rifle	£10K/12 mo	£25K/12 mo	4 yrs
(G) Automatic Weapon	£20K/18 mo	3 yrs	10 yrs
(H) Heavy Weapon	£30K/2 yrs	5 yrs	20 yrs
(I) Explosives	1 yr	5 yrs	20 yrs
(J) Military Weapons	1 yr	5 yrs	25 yrs
(K) Military Armour	£7,000	—	—
(L) Ammunition	£5,000	—	—
(M1) Controlled Subs/Biotech	£10K/18 mo	—	—
(M2) Nonaddictive Substance	£1,000	—	—
(N) Unlicensed Magical Items	£1–20K	—	—
(CA) Class A Cyberware	£25K	—	—
(CB) Class B Cyberware	£20K	—	—
(CC) Class C Cyberware	£60K/2 yrs	—	—
(CD) Unlicensed Decks/ Matrix Software	£5–40K/1 yr	—	—

SPECIAL CONSIDERATIONS

The following distinctions for U.K. law apply:

Parole

A parole is significantly harder to get in the U.K. A first offender is considered for parole after he has served half his prison sentence; for a repeat offender, this is three-quarters time.

Fines for Other Offences

Fines are roughly five times the North American counterpart.

Sentences for Other Offences

Sentences are roughly 150 percent of the North American counterpart.

Unauthorized Access to Computer Resources

Because this is a highly variable crime, the penalties are likewise variable. Major offences (data theft, industrial espionage, major data destruction, and so on) are punishable by fines of up to £100,000 and sentences of up to ten years imprisonment. The fine may be levied at a punitive rate if government data are damaged or accessed, bankrupting the criminal.

Unlicensed Cyberware

This is defined with extraordinary strictness in Britain. Any form of personal-enhancement cyberware (skillsofts, wired reflexes, even cybereyes) must be licensed by the Lord Protector's office. Licenses for such enhancements are readily available for a nominal sum (£10–52). Licenses for aggressive bodyware (smartgun links, dermal plating, and the like) are hard to come by, however, as are licenses for any really powerful skillsofts. Only major corporate influence can get licenses for this kind of enhancement.

Visiting foreigners will be issued a temporary license, allowing them to stay for 30 days with their cyberware, but after this time, they must either leave the country or visit a government clinic that will deal with the problem.

Unlicensed Magical Activity

This is a superb catch-all. Any practitioner of magical arts, hermetic or shamanic, must be registered as such at the Lord Protector's Office in Chancellery Lane. A fee of £500 per annum, plus a DNA sample taken on the spot, are submitted together with a very, very lengthy form. In the case of foreigners, processing can take many weeks, so it is best to apply well in advance of any need to use magic. Applications may be refused without explanation. The penalties for the unlicensed practice of magic and magical items (in addition to possession), can vary considerably. Minor transgressions such as the use of magical healing may result in a trivial fine; £50 or so. Whacking out a massive mana bolt spell at security personnel can get 20 years, in addition to any prison term for injuries the spell causes.

Even if a mage is licensed, many elements of magical operation are proscribed. Magical intrusions and spying, such as the deployment of watchers, are considered to be serious offences, as are magical control of the minds and actions of others, including the use of magical illusions. Fines of up to £25,000 (possibly more for magical industrial espionage) and sentences of up to 5 years imprisonment are applied in such cases. However, given the difficulty of establishing proof (especially if no state-employed mage is to hand to give expert testimony), these cases are a real headache for British courts.

ROYALTY AND NOBILITY

The death of George VII in 2021 brought about a three-year power struggle over the royal bloodline. The king died without issue, and all members of the Royal Family who suffered goblinization were deemed unacceptable heirs to the throne. This was not so much anti-metahuman as a deep anxiety about what the public would accept and whether a goblinized monarch would inflict terminal damage on the monarchy as an institution. There were also serious medical doubts about how long the goblinized would actually survive in their changed form.

Through a haze of genealogical calculations, DNA typing, historical researches, paternity checks, and general political machinations, two rival claimants to the throne gradually came to the fore.

George Edward Richard Windsor-Hanover, born in 1998, was the candidate backed by corporate interests. The 19th Earl of Worcester, as he then was, had the added advantage of his charismatic and extraordinarily attractive wife Lady Diana Maugham, eldest daughter of Baron Stratford. The earl was popular with the public, and had the great advantage (very rare among British royals) of being neither unusually stupid nor prone to behaving like a drunken oaf in public. Windsor-Hanover was desperate to become the next king, and he sold his soul to corporate backers, including many of the nobles of the time, to become George VIII.

His one serious rival was Edward Arthur Charles Gordon-Windsor, the 27th Duke of Cheltenham and Bath. A quiet, studious, and somewhat shy man, Gordon-Windsor was closely associated with the New Druidic Movement. His backers included many of these new druids, who may well have used him in the short term as a lever to gain more power for themselves.

The final resolution of the rival claims was a typically British compromise. Windsor-Hanover became George VIII. The Birthday Honours list handed out titles to many of his backers and cronies, with the druids tacitly agreeing not to challenge the successful corporate interests politically for a while. But the druids got the better long-term deal. The Constitution Act of 2025 established the office of Lord Protector, and their man Lord Marchment became the first (and so far only) Lord Protector. Since then, the Lord Protector has become very powerful, indeed, and the druids have had further success with the Green Party, of which Gordon-Windsor is an enthusiastic supporter. His second wife, Mary Carrington, second daughter of the Earl of Swanage, is a political activist for the Green Party and is a rival to Queen Diana for the public's affection. The two compete for how many thousands of pounds they can spend on their new dresses for The Season.

The British public still holds the Royal Family, and the institution of royalty, in the greatest esteem. Even the most jaundiced LCZ street gang member might leave you alone if you keep your mouth shut and your eyes to the ground, but say anything against Queen Di and you'll get your teeth knocked down your throat. The one royal

SWITHIN'S
Public House

Glouster Court, off Tower Hill
BTG# 711 (226-2380)

offspring, Princess Caroline, is also a public favourite, despite a notorious series of love affairs. Only her recent marriage put a stop to the more scandalous of these.

George VIII's actual political power is weak. Given the burgeoning support for a stronger monarch, he is more in thrall to his corporate and noble backers than ever. With his connections, Gordon-Windsor could have been much stronger than the current king (especially if he knew which of his connections were untrustworthy). This is proof that the source of power is more the king's contacts and friends than the actual institution of monarchy. It is true that, technically, the king can declare war, dissolve Parliament, issue a Royal Pardon to release someone from jail, and dish out honours, but any king who tried to use these powers to their full extent would soon find himself deposed. Brits love their royalty, who are a source of national pride and good for the tourist trade, but they also love the illusion of parliamentary democracy that capitalist society gives them.

>>>>>[Has anyone actually vidied Gordon-Windsor lately? One story says that he's Elvis after he had himself an "accident."]<<<<<
—Georgo (20:52:32/17-FEB-52)

>>>>>[Nobody's seen him for a bit. I hear the same about his "accident," but I also hear he's still kicking, though kicking may not be the right word for the shape he's in.]<<<<<
—Ringer (05:13:52/3-MAR-52)

ARISTOCRACY AND NOBILITY

SOCIAL CLASS

The British class system is extremely complex and subtle. Britain has plenty of subcultures, especially ethnic and street-defined, but there is also a national understanding of the class system. There are official grades of social class: A for aristocrats at the top of the pile, A2 for highly skilled professionals (medics, professors, exceptional artisans, and so on), but this is not the key to dealing with Brits. What matters are the ideas and understanding behind the notion of class. So, while a top surgeon and an exec each making 100,000 nuyen a year may both be social class A2 in the official scheme of things, this is not true in the eyes of most Brits. In Britain, the medic is of a higher class because he does something worthwhile. Making money in business is slightly sordid. Money has nothing to do with social class in Britain and is also the key difference from the government classifications. A knight who is a pauper is higher in social class than any corporate executive without a knighthood.

Social class is defined partly by heredity, but that is true only for the nobles and peers. For others, education is the key factor. The better educated one is, the higher his or her social class. Education is not defined as simply learning skills and acquiring knowledge about economics, the Matrix, neurophysiology, or what-have-you. It also includes learning decent manners, improving the outer person, and eliminating any trace of regional accent. Having a strong accent is common and vulgar. Social class is also defined by what one does. Professionals are higher than blue-collar workers, people in business are of lower class than those who teach, heal, practice performing arts, and generally express a healthy disdain for nuyen.

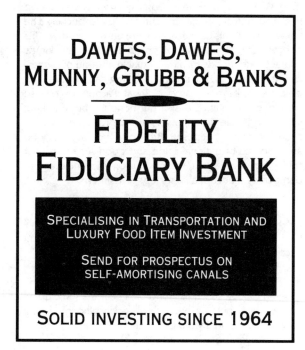
NOBLES

The individuals at the top of the social pile are the titled aristocrats. These are the peers of the realm, which include five grades. In order, these are dukes, marquises, earls, viscounts, and barons. They all get to call themselves Lord so-and-so, but the serious, long-standing hereditary peers have titles that speak of the properties they own (or used to). Hence Lord Cambridge, the Duke of Kent, Lord Marchment (an area of Edinburgh). In most cases, the place names are now hopelessly dated. These five grades of title are hereditary, passed from father to son (or nearest male descendant). Females do not inherit titles. To complicate matters, the most important nobles actually have an array of titles, the least of which tend to get passed on to their male offspring before their father dies. Thus, the Duke of Monmouth (south Wales) is also the Earl of Caerleon, and his eldest son is known by the latter title before he acquires the ducal title on his father's death. If the duke has no son, he retains both titles, but usually is addressed only as a duke unless the social situation is the most formal.

>>>>>[I don't understand this. When's a duke called a duke and when's he called a lord? When's the duke an earl as well? What's the point?]<<<<<
—Clyde (18:43:05/7-JAN-52)

>>>>>[It's quite simple. The Duke of Monmouth is the Duke of Monmouth when he feels like it. If he'd rather call himself Lord Monmouth, he can. But it's rude to call him Lord Monmouth. The correct address is, "My Lord Duke." He's an earl as well because these people collected titles the same way they collected property—through theft and swindling. Oh, and just to get you absolutely straight, the wife of a duke is a duchess, the wife of a viscount is a viscountess, and the wife of an earl is a countess. But we don't have any counts. I hope that's clear.]<<<<<
—Sir Peter Mainwaring, KMV (18:44:48/7-JAN-52)

>>>>>[KMV?]<<<<<
—Clyde, again. (18:44:53/7-JAN-52)

>>>>>[We'll get to that.]<<<<<
—Sir Peter (18:45:52/7-JAN-52)

KNIGHTS AND HONOURS

Below the peers come the baronets; these are the highest echelon of the orders of knighthood. There are several orders of knighthood below that, but not even Brits bother distinguishing these.

The system of honours is a vital cog in the British social class system. Knighthoods are part of this. For the 99.99 percent of the population who are not hereditary aristocrats, the knighthoods awarded by Crown and government are an elevation to an exalted class. They are distributed sparingly as rewards for toadying and sycophancy, and for clandestine transfers of funds to the political party in power at the time. Captains of industry, editors of newspapers and trideo news systems friendly to the government, and a few personal hangers-on of Ministers of State get knighthoods, for example. About 60 or 70 knighthoods are awarded each year.

There is also a weird array of other civil honours awarded twice a year (the New Year Honours List on 1 January and the Birthday Honours List on 25 June, the King's "official" birthday). Gloriously outdated awards of minor titles and medals are given to swell the egos of selected grateful recipients: media personalities and sportsmen, civil servants and industrialists, long-serving minor politicians, artists, and others who have achieved some prominence. These awards do not allow the recipients to use a title, but they can use the letters after their names.

Their function is mainly to sustain the entire system of titles, nobility, and honours. By spreading it wider among the lesser beings, it generates wider respect for the system, all the while keeping the real power and recognition concentrated in a very few hands. This is a typically British resolution of a problem. The most important of these minor honours, after a rationalization of 2025, are (in order of increasing kudos):

MBE = Member of the British Empire
OBE = Officer of the British Empire
CBE = Commander of the British Empire
KMS = King's Medal for Service
KMH = King's Medal for Honour
KMV = King's Medal for Valour

HOW TO ADDRESS BRITISH NOBILITY

Person	Start letters	Address as	Refer to as
Baron	The Rt Hon Lord… or The Lord…	My Lord	Your Lordship
daughter	The Hon…	Madam	
son	The Hon…	Sir	
Baroness	The Rt Hon Lady… or Lady…	Madam	Your Ladyship
Baronet	Sir (name) Baronet	Sir	Your Lordship
wife	Lady…	Madam	Your Ladyship
Duke	His Grace the Duke of…	My Lord Duke	Your Grace
daughter	Lady…	Madam	Your Ladyship
eldest son	(usually takes one of father's secondary titles, e.g. earl)		
other son	Lord…	My Lord	Your Lordship
Duchess	Her Grace the Duchess of…	Madam	Your Grace
Earl	The Rt Hon Earl of… or The Earl of…	My Lord	Your Lordship
child	(first son has father's secondary title, others as Baron's son; daughter as a duke's daughter)		
wife	The Rt Hon the Countess of… (Countess)	Madam	Your Ladyship
King	The King's Most Excellent Majesty	Sire, may it please your Majesty	Your Majesty
Queen	The Queen's Most Excellent Majesty	Madam, may it please your Majesty	Your Majesty
Marquis	The Most Hon the Marquis of…	My Lord Marquis	Your Lordship
child	(as duke's)		
Marchioness	The Most Hon the Marchioness of…	Madam	Your Ladyship
Prince	His Royal Highness Prince…	Sir	Your Royal Highness
Princess	Her Royal Highness Princess…	Madam	Your Royal Highness
Viscount	The Rt Hon the Lord Viscount…	My Lord	Your Lordship
child	(as baron's)		
Viscountess	The Rt Hon the Viscountess…	Madam	Your Ladyship

NOBILITY AND POWER

A small number of noble families have considerable power in Britain. This power is partly economic; a handful of noble families own astounding wealth and have major ownership of several megacorporations and even outright ownership of a few. Their power is also political, although not strong as it could be, mostly because it is divided. While the House of Nobles does not formally have much power, nobles can get a long way through networks of mutual contacts and shared privilege, plus the old British habit of groveling to anyone with a title.

THE MOON AND SIXPENCE

A PUB FOR YOUR DRINKING AND DINING PLEASURES
home of the
miraculous,
marvelous

CYBER-COW!

An important division exists within the noble families: humans and elves. Astonishingly, 27 percent of the male heads of noble families (as of 2051) are now elves, and Berk's Peerage (accessible on C-net), the standard reference work, estimates that more than 40 percent will be elven by 2065. This reflects the extent of UGE within British noble families. Elven nobles tend to be fairly arrogant, but beautifully mannered. They do not necessarily form a cohesive wedge of power, for elves have a diversity of goals just as humans do. But they are somewhat united against anti-metahuman forces in society, and elven nobles will avoid corporate conflicts between their ownership interests if they know of them.

Generally, elven nobles remain aloof from druids, whom they tend to distrust, and take an independent political line. They have become gradually more cohesive over the last 15 years as more elves have assumed titles and as their contacts through shared gentleman's clubs, country retreats, and The Season become firmer and of longer standing. If there is a shared elven agenda, it includes keeping an eye on the druids, snooping on the Lord Protector (who is mostly distrusted), quietly funding those who practice direct opposition to anti-metahuman groups, broadly Green issues (so they vote with the druids on these, minimizing open conflicts), and establishing links with Tir Tairngire. These links are kept very quiet, but are increasingly strong. British public schools that specialize in catering to elven noble children take an increasing number of young elves from across the Atlantic. Elven university lecturers, especially in magical studies, take frequent sabbaticals in the other country. There are rumours of information-sharing between the government of Tir Tairngire and British elven nobles. Finally, the jealously prized orichalcum from the Wild Lands finds easier export licenses to Tir Tairngire than elsewhere.

Human nobles mutter about the elves as a secretive, arrogant lot, but they do not organize against them (this would be very un-British). They, too, have their own goals, with conflicts sometimes occurring between them. Human nobles are mostly conservative about the status quo in society and few have real ambition or drive.

A handful of nobles in the U.K. are particularly powerful, and their actions and words have especial influence. The most important of these, apart from royalty and the Lord Protector, are the following:

Justin Carmichael, Duke of Oxford

Justin is an elven noble, 37 years of age, with major industrial holdings (in British Industrial PLC and IWS, among others) as well as extensive landholdings. Carmichael owns a string of commercial properties on prime sites in north London, which he leases to hotel chains and the like. Like other elven nobles, Justin Carmichael has not altered his birth name to a more "elven" one. That would diminish his family heritage, and thus his power. Carmichael is a highly independent political force who is indifferent to many issues but very involved with others. He is known to be actively hostile to the burgeoning power of the Lord Protector and very suspicious of the Druidic Hidden Circles.

>>>>>[Carmichael is also known to be the (well-hidden) owner and funder of the Oxford Astral Workshops, which conduct high-power research and training into astral space and metaplanes. There is also a powerful hermetic circle here devoted to the study of metamagic. What no one knows is why Carmichael is the person behind this research and what he intends to do with the knowledge and power acquired.]<<<<<
—Magister (05:23:49/15-FEB-52)

Daffyd Rhys Williams, Earl of Pembroke

Daffyd has been earl for 11 years. Now age 41, he was one of the first noble-born elves. Daffyd is a passionately Green politician, and uses his great influence in the House of Nobles to further environmental causes. His popularity with the Green Party and the druids is distinctly low, however. For one thing, he has powerful political links with Tir Tairngire, and his association with his cousin, the unpredictable Duchess of Snowdon, makes him untrustworthy. He is also known to have long-standing family investments in Germany and Japan, and has a reputation for being a skilled and somewhat devious operator despite his apparent political naiveté. His dynastic marriage to Alicia, eldest daughter and only child of the aged Baron of Cheshire, is also seen as a shrewd way to expand his power and influence.

Rhiannon Glendower, Duchess of Snowdon

The brilliant and dazzling figure of this wild elven noble has broken the hearts of half the male nobles of Britain. Rhiannon is certainly a powerful hermetic mage, with great enchanting skill, but her personal magic also weaves its spells. At 27, she is a young noble, and her adopted name reflects her identification with the wild elves of north Wales and their heartland Gwynedd. Within her domain are the orichalcum deposits of Snowdonia, fiercely protected by elves and mercenaries in her service. She is known to have many personal links with powerful elves and mages in Tir Tairngire, possibly with the Shidhe of Tir Nan Og, and even the wild shamanic druids of Caithness and Moray. She uses her personal wiles to influence nobles to support Welsh, metahuman, and environmental causes, but is not a tactful or patient person.

>>>>>[Ah, sweet lady of my dreams. I once beheld her standing alone on her balcony at Harlech Castle, looking out over Tremadoc Bay on a cloudy, starless night; and as I looked, a single moonbeam shone from a tiny parting in the clouds and wreathed her face in its glow. Not even John Donne could have done justice to what I felt. She's a true free spirit.]<<<<<
—Admirer (23:15:44/9-FEB-52)

>>>>>[Does this man realize what he just said?]<<<<<
—Gwalchmai ap Gwyr (23:16:12/9-FEB-52)

>>>>>[Of course not. He's too romantic for that.]<<<<<
—Deborah D. (23:16:55/9-FEB-52)

>>>>>[Ha! Romance is just love before it's had time to go wrong.]<<<<<
—Slammer (00:08:07/10-FEB-52)

Edward Symington, Marquis of Sherwood

Owner of considerable tracts of land in the Birmingham industrial district as well as a major shareholder in IWS, Symington is an elf manqué. In his padded silk smoking jackets and formal tuxedos, he is the English gentleman par excellence. Some elves consider him a traitor to elven interests. On the other hand, it is undoubtedly true that this soft-spoken and persuasive elf has more influence with human nobles than most of his race. He also has a "personal staff" of mixed metahuman blood (including at least three orks) who have a reputation for being vigilant and loyal researchers. Certainly, Symington is rich and unusually well-informed.

>>>>>[Don't be fooled by the image. Symington is one sharp pixie. He knew about the Mogadishu supergun even before British Intelligence did, and he had the plans by the time they knew about it. His use of money to support metahuman causes across the developing world is equally clever and well-hidden. Not all of it is his, either, but that's another story.]<<<<<
—Mole Man (13:06:33/11-FEB-52)

Hamish Campbell, Earl of Dundee

The irascible 77-year-old 17th Earl is a legend in his own lifetime. Through his father's and his own efforts, he owns half of Scotsprawl, and many of the great castles of Scotland—as long as tourists are willing to pay to see them, that is. Although a Scot, Campbell has little time for the Scottish shamanic druids, whom he views as feckless amateurs. He has also had run-ins with them over their transformation of his coniferous forests. Campbell is actually a high-ranking member of the English druidic groupings.

George Matthews, Duke of Newcastle

This dashing young noble, in his 25th year, is the heartthrob of young debs everywhere. Immaculately groomed and manicured, he is the archetypal charming Englishman. Obviously, he doesn't live in the grime and squalor of Tynesprawl, preferring a Hampstead residence, where his existence is cushioned by some 28 servants. Matthews looks smooth and somewhat vacuous, but he is a vicious racist and a cutthroat businessman. His anti-metahuman instincts are a well-kept secret, but he certainly channels funds to Alamos 20,000, the Spanish Racial Purity Commandos, and other equally squalid groups. His major investments are in ATT, IWS, and other communications and armaments corporations in Europe and the Far East. He is known to be an important supporter of George VIII.

>>>>>[This roller is slime. He's a straight emotional fascist; he beats up on women, he's a racist and metaphobe, and he's got a collection of guns you wouldn't believe. The dogs on the country estate in Cumbria are brainchipped for maniacal aggression. This man needs wraithing.]<<<<<
—MesoStim (22:05:21/11-FEB-52)

>>>>>[You're too kind to him. I got a word for his friends. TOXICS.]<<<<<
—Mole Man (14:42:53/12-FEB-52)

>>>>>[Mention that again and it won't be Newcastle who gets wraithed, friend. Keep your head together here.]<<<<<
—Phantom (15:32:02/12-FEB-52)

Francesca Hamilton, Duchess of Cambridge

Tragically widowed by the death of her husband Charles in 2050, the Duchess of Cambridge is one of the most eligible ladies (at 32) in the land. Although not politically powerful or influential, she has a string of excellent commercial and stock holdings in powerful megacorporations such as Transys Neuronet and Zeta-ImpChem, and in foreign corporations on the cutting edge of technological advance. Her younger brother Simeon is a financial whiz kid who has made her one of the three richest women in Britain.

LIVING THE NOBLE LIFE

Nobles who do not have much money are still nobles, still regarded as aristocrats by the general population. But those nobles with serious money live a unique lifestyle, and some of them have truly serious money (the Duke of Oxford earns more than 7 million nuyen a month in rents from his London properties alone).

These rich nobles divide their time between their London homes and their country homes, which occupy vast acreages in the few unpolluted areas of the British countryside. The London "Season" begins on the first day after Easter Monday and lasts until late July; this is much the same as the first session of Parliament (although it extends later). If one is an important noble or someone aspiring to that status, this is the time to Be Seen. The most important events of The Season are a series of glitzy private (and ultra-select) balls at private homes, ultra-luxury hotels, and gentlemen's clubs, the new productions of major operatic and ballet works, Royal Academy exhibitions, Ascot and the Derby (horse racing), and the Eton versus Harrow cricket match (played between the two British public schools).

The balls are the main events, serving primarily to provide the daughters of the nobles, usually cocooned in the safety of country homes (not least because of kidnappers), with the chance to "come out" (as debutantes, or debs, in semi-vulgar parlance) and meet eligible young men. Marriages contracted usually have less to do with love than with dynastic suitability and political advancement. There is also an element of old heredity meeting new money, as some recently titled and very rich folk get invited to some of the lesser events, where their offspring may be able to buy the hand of some hapless offspring of an impoverished old noble house. Even the odd American might get in if he is extraordinarily rich and has a pretty enough daughter.

The daughters of the wealthy also get presented to the king and queen at Court. This happens at The Palaces, and is done through an introduction from someone who has, in turn, already been presented. The etiquette relating to such introductions is complex, indeed, and requires days of expert coaching.

>>>>>[Runners are not likely to find themselves within sniffing distance of an invitation to one of the events of The Season, but because balls and celebrations require a small army of casual labour for support (people to erect marquee tents for outdoor dances, caterers, and footservants, and so on), there is always a way to get into them. Alternatively, runners can always try entering domestic service as footmen or butlers!]<<<<<
—Woggle (06:25:44/13-FEB-52)

>>>>>[Oh how obvious.]<<<<<
—Stooge (22:13:55/17-FEB-52)

Out in the country, the ancient pursuit of fox and deer hunting (in the handful of estates where foxes or deers still exist and the terrain is unpolluted) is still practiced. The colourful sight of red-jacketed sportsmen riding out on horseback in jodhpurs and peaked caps, their hounds baying, is still a much-photographed sight and one that attracts sightseers.

>>>>>[So it's great to hunt down and butcher some wretched, defenceless creature, huh? Well, this pastime has lost popularity since the spectacularly successful Deep Green action of 2049 in which 31 members of the nobility were killed by the forests of Dartmoor. The successful use of airburst frag grenades with nerve gas droplet spray augmentation marked a striking escalation in Deep Green technological application. So, nobles now tend to stay in their well-secured country houses, eating and drinking too much and indulging in recreational BTL chipping and pharmaceutical abuse, emerging only for a half-drunken game of croquet or some similarly effete pastime now and again.]<<<<<
—Grenadine (01:16:43/3-APR-52)

>>>>>[And last year the Bodmin Hunt happened to ride right into a pack of those nice paranormals, black dogs, hell hounds, whatever you want to call 'em. Not much left of the bleeders after that. I felt a bit sorry for the horses, though.]<<<<<
—Deep Green (01:18:11/3-APR-52)

COUTTS &

FitzHerbert

DOMESTIC PLACEMENT AGENCY

Where Good Breeding Counts.

GRAZERS
ELECTRONICS
BTG# 715 (895-0779)

Peppermint
T·w·i·s·t

114 Knightsbridge   BTG#715 (909-3890)

UNLEASH YOUR INNER ABILITIES!

JOIN THE UNIVERSAL BROTHERHOOD TO BUILD A BETTER TOMORROW!

 VISIT ONE OF OUR U.K. BRANCHES TODAY FOR A FREE
TOUR AND SEMINAR. LEARN HOW TO FEEL GOOD ABOUT
YOUR LIFE AND THE PEOPLE AROUND YOU.
MAKE THE BEST DECISION OF YOUR LIFE TODAY!

THE DRUIDS

The druids are major players in the British political game. They control the Green Party, have stakes in many megacorporations, have sympathizers among those nobles not actively hostile to them, and have very powerful mages and rich resources. British druidism is a complex entity, with its own strong divisions and schisms.

>>>>>[What exactly is a druid anyway? Are they politicians or guys who run around stone circles in weird white frocks on Midsummer's Day?]<<<<<
—Chuck Odom (19:13:07/15-FEB-52)

>>>>>[Good question. The English druids are politicians and powermongers first and foremost. They're a sort of Masonic group, with lots of orders of initiation and occult trappings and lodges. Well, they're called lodges, but the mages among them are hermetics, not shamans with medicine lodges. At least, most of 'em are. They're into magic pretty heavily, but not shamanic nature magic; that's strictly for tourists, so far as English druids are concerned. One or two of them are a bit esoteric, but it's not compulsory. The Welsh, or Celtic, druids are strange. They're very friendly with the elves and the Awakened of Gwynedd and they have a lot of shamans with odd totems. They say there are Welsh Grand Druids with a Dragon totem, and they are serious people. The Scots druids, up in the Wild Lands, they're crazy men, shamans and avengers, promising uprising and regrowth and renewal of the land through blood. They're the least organized, but there are some weird paranormal creatures in the lochs up there and you don't want to get too close to what they do with them.]<<<<<
—IC-Hammer (19:16:44/15-FEB-52)

>>>>>[Oh, be reasonable. The druids are also concerned with education and philanthropy; they organize a lot of adult education and literacy classes for the underprivileged.]<<<<<
—Seer (21:25:23/15-FEB-52)

>>>>>[Looks like one of the druids' media officers just crawled into the Matrix. Got a good trace and some hot black anyone? Fancy a whiteline around here?]<<<<<
—Hal (21:33:32/15-FEB-52)

>>>>>[That's not funny. Not even with a druid.]<<<<<
—Slammer (21:35:11/15-FEB-52)

NEW DRUIDIC MOVEMENT

The New Druidic Movement (NDM) of Britain is the governing force of the ruling Green Party, and the druids have a thorough grip on Parliamentary power. The NDM is a British movement, with the vast majority of its members English; the Celtic druids stand outside of this structure. The NDM recruits by invitation only, and power radiates from the central circles of power to the outer fringes. These outer fringes are composed of people of some rank, (professional) skill, influence, or wealth who are invited to join the Druidic Lodges that exist in almost every town or city of any size at all. At this level, druidism has three orders of membership (initiate, member, and adept) with rituals for attaining each order. It bears a notable resemblance to the Freemasons, which it has superceded. The emphasis is on sharing resources with fellow NDM members in need, and also a reverence for the British (really English) heritage and the need to protect the land. An ever so slightly esoteric doctrine is pumped out to the adepts; this revolves around Sun/Moon symbolisms, the notion of the Inner Sun of Man and the Inner Moon of Womanhood. It's faintly nostalgic, vaguely chauvinistic, and not very authentic in terms of its symbolisms, but is relatively harmless and lets middle-aged men eat and drink too much in fairly convivial surroundings once a month or so.

Of far more importance are the Inner Circles of the NDM. Membership in these is also by invitation only and most of the outer fringes (and most of the general population) are not aware that these Inner Circles exist, or at least have little idea of how powerful they are or what form they take. The Inner Circles are the real powerhouse of the druids, being comprised of some nobles, men of major political and economic power, and others with military or informational resources or magical skills. The term druid is really only correctly applied to the leaders of the Inner Circles; these men are known usually to each other, and always to the so-called Grand Druid of Britain, currently the Earl of Dundee. The "Grand Druid of Britain" is not really the major force in the NDM, however, because the non-English druids do not affiliate with the Inner Circle groupings. Besides, the Earl of Dundee is an old man now. Lord Marchment, the Lord Protector, is the effective leader of the British druids. Members of the Inner Circles, each with some 6 to 20 members, are secretive about their membership. A coded system of secret hand signs stolen from Freemasonry allows them to recognize each other in public if the need is dire.

The Inner Circles are what English druidism is really about. The same themes of English nationalism, preservation of the land, and group fraternity (plus the frisson of magical power) are the apparent basis for the druids' existence. But the truth is that power is what the druids seek most, often for its own ends.

And the political and economic power held by the Inner Circles is very great. Probably some 20 percent of the Green Party's noble and MP support, including at least three ministers of state, are members of druidic Inner Circles (and many others are members of the outer fringes). Company directors and major stockholders of all major U.K.-owned megacorporations are members of Inner Circles. As usual in Britain, it is impossible to get exact figures and lists of names.

>>>>>[But you can try. Look at the Foreign Office for one sure-fire druid; he's one of the Primrose Hill Lodge. The druids have Grenville-Adams in their claws, that's for sure, because they runaround stick ownership among themselves—actually that's a good way to catch them if you can follow the cascades fast enough. Three of the eight corporate-division directors of HKB are druids. And isn't it funny how weapons testing by IWS is subject to special restrictions on certain dates of the year? You know, those festival days when the big noises are all down at the country estates and stone circles. Oh, and the UCAS ambassador got invited to Lugnasad down at Stonehenge last week. Don't those people make the nicest tourists?]<<<<<
—Mole Man (18:32:05/16-FEB-52)

DRUIDS AS MAGES

It is certain that many Inner Circles contain a number of practicing mages, and in other cases, hermetic circles are maintained permanently at Druidic Grand Lodges (where Inner Circles meet). The British government actually pays the salaries of many of them via the Lord Protector's office. The identities of these unusual wage mages are protected for reasons of "national security." As a group, the Inner Circles have the following profile:

MUSIC• DANCING • REGURGITATION • 2 •EXCESS

London falling...
...nightly.

Type: Conspiratorial (temporal power)
Members: U.K. total, estimated 870 (mages only)
Limitations: Biological (humans only). Moral limitations are actually very weak with druids; English druids are highly pragmatic.
Strictures: Attendance. Fraternity. Obedience. Link. Secrecy.
Resources/Dues: Luxury. Actually, resources beyond luxury. Being able to call on some 2,000 mercenaries and tactical air support count as better than luxury. Dues are high, and special funding may be requested.
Customs: See below.

Druidic mage groups have grades of initiation. The preferred ordeals are those of oath and thesis, with research into metamagic an especially preferred form of thesis research. Asceticism is acceptable only for those druids who live unusually sheltered lives (e.g., as directors of research laboratories). The Lord Protector is believed to be an eleventh-grade initiate, and the Earl of Dundee a tenth-grade initiate. Druidic circles dislike geasa because of its limitations on the individual mage's freedom of action (and thus on how he may best serve druidic interests).

DRUIDIC GRAND LODGES

A certain number of druidic lodges are Grand Lodges that are foci for powerful magical Background Count. (For more on Background Count, see p. 145). These lodges are located on ley lines, and usually at such sites as ancient stone circles, barrows, and great castles that lie on these ley lines. Ley lines are straight lines connecting a number of such ancient sites along a line of magical power, visible to the astral perceiver as a sinuous and pulsing artery of raw, potential, magical energy. Only when a ley line is focused at an ancient site of power is Background Count effective, and only druidic mages know the secrets of its use. A druidic Inner Circle member must be at least a second-grade initiate to be able to use this Background Count. Other mages cannot use or even affect the energies of ley lines. The magical force of these lines is endless centuries deep, and though the Sixth World may be able to recognize their energies, no one can affect them much.

These Grand Lodges are in turn divided into two groups. A small number are aligned on the great leys of England and Wales, shown in the ley map in this book. Four great leys are known to the English druids: the Stalker ley, the Royal ley, the Stonehenge ley, and the May ley.

At each named site there is a Druidic Grand Lodge protected by heavy security; a force of at least 20 well-armed and armoured men, a forest of electronic surveillance, and a strong hermetic circle. The place swarms with watchers. Warwick Castle is the best-defended site in the whole of Britain, including the Royal Palaces. The other Grand Lodges are all aligned on minor leys, ley lines that extend for significantly shorter distances than the hundreds of miles of the great leys and do not have the same magical charge (and hence the sites on them have a lower

Background Count). The most important other Grand Lodge is the central headquarters of the London druids in Primrose Hill.

All the Grand Lodges are located on unpolluted terrain (for a radius of at least one half-mile around; 4 miles in the case of Stonehenge). The sites, like the lodges themselves, are guarded by impressive security and are not open to the general public.

Stalker Ley

The Stalker ley runs from Beaumaris Castle in North Wales, through Blaenau Ffestiniog and its orichalcum mines, to Llandridnod Wells, where the Welsh Grand Druid holds court, to Caerleon, which is a ley nexus, down through Glastonbury Tor (a second ley nexus), the Naked Giant of Cerne Abbas, and then to the Sunken Island in the English Channel (another ley nexus).

Royal Ley

This ley runs from Tintagel and Merlin's Cave in Cornwall, to Caerleon once again, through the site of the Banbury (standing) Stone, and on to Warwick Castle, the First Lodge of the English druids and the residence of the Lord Protector.

Stonehenge Ley

The Stonehenge ley runs from the Sunken Island through the steep-mounded Corfe Castle (rebuilt between 2005 and 2027), through the Knowlton Circles and Stonehenge and on to the Rollright Stones of Oxfordshire.

May Ley

This ley runs from Marazion in Cornwall, through Glastonbury and the stone circle at Avebury (where the druids have a particularly fine guarded manor house), and on to Royston, where an exceptionally powerful druidic hermetic circle is located at the site of an ancient burial ground. This ley lies on a meridian that exactly matches the point on the horizon at which the sun rises over the East Coast on May Day (1 May).

DRUIDIC HIDDEN CIRCLES

A tiny fraction of the Inner Circles are more correctly termed Hidden Circles. They feign acceptance of general druidic organization and principles, but are secretly contemptuous of the Lord Protector. They believe that English druidism has become too concerned with temporal power for its own sake, having lost sight of its sacred mission to renew the land. The Hidden Circles strive to do just this by more radical means than orthodox druidism allows. First, they covertly support eco-terrorism, including the funding of foreign groups. Second, they fund and support Deep Green groups, including propagandists, direct-action activists, and Matrix anarchists (who specialize in random data-destruction, virus seeding, and so on) and information-gatherers. The Hidden Circles may support the Deep Green because their nature is truly radical or perhaps because they want Deep Greens to create a backlash against weak government that could sweep a draconian one (with their man the Lord Protector at the helm) into power. There is a further dangerous side to these Hidden Circles: just as they wish to purge the British

land of impurities, so many of them also wish to rid British blood of the "impurity" of metahuman genes.

Last, these Inner Circles include a minority of shamanic initiates of an especially dangerous kind: the toxic shamans. Usually, these are avenger shamans who live on the country estates of rich (usually noble) Inner Circle druids, directing their magical arts from this base. A handful are poisoner shamans who direct retributive magical strikes against targets perceived as hostile to the health of the environment, exploiters and defilers. Given that the more extreme toxics have only the shakiest hold on sanity, their strikes have sometimes generalized into an attack on populations generally. One Inner Circle is known to hold the view that, because overpopulation is the prime cause of pollution, some rapid biological action to reduce population drastically is the most effective Green action possible. The Chancellery Net contains data pertaining to the para-VITAS outbreak in Tynesprawl of 2047 that strongly suggest that toxic shamans associated with a prominent English druid were responsible. Bringing the criminals to justice would have exposed the druid and scandalized the population against the Green Party; the druids could not allow that, so the affair was carefully hushed up.

The Inner Circles are dangerous, even deadly opponents for runners. The insanity of their toxics and their possible manipulation by or association with sinister paranatural forces (the involvement of wendigos, vampires, and vengeful spectres have been rumoured), allied with their resources of money, influence, and muscle, are a frightening combination, indeed.

>>>>>[Word is that one of these Hidden Circles is allied with the rival bloodline to the throne, or at least is using this as a pretext for furthering its own ends.]<<<<<
—Debrett (11:17:45/14-FEB-52)

>>>>>[I heard that, too. I also heard that this group is involved in human sacrifice, blood to be spilled to save the earth and all that sick stuff.]<<<<<
—MesoStim (17:32:56/14-FEB-52)

DRUIDIC FESTIVALS AND INSIGNIA

Druids celebrate four major feast days during the year. These are: Imbolc (February 1), Beltane (31 April), Lugnasad (1 August), and Samhain (1 November). The backbone of these celebrations are bardic recitals, the celebration of dawn at stone circles and standing stones and other sacred sites, and feasting. The Inner Circles perform their rituals secretly, and these almost certainly involve ritual magic: at any site on a ley line, the Background Count is increased by +1 from dusk to dawn on these dates. Other druids perform nonmagical ceremonies that are usually open to public attendance. The celebration of Beltane at Glastonbury Tor (a ley nexus on the May ley, so the sun rises over the ley meridian at dawn) is the most important single event of the druidic calendar.

>>>>>[Good for the tourist trade. I love those cute little pointy hats the old ones wear and they do look cute in those long white robes.]<<<<<
—AKA-47 (19:19:42/17-FEB-52)

>>>>>[CUTE? We've got a sep jacking in here. But he obviously has a soft spot for the sandals.]<<<<<
—IC-Hammer (20:32:42/17-FEB-52)

The Inner Circle wear simple, functional white robes at these events, marked with their grade of initiation. This is denoted by a simple symbol displayed on the left breast within a simple circular patch design:

Grade 0 initiates display a blank, sky blue circle.

Grade 1 initiates wear a sky blue patch with a golden sun just right of centre.

Grade 2 initiates wear a deep azure patch with a silver crescent moon just left of centre.

Grade 3 initiates wear a black patch with a single seven-pointed star at the zenith.

Grade 4 initiates wear a royal blue patch with a central golden sun.

Grade 5 initiates wear a blue-edged white patch with a central golden sun eclipsed by a silver full moon.

Grade 6 or higher initiates wear the same design as Grade 5 initiates, save that the eclipsed sun is displayed below the horizontal meridian of the badge, a yellow seven-pointed star is displayed above it, and the two symbols are contained within the figure-of-8 of a multi-coloured snake swallowing its own tail.

>>>>>[Very pretty, too. But what does it mean? Just some iconography for the tourists, huh, chummer?]<<<<<
—AKA-47 (21:16:24/17-FEB-52)

>>>>>[Spot the sep, OK. Well, no, try checking the standard interpretations of the Tarot major arcana sequence 17 through 19 and then 21 and 0. At least it'll keep you off the net for awhile.]<<<<<
—Spacer (21:19:32/17-FEB-52)

THE LORD PROTECTOR

The Lord Protector, sitting in his offices in Chancellery Lane or relaxing in the sumptuous surroundings of Warwick Castle, is the most powerful man in England. He is also the most powerful druidic mage in England, and can command unbelievable resources. The 17th Earl of Marchment, born 1994, is a man still at the peak of his powers.

Marchment himself is an imposing man: just over 6'4", he is aquiline, slim, elegant, and always immaculately (and conservatively) groomed. He rarely appears in public, save to make a speech on major occasions of state in the House of Nobles. When he does, his carefully coifed blond locks and blue-grey eyes make him look some 15 years younger than his real age. He has few friends outside the major Inner Circles of the druids, save for such mundane folk as the King, the Prime Minister, the ambassadors of several major world powers (including the Republic of Moscow, UCAS, and the CAS), and major corporate powers such as Paul Bernal, Jr. of the HKB megacorporation.

The Lord Protector's Offices have five different divisions. These are usually referred to as Bureaux, but in one case as a Directorate and in another as a Board (just to keep things slightly confused). All have their headquarters in the Chancellery Lane complex. These five divisions are the Licensing Bureau, the Oversight Board, the Information Directorate, the Education Bureau, and the Administrative Bureau.

LICENSING BUREAU

This division is responsible for administering all forms of licensing of restricted products and services. That includes the licensing and registration of mages and the collection of DNA samples (allowing the use of ritual magic, evocation, and commandment of watchers to follow the mage, and similar activities that may be useful to the security services), licensing of personal cyberware, the registration of patents relating to all forms of cyberware, personal-enhancement technology and Matrix technology, biotechnology, and lots else besides. Listing all the restricted products and services in Britain today would be almost an impossibility. If in doubt, it is restricted. And if it is restricted, the Licensing Bureau (or the Administrative Bureau) deals with it. If someone is not sure whether he will get a license for what he wants, the probability is 90 percent or more that he will not. And no, these people cannot be bribed at all easily…

OVERSIGHT BOARD

The Oversight Board is a rather sinister organization that investigates more or less anything it chooses in the interests of "national security." While the SAS are officially under the jurisdiction of the Ministry of Defence, it is an open secret that they act as one of the active arms of the Oversight Board when direct action (i.e., killing people) is considered necessary. The Oversight Board is usually brought into play when British law cannot actually stop someone from doing what he wants to do, but who the Lord Protector (or someone important who appeals to him for a favour) would like to put a stop to. This can be anything from building a chicken shed at the back of a sleazy hovel to owning some software for which a license was given (perhaps as the result of a bribe). The action the board takes can vary from drowning its victims in paperwork to sending the SAS after them. The Oversight Board is perfectly capable of functioning in error ("Oh, that's Thompson without a 'p'? Dreadfully sorry, Mrs. Thomson. We'll look after the hospital bills.").

INFORMATION DIRECTORATE

This division is responsible for the maintenance of the Chancellery Net, the part of the Matrix containing supersensitive information and a great deal more. Anyone who manages to get into this system has the major problem of avoiding the unimaginably vast areas of mundane information and getting to what he actually wants to find.

>>>>>[Ha! You'll never get anywhere near, not even a sniff. The black IC is unreal. It's layered in cascades, with a positive feedback subroutine system—several of the rakking things. Get past one death trap and four more are triggered; get past those four and you've got sixteen more hammering in at you. You can have all the enhancement implants, reflex-boosting, and skillsofts you like, the best cyberdeck out there, and real banging software, and you're still whitelined in milliseconds. Forget this one.]<<<<<
—Razzz (03:17:54/18-FEB-52)

>>>>>[Razzz does not, repeat NOT, spend time here, gentlemen. I know him from elsewhere and can vouch for his skills. If he says it is so, then believe that it is.]<<<<<
—Hampstead Hi-Jack (10:24:13/19-FEB-52)

EDUCATION BUREAU

This bureau oversees the approval of all secondary school (age 11–17) and university/polytechnic (higher education, 18+) syllabuses in Britain, appoints examiners for competitive examinations, and awards (or approves the awarding) certificates of achievement, degree titles, and the like. It is also ultimately responsible for appointing the most important figures in the educational system (headmasters at major secondary schools, including public schools, and senior/administrative professors at universities and state-sponsored research institutes). It is also responsible for the allocation of funds to different educational establishments, which gives it enormous power. This power is used for many purposes, not least to make sure that the Lord Protector's offices stay fully informed and have complete up-to-the-minute news of all forms of advances in research at higher education and research institutions. The notorious British "old-school-tie" network is maintained through this mechanism. Ex-pupils of public schools get jobs in this division and then use their power to further the interests of their schoolmates within the educational system (and usually this also has a strong overlap with membership in the NDM; it's a prime way of recruiting ex-public schoolboys into the druidic network).

ADMINISTRATIVE BUREAU

This is a living nightmare. The U.K. Constitution Act of 2025 defined the duties of this division so amorphously that almost anything is possible. How far these people stick their noses into other people's business depends on how aggressive and pushy the director of this bureau is at the time. The current director, Rupert Symonds, is an ambitious and punctilious man who treats self-advancement with all the serious dedication one would expect of a graduate of Eton and Oxford. The distinction between these people and the Oversight Board is fairly straightforward: the Oversight Board needs some kind of justification on paper for its actions. The Administrative Bureau does not. It can be nosy whenever it feels like it. But it is very slow, and certainly inefficient.

The Administrative and Education Bureaus jointly deal with the training of all governmental civil servants for an initial 12- or 24-month period. This ensures that these people (78 percent of whom are from public schools) have their group ethos even more tightly knit. It also develops the old-boy network throughout government departments, and ensures that the Lord Protector is well-informed about activities in all departments of national government.

The Administrative Bureau is headed by Sir Damian Green, the Lord Protector's PPS (Permanent Private Secretary). Green is a druid, a man of 48 years with perfect manners and grooming, the scion of a family from Somerset that can trace its ancestors back over 600 years. Below Green come six junior PPS (Personal Private Secretaries), and then the other myriad clerks, pen-pushers, and dogsbodies.

>>>>>[Rakk these guys. Here are some time-honoured ways of slowing them down so they operate on geological time:
—Write them (never fax or Matrix-page them, it's too fast), using made-up reference numbers to refer to the letters you never sent. It takes them weeks to find they haven't got them and then they think they've lost them so they get paranoid and scared.
—Write them and say you'll reply to their letter of (whenever) after you've buried your poor mother/father/wife/husband/girlfriend/boyfriend/goat because you're too distraught right now. That gets you an extra two weeks every time.
—Write and claim you have to be abroad on business vital to British-export interests for the next month. They never get round to checking it and everyone knows Britain lives by trade. This buys more time.
—Write and query their communication of (specify date, specify reference number). Use a reference number within their coding system, but make sure you don't have one the same. The effect is much the same as in option #1 above, although they tend to clear this one up faster. It's hilarious when they actually send a communication with the number you dreamed up.]<<<<<
—Mole Man (23:27:02/18-FEB-51)

THE DARK SIDE OF INSECTICIDE.

>>>>>[Some good hints there, people. Especially the quote-their-reference-number bit. Last time a friend of mine tried that, he got a copy of the reference communication, which turned out to be very sensitive material. Pertaining to someone's medical history, fascinating stuff. You wouldn't have expected a person in that position to have acquired something as distasteful as…let's just say my friend earned a few thousand sterling with no questions asked.]<<<<<
   —Snakeskin (02:04:06/19-FEB-52)

THE TEMPLARS

The popular slang term for agents of the Lord Protector's office is Templars, but this also corresponds to a far more sinister truth. Somewhere in the myriad complexity of the offices in the Temple is a subdivision of "Field Officers," which is never referred to among the other divisions. Even its funding is almost impossible to trace within the Chancellery Net itself. The field officers are directly responsible to Sir Damian Green. Their own head of operations and their identities are absolutely secret.

The Templars' official duties are to deal with all instances of reported illegal magical activities that may threaten national security (the usual catchall that allows them to do whatever they feel like doing). It is certain that among the Templars themselves there is a hermetic circle of major power, although whether they are actually druids is disputed. Any significant unlicensed magical operations will attract the Templars eventually. Many such operations cease without the people who performed them ever being visible again.

>>>>>[It's worse than that. If you ever manage to put together some idea of their operations, simply by keeping your neurons to the Matrix when reports of mages being boxed swirl around, you realize that a very, very high percentage of them are metahumans. These Templars have some very dubious ideas about Good Old English Racial Purity, right? Sometimes they are alerted by magic, but sometimes they go hunting, and if they catch a licensed elf mage or an ork shaman, so much the better. That's the word out, anyway.]<<<<<
   —Carol K (07:11:45/25-FEB-52)

>>>>>[The lady talks sense. Rhiannon's Knights of Harlech were created in part to keep the Templars at bay and to keep Gywnedd safe for us. Our people need other orders of protection of the same kind.]<<<<<
   —Aoibheil ap Laochilain (11:52:45/25-FEB-52)

POLICLUBS IN BRITAIN

Policlubs in Britain are a peculiar and diverse bunch. For the most part, they inflict severe cultural disorientation on foreign visitors. British people have no real tradition of political lobbying, pro- or anti-metahuman violence (outside of isolated racial ghetto areas and pockets of violence), and single-issue politics has never been an important feature of British political expression. So, British "policlubs" almost stretch the definition of this term to its wildest extremes; they are more refuges for eccentric hobbyists rather than anything else. Some have rich and/or influential backers and members, though, and visitors should be aware of them. Following are brief descriptions of the most important ones.

FRIENDS OF MARYLEBONE

This policlub seeks to preserve traditional forms of the ancient English game of cricket. It vigorously opposes all forms of skillsoft use in cricket, attempting to block such pollution of traditional sportsmanship by persuading owners of suitable venues not to lease them to cricket teams with skillsoft-augmented players, promoting "true, amateur" cricket, and generally appealing to the British sense of fair play. The membership is 100 percent male, has 17 percent noble membership, and owns sumptuous club premises in Primrose Hill. Membership is by invitation only and only true gentlemen are ever invited.

HEALTHY EATING GUIDE

This annual publication has become mandatory reading for almost the entire British population, and with a total staff of 355 researchers (and endless hangers-on involved in fringe activities and fund-raising), it is now a policlub, with nightly lectures, seminars, and learning experiences at country retreats for the more financially well-to-do. No British people actually base their eating habits on the HEG, but everyone buys it, and many people attend some of its activities because it makes their environmental sensibilities feel better.

Take one as needed for your good health

HEALTHY ◆ EATING
G ◆ U ◆ I ◆ D ◆ E
Eye on Potatoes

>>>>>[They're deeply nice people aren't they? Bunch of mellow rakkies. The truth is, if you read the guide what you get is all the obvious stuff. They publish fearless exposés of food contamination everyone knows about anyway, but they cover up the subtler things like the photochemical carcinogen hazard in United Meat Products' filth in 2044, the neuromodulator-inhibiting algal residues in Soy Joy pastas and pizzas in 2047, and the aluminium saturations in that tofu drek last year. Well, hell, if these people eat tofu, they deserve all they get, I reckon. But don't be fooled: Zeta-ImpChem secretly fund these people through a couple of their noble sponsors. Check it out.]<<<<<
—Deep Green (10:13:17/5-FEB-52)

GENEALOGY SOCIETY

Outside of private paramilitary organizations supported by fascistic anti-metahuman nobles and their ilk, this is the closest Britain gets to an actively anti-metahuman society. Nominally, this policlub is comprised of people who share an interest in tracing back their own ancestors and those of traditionally respected and/or noble British families (especially Men Who Made The Empire Great). They have branches in most major British cities, and though their membership is small (nationally some 14,000), their influence is felt and their resources are good. Once again, shadowy corporate and noble backers provide this policlub with a good supply of money and resources. An especially unpleasant and dangerous aspect of the Genealogy Society is its immense popularity with the agents of law enforcement in Britain; at least two chief constables, several deputy chief constables, and an uncertain number of the SAS hierarchy are, at the least, strongly sympathetic to this policlub. Terrorist bombings against metahuman properties and homes may very well reflect the logistic support such contacts can provide to the Genealogy Society.

The Genealogy Society is known to have particularly strong links with neo-Nazi German policlubs and paramilitary groups. It also, at the least, shares information with the notorious Humanis Policlub and uses its influence in certain quarters to obtain visas for North American visitors whose presence the U.K. would be better off without.

ANGLO-AMERICAN FRIENDSHIP SOCIETY

This policlub exists to maintain links between British citizens and those of UCAS, the CAS, and other North American states. Cultural exchanges, cheap group-purchased air travel, negotiated cheap rates on trans-Atlantic vidphone and other communication services, publishing, and similar "contact" activities are furthered by this apparently innocuous society. In its way, this society is almost a mirror-image to the Genealogy Society because its links with Tir Tairngire, the Salish-Shidhe Council, the Sioux nation, and other states fosters cultural tolerance and understanding. Several elven British nobles are known to fund this policlub.

BRITISH FOREIGN RELATIONS

Britain's political links with the rest of the world are obviously important in the global village of the current era. It is impossible to describe Britain's political relationships with every state in this fractured world, so this section focuses on the most important relationships Britain has in North America and Europe.

BRITAIN AND EUROPE

France

The traditional enmity between England and France is reflected in their current political relations, which are a form of cold war. The Chunnel is heavily guarded at both British and French ends, and security checks are fierce. Security and monitoring of airspace and sea space across the English Channel are extraordinarily strict.

The recrudescence of this ancient enmity came with the withdrawal of Britain from the EEC and the events of the Euro Wars. No one can be certain from where came the *Nightwraith* bombers that ended the major European involvement in these wars, but Anglo-French relations became glacial from then on. The French are widely believed to have covertly supported the alleged Pan-Europa strike against London in 2039, if it was not actually the work of their own agents. The Green Party and the druids are very suspicious of French ruling aristocrats forming some kind of alliance with British nobles to strengthen general noble rule; very few British nobles, however, regard their French counterparts with any positive feeling. As always, the general population of Britain dislikes French people, and such anomalies as French restaurants and businesses need to pay high premiums to their insurers.

Germany

Britain has reasonably cordial ties with the fragmented German states. Industrial ties are strong, and Britain imports a significant quantity of manufactures and consumer goods from North Germany in particular. Intelligence-sharing between Germany and Britain is practiced so far as anarchist and neo-anarchist German decker/rigger groups are concerned, and general anti-terrorist surveillance is shared. Britain is ever alert for any sign of Germany becoming politically over-powerful; however, current cordial relations depend on the relative weakness of the German state.

Switzerland

Links with Switzerland are of major importance to the city of London and the financial corporations there. Switzerland is the focus for international control of the money supply and stabilizing the value of the nuyen, and so has a pivotal role in worldwide economics. The semi-invisible Swiss banks, clearinghouses, and financial institutions have considerably greater power than they care to use, and if the financial data one seeks is not somewhere in the Swiss Matrix, then it almost certainly does not exist. Britain has cordial relations with the Swiss, and the marriage in 2051 of Princess Caroline to Jurgen Meier, a Swiss banking magnate, has helped strengthen these links.

Italy

Governmental links with Italy are polite, but marked by suspicion on the British side. Trade links are weak, but there is a burgeoning black market for imports of Italian demi-tech, BTL chips, and general consumer goods. Save for the BTL chips, this will never be a major market attracting high-profile British criminals because there is not much money in demi-tech. There is a more sinister and growing market for body tissues imported into Italy from cheap sources in Africa and the Islamic states; Italy is the prime European import country and distribution centre for these grisly products.

The Papal state shares with British royalty a love of pageantry and ceremony and its links with British human hereditary nobles (many of whom are still at least nominally adherents to the Catholic faith) are long-established and powerful.

>>>>>[Word is, those nobles who are also druids are into the whole Templar thing up to the elbows. The kind of druids who don't like metahumans, right? The really serious hermetics are in with these kiss-the-tarmac clerics. Heavy magic.]<<<<<
—Orange Man (17:32:15/4-MAR-52)

>>>>>[Gentlemen, don't believe everything you read here. As but one example, the Earls of Camarthen have been devout Catholics for over 400 years, so it's not so surprising that the current earl seeks an audience with the Pope from time to time. Certainly, the Templars have friends among the British nobility. But it would be most surprising were it otherwise.]<<<<<
—Hampstead Hi-Jack (11:11:27/5-MAR-52)

The Eastern States

Relations with the Polish Union and the various former Soviet nations are cordial, but detached. Some industrial trading on a technological level occurs with Poland, but little beyond textiles and liquors actually exchanges hands. Moscow and her associated states continue to smile diplomatically, but nothing is accomplished beyond the pleasantries because of Moscow's lingering concern over the *Nightwraith* affair.

NORTH AMERICAN STATES

The most important of these, for business and politics, is the United Canadian and American States, UCAS. Historically, Britain has strong links with Canada and a "special relationship" with the old U.S.A.; and British corporates still own about 10 percent of UCAS economic capacity. The neutrality of American forces during the Euro Wars did not help this relationship, but it did not destroy it either because Britain was only a reluctant participant in that conflict. The British still use American military technology, and they continue as favoured clients for high-tech arms sales in specific areas such as anti-missile-missile killing systems. The UCAS remains a major import and export market for Britain, and many people in each country have relatives and/or ancestors in the other. The same is true of the Confederated American States (CAS), but to a somewhat lesser extent (except for British tourists, a common sight in the sunshine belt there). Of the other North American states, the most important relationship is the well-known affinity between British elven nobles and Tir Tairngire.

CARIBBEAN LEAGUE

Britain has historical links with these states, having been responsible for importing much of their population as slaves way back and then re-importing them into Britain as cheap labour for menial jobs in the 1950s and early 1960s. This wave of immigrants are the ancestor of many of the blacks living in London and inner-city areas of other British cities (an exception is Liverpool, where the black community is of much longer standing). Britain still provides a major export market for Caribbean products, provides some economic and development aid, and most important of all, still competes with the Caribbean League at cricket.

RACIAL POLITICS AND RELATIONSHIPS

Britain has two categories of racial divisions: human-metahuman and human-ethnic. In both cases, British attitudes and behaviours are quite different to those that exist in American states. There is no significant history of extreme attitudes or overt violence in Britain. It is not conceivable that, in the U.K., the Awakening could have fractionated the nation into a whole variety of states, as in the American states. British elves are happy to keep "human" names and their positions in society, and feel no need to form a new nation. The northern dwarfs do not want a separate society, but rather to transform the one in which they live. The London orks have found various niches of their own. And so on.

On the other hand, institutional racism is endemic in Britain. Elves suffer least, because of their concentration in the nobility and because their physical appearance is most appealing to humans. Trolls actually do rather well in employment, their extraordinary physical powers guaranteeing them good work and a fair standard of living, but they suffer social discrimination. Such discrimination is always well-mannered and polite, but it is ostracization all the same. Dwarfs have managed to get into positions of some authority and power in the north of England, where they are most common, and the Lord Mayor of Tynesprawl is a dwarf, as are six of the twelve members of Parliament elected from central Tynesprawl. The general (human) British public regards dwarfs as good workers who earn what they get in life, and therefore accepts them (faintly grudgingly). Orks are the bottom of the pile. They do not have the brute strength of trolls, they are not especially smart, and they are not pretty to look at. Nobody likes orks all that much.

Though these are generalizations, they represent widely held views among the Brits. Such opinions are not usually expressed publicly and/or vehemently, but most Brits are closet racists, just as most are actually awful snobs.

There are also "metahuman-racial" communities, metahumans derived from ethnic subgroups who have a distinct identity of their own. The Black Orks of Merseysprawl and the Indian Orks of Covent Garden are two examples of this. These groups seem to possess a strong, vibrant cultural identity, but they tend to be clannish and self-sufficient. Human reactions to them are, if anything, slightly less prejudiced than toward the racial or metahuman strain to which the group belongs, perhaps because these folk are so truly different that they are dismissed as a threat.

THE BIG PICTURE

It is impossible to calculate the British gross national product. The government does not publish exact figures for tax revenues and levies for reasons of "national financial security." This also helps the government to practice covert expenditures without their being traced. Megacorporations can easily shuffle monies around national boundaries, and Anglo-Swiss contacts are particularly vital in this context. Nobody can be sure what the Brits are worth.

>>>>>[Yeah, and that's before you get into looking at foreign sterling balances, Brit ownership of foreign economic production—HKB and Grenville-Adams own an estimated 6 percent of UCAS productive capacity—or the cascade chains of GA or a hundred and one other indirect control paths. You can't know what these people own half the time. Try jacking and you can get brain-fried before you even figure out how to ask the right questions.]<<<<<
—PRN (05:15:43/7-JAN-52)

Britain has some heavy manufacturing industry, mostly localized in the West Midlands and the north of England. The weakest industries in the U.K. economy are: motor (car/automobile and bike) manufacture, steel manufacture, large electrical goods (trideo, freezers, washing machines, and so on), and heavy industrial component industries. These are mostly imported, partly from Germany and Poland and partly from the Far East and North American sources. On the other hand, heavy industrial plants for U.K. use, experimental and highly technical machine-tooled equipment, and quality/prestige manufactures are made at home. These are exported largely to the European and richer southern-hemisphere countries. Less than 5 percent of the working population has employment in heavy industry.

Light industry and research installations are a major feature of the U.K. A skilled labour pool at "white collar" manual (and controlled-robotic) tasks has traditionally been strong. Though U.K.-based megacorps at times seem insular, they are usually well-entrenched in covert linkages and often have their elite skilled work force trained outside the U.K., and/or trained by top foreign technical instructors imported for the purpose. Research obviously shades from technical into service (hardware into software and logistics, ergonomics, and the like), where Britain is also economically very powerful. The traditional British supply of economic services in the City of London has expanded and grown, not least through strong Anglo-Swiss cooperation. It is also diversified and interlinked with software design, experimental cyberware design and testing, and a dozen other research areas. Pure research tends to be conducted mostly in the south of England, at certain northern universities, and at Silicon Glen in Scotsprawl.

Major areas of British economic strength are: armaments (manufacture and design), cyberware (manufacture and especially design), and experimental cyberware and communication systems (all aspects). British arms are highly reliable and durable and shipped to anyone and everyone who can afford to pay for them. British expertise covers the full range, from pistols to APDS ammo to tanks, laser cannon, and chemical weaponry. Finally, the major strength of the British economy is its extraordinary spread across the world. The British government and U.K. megacorporations own little chunks of people everywhere.

Britain's economic weaknesses are its feeble manufacturing base, leaving it at the mercy of foreign suppliers, and the fact that it now grows only enough food to feed about 80 percent of its people. This is a consequence of gross pollution of agricultural land. The worst case is the destruction of the East Anglian grain belt, where nitrate poisoning and chemical dumping have destroyed huge regions of farmland in the last 40 years. The fact that the chemical dumping has usually been of low-grade waste suggests very strongly that one aim was to open up the farmlands for construction of research installations in the area. Since much light industry, U.K. (and old UCAS) air bases, and major university sites were already in the area, this made excellent economic sense. After food prices went up generally, it also gave the same megacorps the financial room to produce and market synthetic and algae/fungal-based products at economically viable prices. Nothing pays like a little economic stimulus, after all.

>>>>>[Yes, but Zeta-ImpChem went a little over the top with the North Cambridge dumping of 2012–13. They messed up the nitrate saturation by an order of magnitude, and the stuff got stored somewhere a little messy and they got a whole sludgeful of free radicals, nitrosamines, and every kind of chemical crap. They used to say it was hard to understand the Fenlanders round there because of inbreeding—like they usually say about any rural community, let alone the poor bastards in the Stinkfens. But I reckon if I hear anyone making a jokey comment about one of their children without proper limbs, that comedian will get some teeth knocked down his throat. This is where corporate profit really comes from.]<<<<<
—Deep Green (11:16:37/15-JAN-52)

MAJOR CORPORATIONS

Major British corporations fall into two categories; the foreign-based megacorporations and those primarily U.K.-owned and managed. The intense secrecy of British corps and the absence of statutes forcing them to supply information serve to restrict access to knowledge of their operations and makes exact figures, information on subsidiary ownership, and the like very hard to come by. Corporations and companies do have to register with and supply information to the Companies Directorate of the Lord Protector's Office, but the Lord Protector does not have to supply this information to anyone else (except for the prime minister and the Minister of State for Trade and Industry).

FOREIGN-OWNED CORPORATIONS

Of the major multinationals, virtually all (except Gaeatronics) have some presence in the U.K. With only three exceptions, however, they are not of major importance and their U.K. operations are both small-scale and not innovative. The exceptions are Aztechnology, Fuchi, and Renraku. For political and espionage reasons, ATT, a German-owned subsidiary, is also important.

As for corporate militaries, the Brits don't like corporate armies, and so such forces have to be kept small, clandestine, or very much in-house as security organizations. The few exceptions are noted below.

AZTECHNOLOGY (AZTECHNOLOGY, U.K. DIVISION)

Home Office Location: Mexico City, Aztlan
U.K. Division: Aztechnology Habitat, City of London
President, U.K. Division: Diego Cuauhtemoc
   Chief Products/Services: Electronics, surveillance systems, light and personal armaments

Business Profile:
Aztechnology's presence in the U.K. seems small, with less than 20,000 employees in its habitat housing. However, Aztechnology is rumoured to have fingers in many pies and to have many subsidiaries, particularly within the U.K. arms manufacture and surveillance indus-

tries. Aztechnology is also known to have funded several chairs of occult and magical studies at U.K. universities, most notably the Teochithlan Chair of Experimental Hermetics at Cambridge.

Security/Military Forces:
Aztechnology maintains small cadres of seasoned veterans as "security advisers." Many of these are ex-police or ex-military personnel, and their employment gives Aztechnology links with certain elements of the state (notably those of right-wing persuasions).

>>>>>[But there's more. Not so much as the paranoids claim, but definitely a chunk. Aztech is in with some of the big players in the NDM, one of the Hidden Circles. The company seems to get orichalcum more easily than most—not the Welsh stuff, but some from secret Lake District sites. They've got piles of it salted away in that nasty little pyramid, is what I've heard. What are the druids getting in return? Who knows? Access to firepower they can call on? Could be.]<<<<<
—ZapLox (22:25:17/16-FEB-52)

>>>>>[More than that, matey. Think about it this way: druids and nobles, lots of antagonism, right? Think elves: think nobles and Tir Tairngire. Now think druids and Aztechnology. Then think Aztech and elves: no great warm feeling, right? Now you've squared the angles. Smart boy.]<<<<<
—MesoStim (00:08:23/16-FEB-52)

FUCHI INDUSTRIAL ELECTRONICS (FUCHI INDUSTRIES U.K.)

Home Office Location: Tokyo, Japan
U.K. Division: Cambridge, U.K. Sprawl
U.K. Division President: Charles Nakatomi
   Chief Products/Services: Research and development on advanced cyberware and related technology for governmental, corporate, and military markets

Business Profile:
Fuchi Industries U.K. is headed by Charles Nakatomi, an Anglo-Japanese whiz kid of the Nakatomi family, one of the three families in co-ownership of this high-flying corporation. Fuchi Industries U.K. specializes in recruiting the best graduates from Cambridge and other British universities for their sprawling complex of research laboratories extending over almost 16 square miles. Fuchi is responsible for many government security installations and for cyberware installed at major government sites.

Security/Military Forces:
Fuchi is licensed to maintain up to 2,000 security staff to protect its research secrets in its various U.K. installations.

>>>>>[And they don't take prisoners, either. Regular weapons practice is held every Friday morning, and that includes heavy weapons, tasers, lasers, experimental neural weapons, everything under the sun. And as for security, well, they take retina scans before you even sniff the razor wire.]<<<<<
—MesoStim (01:17:40/17-FEB-52)

RENRAKU COMPUTER SYSTEMS (RENRAKU U.K.)

Home Office Location: Chiba, Japan
U.K. Division: Dagenham, London Sprawl
U.K. Division President: Frank Butcher
   Chief Products/Services: Data storage and manipulation devices, dedicated expert systems, mainframe hardware

Business Profile:
   Renraku has a fairly powerful corporate presence in the U.K. It has a low profile, in that it supplies "enabling technology" to other more ambitious and innovative corporations. This creates useful economies of scale and product standardization, the latter being Renraku's best hope for major future profitability. Renraku U.K.'s image is reliable, stolid, and rather dull, an image reinforced by its slow-witted U.K. president, who allegedly used to sell second-hand cars in East London.

Security/Military Forces: Information not available.

AMALGAMATED TECHNOLOGIES AND TELECOMMUNICATIONS (ATT)

Home Office Location: London Sprawl
President/CEO: Sir Arthur Gordon
   Chief Products/Services: Telecommunications and allied systems, newsnet services, data archives, electronics, industrial robotics

Business Profile:
   ATT is 57 percent owned by Saeder-Krupp Heavy Industries; the remaining 43 percent of share issue is owned by a range of U.K., Japanese, and North American corporate investors. ATT deals in information technology and also in information. It has a happy knack of acquiring data archives shortly before they become highly important for unexpected reasons—such as demographic and cyclical time-series data, which form the basis for predictive extrapolations. Just how ATT manages this almost precognitive investing is far from clear. It is also well-known that ATT recruits a high percentage of its executives and high fliers from English public schools, and that a fair percentage of them, in turn, are druids or those sympathetic to druidic ambitions. They are also often aristocrats. Thus, ATT specializes above all in influence through contacts and information.

Security/Military Forces: Information not available.

BRITISH-OWNED CORPORATIONS

BRITISH INDUSTRIAL PLC

Home Office Location: Angel Towers Arcology, London
President/CEO: Clive Woolford
Principal Divisions
   Division Name: British Electrical
   Division Head: Sir Alan Fitzsimmons
   Chief Products/Services: Electrical and general consumer goods
   Division Name: British Food Products
   Division Head: Walter Crowther
   Chief Products/Services: Processed foods, additives, general synthetics, fast foods, and fast-food stores

Business Profile:
   British Industrial is a sprawl in itself. The electrical division manufactures and imports consumer appliances of all kinds, while the food products division owns vast factory farms, chemical plants, chains of fast-food operations (including Regal Burgers, the home-grown and terminally loathsome alternative to the Stuffer Shack import), trivid-shopping agencies, street chemist stores, and much more. Some 5 percent of this company's products and services is of good quality, and its elite range offerings are generally underrated. The other 95 percent is generally mediocre and banal, but not usually actually vile or dangerous.

Security/Military Forces: Information not available.

NERPS.
FOR ENDOMORPHINS.

>>>>>[These guys make real plazzy stuff, just ace. They get away with it because Brits are generally too polite to complain when they're sold rubbish.]<<<<<
　　—Slammer (01:16:32/18-FEB-52)

>>>>>[It's not really rubbish, just demi-tech. Lots of it comes from Far Eastern sweatshops and gets stuck in a plazzy box somewhere in Brum.]<<<<<
　　—Rosie Posie (01:17:22/18-FEB-52)

>>>>>[Check out what else they get in from the Far East. You think Korea just ships out cheap electricals and ginseng sherbet? I hear there are a few trancers around the import house down in Gunnersbury.]<<<<<
　　—MesoStim (01:20:32/18-FEB-52)

GRENVILLE-ADAMS PLC

Home Office Location: Unknown/inadequate data
President/CEO: Unknown
Principal Divisions: Unknown/inadequate data
　　Division Head(s): Unknown/inadequate data
　　Chief Products/Services: Unknown/inadequate data

Business Profile:
　　Grenville-Adams PLC (often known as GA) is an unusual corporate entity. In some ways, it does not actually exist. That is, it has no offices that anyone can find. And the corporation apparently produces nothing. It does not create or manufacture any product. It provides no services. It seems mainly to own slices of other people, usually without their knowing about it. GA owns shares and chunks of people and corps all over the place through a string of holding companies in tax havens such as the Isle of Man, the Channel Islands, Switzerland, the Cayman Islands, and a dozen places even HKB knows nothing about. In addition, algorithms of fearsome complexity reroute the cascade chains of ownership and control into increasingly baroque hierarchies by the day in a weird fractal dance. This untraceable network spreads its tentacles of influence and control into many foreign corporations. GA is owned by druids, though which group(s) is unknown. Their aims, beyond the acquisition of funding, are unknown. But they are past masters at making GA rich.

Security/Military Forces: Information not available.

>>>>>[This doesn't make sense. I admit it, I'm confused...]<<<<<
　　—Lulu Doom (23:08:35/25-MAR-52)

>>>>>[I agree, but vidie this extract from a lecture by Professor Rachel Lewis to the Seattle Economic Institute, online, 13 May 2051:

GRENVILLE-ADAMS AND COMPETITIVE MONOPO-LIZATION

　　Grenville-Adams uses a standard corporate strategy: competitive monopolization. GA effects ownership of all competing firms in one key manufacturing area and then sustains apparent competition between them while receiving the benefits of monopoly power. How does this work? Unlike a normal monopoly, the employees are not allowed to get fat and lazy. They think competition still exists in the market, and they have to keep working to keep their jobs and take home credsticks. Because GA owns different firms without the latter knowing it, the illusion of true competition is maintained. This keeps people lean, mean, and scared, and keeps costs down. The monopoly is price-competitive, while profits remain good.

　　What's more, this strategy keeps outsiders out; the range of owned companies produces such a plethora of variants on the product theme that outsiders can find no entry into the controlled marketplace. The pseudo-competition of the subsidiaries guarantees this spread of differentiated products. Indeed, the existence of such a spread is a good sign that GA-stimulated competitive monopolization is operating, most especially when the board of directors expressly orders manufacturing that the company accountant believes is not commercially justifiable.

　　Next, we need to consider which product ranges within the U.K. and localized European markets show evidence of GA-stimulated competitive monopolization in the last ten years. This is the subject of our next lecture...

Does that help?]<<<<<
　　—Kudo King (06:22:51/27-MAR-52)

>>>>>[Well, that certainly explains a few things. Recently, I determined that a particular Johnson I'd jazzed with was on the GA payroll. Odd part was that the target company was also associated with GA. The job was fire-bombing a warehouse. Guess they were keeping inventory down. Too strange for me.]<<<<<
　　—Aplomb (03:46:04/2-APR-52)

HILDEBRANDT-KLEINFORT-BERNAL

Home Office Location: London Sprawl
President/CEO: Paul Bernal, Jr.
Principal Divisions
    Division Name: HKB Financial Services
    Division Head: Anthony Hildebrandt
    Chief Products/Services: Insurance brokering, commodity brokering, investment management
    Division Name: HKB Data Services
    Division Head: Meredith McAlpine
    Chief Products/Services: Data management, software security systems

Business Profile:

HKB is an aggressive, dynamic U.K. corporation that has a stranglehold on British and London-based financial services since Paul Bernal's brilliant and daring takeover of Lloyds in 2020. HKB handles all forms of risk insurance and commodity brokering and is reputed to have some distinctly original ideas on stimulating demand in the market. HKB also has subsidiary companies carefully selected to produce an extending portfolio of linked businesses. For example, HKB Data Services also owns Risk Protection Factors Inc., which handles "private security" (i.e., muscle), so a customer can buy software protection and muscle at the same time. Word is that Renraku has some links with HKB, which would be surprising if true, given the caution of Renraku and the aggressive nature of HKB.

Security/Military Forces:

HKB Data Services is rumored to have access to corporate muscle with major firepower in less than ten minutes at any given time, though just how they can do this and who they are calling up is very uncertain. This is only one of HKB's well-kept secrets.

>>>>>[Here's another juicy one. HKB makes good money insuring people against terrorism, right? Right. Dumb seps who've actually got a better chance of being killed in an auto smash than of being blown up in a plane by some crazy towelhead don't know that, so HKB brings in the money with tasty premiums. Mind you, some high-profile terrorist atrocities sure help up the ante, right? Meanwhile, HKB ships money and arms to Abu Khalid and his Blacksand Revolutionaries. They get money and arms, they blow up some tourists, the premiums go up, and HKB get richer. Then they can buy some more arms for Khalid. Cosy, huh?]<<<<<
    —MesoStim (04:11:27/19-FEB-52)

>>>>>[Better than that. Khalid actually insures the people he blows up with HKB!]<<<<<
    —Mole Man (11:13:48/19-FEB-52)

>>>>>[I'm beginning to take this fellow seriously.]<<<<<
    —Hampstead Hi-Jack (14:42:17/20-FEB-52)

>>>>>[You'd better believe it, dweebhead.]<<<<<
    —Mole Man (14:43:17/20-FEB-52)

INTEGRATED WEAPON SYSTEM PLC

Home Office Location: Nottingham, U.K. Sprawl
President/CEO: Nigel Wilkinson
    Chief Products/Services: Heavy and military weapons, automatic weaponry, combat-enhancement cyberware, advanced aeronautical research

Business Profile:

IWS is a heavy industrial arms manufacturer. Its products do not rely on subtlety. They like to sell people bazookas, cannons, SMGs, armoured personnel carriers, SAMs, frag-head missiles, and the kind of specialist item they refer to as "personnel-neutralizing gaseous dispersion agents" (that is, poison gas). IWS has many U.K. governmental contracts and a network of reciprocal contracts overseas: foreign corporations supply essential raw materials and/or funds, and IWS sends out the weaponry. IWS will sell to anyone, often supplying both sides in a conflict. It is rumoured that Ares Macrotechnology Inc. owns some 30 percent of IWS stock and that the two corporates routinely share research findings. Ares may well act as worldwide marketer and tub-thumper for the experimental Feith VTOL fighter-bomber currently being tested at the Lake District flying ranges by IWS personnel.

Security/Military Forces:

IWS has small cadres at its research plants. Though small-scale affairs and few in number, they are exceedingly well-armed with excellent logistic (air cover, artillery, and so on) support. Because IWS has contracts with the Ministry of Defence they are also able to call on armed forces personnel.

TRANSYS NEURONET

Home Office Location: Edinburgh, Scotsprawl
President/CEO: Sir Iain Greig
Principal Divisions
   Division Name: Transys Neuronet GB
   Division Head: Johnathan Cooper
   Chief Products/Services: Experimental communication systems, lasers, advanced cyberware and Matrix software

Business Profile:

Transys Neuronet (usually simply Transys) was formed by the merger of four separate British hi-tech companies between 2013 and 2017. Their aim was to form a corporation able to stand up to North American and (especially) Japanese competition. Transys is funded by other corporates and governments; new rumours circulate every week about which ones. Its work is secret and its datanets are notorious for its omnipresent IC, even in innocuous locations. Black IC guards against even a glimpse at its current cutting-edge projects. Manufactures for the military, medical, and personnel-enhancement markets are all under research by the small laboratories Transys maintains in Silicon Glen and in southern England.

Security/Military Forces:

Transys maintains a small, licensed corporate force that boasts formidable advanced cyberware. Their troopers are as much machine as they are meat, if not more.

>>>>>[Believe me, you do NOT want to meet the troll samurai these people keep, with their boosted reflexes and softwires. They can hit a pea at 100 yards. They'll hit you before you even know they're there. Some say they shoot first and ask the corpse questions afterwards. This is based on a simple misconception. They actually don't give a 4X about asking questions.]<<<<<
   —Slammer (12:00:04/20-FEB-52)

>>>>>[These guys are in with Celedyr the dragon, of course. It's their money down at Caerleon with those wild Rastamen. Word is, weird stuff goes down in the Matrix. Anyone gets close, they get brain-fried in ways we don't even know how to understand yet.]<<<<<
   —Phantom (03:57:11/22-FEB-52)

ZETA-IMPCHEM

Home Office Location: Interlaken, Switzerland
U.K. Division: Cleveland, Teesprawl
President/CEO: Harald Meier
U.K. Division President: Michael Carruthers
   Chief Products/Services: Pharmaceuticals, petrochemicals, plastics, polymers, industrial chemicals, cyberware

Business Profile:

Zeta-ImpChem was formed by the merger of the British ICI (Imperial Chemical Industries) with two Swiss-owned pharmaceutical firms in 2017. After its takeover of the German Hoechst in 2022, it became easily the biggest corporate in its field in Europe. Most of its industrial capacity is integrated, save for its cyberware manufacture, a relatively recent expansion for the company. So far, the corporation has concentrated on mundane skillsofts and similar "safe" products. It has only recently begun to step into the territory of experimental and cutting-edge cyberware, where it will be taking on Transys Neuronet. How wise is this move remains to be seen.

Zeta-ImpChem is infamous for its lack of morals in product-testing and dumping, with Africa and Asia its standard victims. The corp is still trying to live down the Polydopa scandal of 2042, and the public treats its official protestations of "environmental awareness" with the contempt they deserve.

Security/Military Forces: Information not available.

>>>>>[These are not nice people. Polydopa; there's a case in point. They knew that stuff was neurotoxic during the four years they were dumping off their stocks to the people of central Africa, claiming that it was a "performance enhancer for men" as well as being a general neurofacilitator. Subtle, huh? Final estimates: 4,000 premature deaths, 35,000 cases of irreversible brain damage. Boycott these people. They're slime.]<<<<<
   —MesoStim (01:25:32/24-FEB-52)

>>>>>[But I like the buzz.]<<<<<
   —Hal (01:32:32/24-FEB-52)

>>>>>[There's always one, isn't there?]<<<<<
   —Slammer (01:34:17/24-FEB-52)

>>>>>[But not for long.]<<<<<
   —MesoStim (01:44:19/24-FEB-52)

>>>>>[A warning on their standard foreign strategy. If they fail to bribe one of the African or Asian local officials who has to decide whether to license one of their hellish products, their local operative simply starts a cred account somewhere in the name of the official, pays in the nuyen for a few months from a Zeta-ImpChem subsidiary so that the link isn't too obvious but could be found by detectives, and then goes back to the man. There's the evidence, he says. See how we've been paying you? You've been taking bribes. Refuse me again and I will have to send this information to your local police—you know, the friendly, grinning guys with the laser prods. The poor guy folds on the spot and ImpChem gets their product license. Know your enemy, people.]<<<<<
   —Phantom (03:03:41/26-FEB-52)

ORGANIZED CRIME

In Britain, organized crime has never become established on a national scale. There are powerful criminal groupings who can operate nationally, but none has ever become dominant over a wide area. Much more common—and far more noticeable—is a patchwork quilt of gangs that are greatly feared in their own localized territories.

Britain does not have a long history of politicians being in the pockets of organized crime. The corruption of British politicians is much subtler than that. It is also rare for law-enforcement operatives to be in the pay of crime bosses, and the police are alert to any yakuza or Mafia attempts to establish their activities within the U.K. They devote intensive monitoring and resources to quickly nipping such activities in the bud. These multinational crime groups have thus never become firmly established in the U.K.

The media often blows up the activities of local gangs in places like the East End of London and Manchester's north side, but these gangs tend to limit their activities to their own neighbourhoods, operating almost entirely without ambition. They are, in effect, little more than street gangs in better-quality clothing.

YAKUZA

The Japanese population of the U.K. is tiny (estimated at fewer than 20,000 inside habitats and corporate territory and below 50,000 outside). The indigenous Japanese have never exerted any significant control over British crime. For decades, the Japanese high oyabuns simply ignored the small island off the edge of Europe. As no local yakuza were operating in the U.K., they would probably have continued in this manner had their advisers not presented a persuasive case for the U.K.'s potential for yakuza operations. Britain was financially robust, had an excellent turnover of tourist trade ideal for such crimes as prostitution, and lacked a major presence of Mafia or other nationally organized gangs.

So, the yakuza have taken a leaf from the book of corporate activities in Britain, putting money into British operations fronted by British criminals. Ryuichi Mitoizumi is the regional oyabun for the U.K., with a penthouse suite in the prestigious Marchment District of Edinburgh and another in The Village. He is an administrator, channelling funds from the yakuza into British criminal activities, then laundering profits back out of the U.K., usually through Swiss financial institutions.

The yakuza usually work like this: one of Ryuichi's henchmen hears of a criminal grouping active in prostitution, illegal chip sales, drug-pushing, or the like. The yakuza then make their approach, offering funding, superior hardware, provision of information about competitors, or leasing of suitable yakuza-owned property. In return, the yakuza receive a share of the profits from the expanded operation. What the yakuza do not broadcast—but the British criminals know very well—is that they will immediately dispatch small teams of assassins to deal with anyone who does not make good on his end of the deal. The yakuza rarely kill in the U.K., but when they do, their assassins never miss. The yakuza death squads are the deadliest in the country, composed only of deeply trusted members of the organization.

This strategy has paid off so well that Mitoizumi has been gradually expanding the portfolio of yakuza-owned properties over the last five years. They are still largely concentrated on operations in London, Glasgow, and Edinburgh, and avoid the Midlands because of Tong activity. If there is one area into which the yakuza are most likely to expand, it is top-of-the-range crime; technocrime, illegal good-quality cyberware, BTL and other addictive chips, and the like. As none of these would bring the yakuza into competition with the Tongs or Asian families, Mitoizumi has recommended this expansion to the Japanese high oyabuns.

MAFIA

The Mafia has never had a significant presence in Britain. This is because 20th-century Britain was merely an offshore dump-off point for drugs that found no market on the European mainland. In this century, security across the English Channel has been so tight since the Euro Wars that smuggling is a dangerous operation.

In recent years, however, Italy has become an important centre for illegal BTL chip-distribution, usually via the Mediterranean to North African and Islamic states, but also to the rest of Europe. The main supply line to Britain is via Spain (and the Santander ferry link) and Eire. The Mafia has a major investment in this distribution network. Even so, they do not have their own distribution network or operatives within Britain itself. A handful of resident Italians are involved in importing the chips into Britain, but no muscle or organized families.

TONGS

The Chinese Tongs are dominant in Nottingham and Manchester, two major cities within the U.K. sprawl, and they also have a significant presence in the Chinatown area of London, in Liverpool, and the whole of Merseysprawl. The Tongs in these cities are mostly family-based, with a structure akin to that of the Mafia. Tong members are noteworthy for their expertise in martial arts, preferring them to the use of firepower. Many are physical adepts. They are notorious for their cruelty and their routine use of torture to extract information and to instill fear in those from whom they extort money. Protection rackets are a staple of Tong activity, a rewarding form of crime because protection involves little risk, capital outlay, or need to store contraband.

Tongs also use intimidation to corner particular areas of commerce for their own monopoly. In the Midlands, Chinese and other ethnic food shops and restaurants are mostly Tong-controlled. Those who resist will be firebombed or attacked by a dozen masked Chinese armed with pickaxes or similar weaponry. Though the Tong prefer to raid when few people are about, they will dispose of customers who might be witnesses for the police. The owners are often burned alive before their properties are set light to.

The Si Peng family of Nottingham and the Xiao Ziang family of Manchester are the powers behind the two most important British Tongs. They tend to cooperate with information, and in one or two special instances (usually to demonstrate their power), they have actually pooled their hatchet men.

>>>>>[Folks, give these people a wide berth if you can. When they torched the Singapore Sling in Nottingham last year, they poured napalm on the head waiter and owner and let 'em writhe awhile before they burned the place down. Then they posted letter bombs to the son who got the insurance money, so that he needed it for the medical care. These are evil people.]<<<<<
—Manta (12:04:22/11-JAN-52)

>>>>>[Yeah, keep well away. All a friend of mine did was make a cheeky remark to a young assistant in a food store and got his faced razored to the bone for it. Tong pride is something you don't want to injure.]<<<<<
—Kondradis (01:57:33/12-FEB-52)

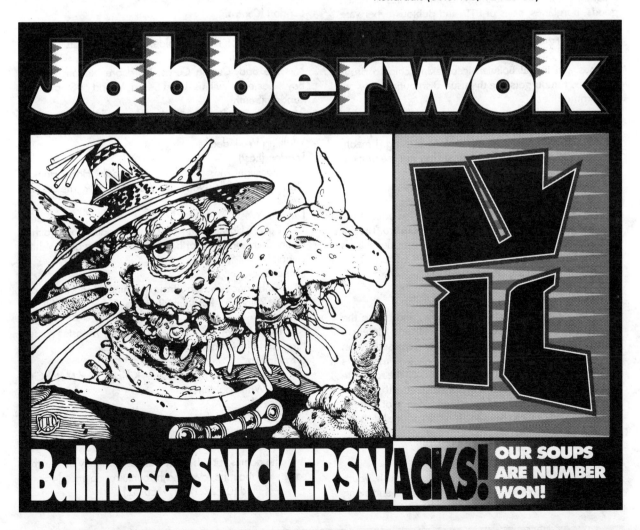

ASIAN GANGS

Large communities of people tracing their origins to the Indian subcontinent and groups of ethnic Indians from East Africa who came to Britain in the 1970s fleeing Idi Amin's atrocities in Uganda have made their homes in Britain for several generations. Nearly 10 percent of the British population is now of Indian ethnic origin. The influence of the strict Hindu and Muslim faiths is fading, but that has not diminished the importance of family even for younger Indians, for even though arranged marriages are a thing of the past, Asian (referring to Indian and Pakistani descent) crime gangs are family-based.

In sharp contrast to Chinese Tongs, conspicuous wealth is a hallmark of respect among Asian gangs. They consider it imperative to flash the best new cybereyes, flashiest wheels, most flamboyant jewelry, the most theatrically sinister-looking personal bodyguards. Asian gang members love to draw attention to themselves, which makes them obvious targets. When the Tongs wiped out the Hirwani family in the famous Nottingham attack of 2048, they had been effortlessly tailing every one of the Hirwanis for days.

Asian gang crime is notable for its lack of subtlety. Prostitution, illegal gambling dens, street sales of stolen goods, burglaries, sales of BTL, and dubious cyberware are staples of their operations. Asian body shops are the last refuge of the gambling man. Under-the-counter sales, through the 24-hour Asian shops, of everything from a dubious and illegal Bolivian icebreaking chip to drug-enhanced tofuburgers, are the usual distribution network for commodities.

>>>>>[It's just another way of making a living. I mean, these people are true entrepreneurs! They just see marketing opportunities, right?]<<<<<
—Bernreuter (03:33:16/16-FEB-52)

>>>>>[True, but it's not as if they are excluded from conventional trading the way so many blacks are. They're well-off folks, they're not forced into crime. And then there's the violence.]<<<<<
—Carol K (09:21:17/16-FEB-52)

Asian gangs are notoriously brutal, and unlike the Tongs, they have no scruples about inflicting violence. Tongs usually resort to violence only when crossed; Asian gangs seem to relish dishing it out. Asian gang members are the ones who will leap out of their cars on the roadside and hack someone to death in public view with axes or knives, preferring cruel and bloody elimination of targets. In this way, no one can miss the fact that justice has been done—or who did it.

STREET GANGS

Toward the end of the last century, British youth became enamoured of the American way of life, and along with the music and fashions, they adopted the idea of street gangs. Of course, there had always been gangs of youths roaming the inner cities, but now they turned rebellion and violent crime into an art form. Individual graffiti, clothing, weapons, slang, and colours are all hallmarks of the modern gang. Every part of the U.K. sprawl has its street gangs. Some become locally famous for a while, before being broken up by the police or inner squabbles, but their fame rarely reaches national level. Gangs still wear typical colours or use only certain types of weaponry or attack tactics, but these change with the times and the badge of recognition a gang wears one week is usually different by the same time next month. Nor are gangs always associated with particular territories. They're mobile, winning territory from other gangs or losing it to those sniffing at their own borders. British street gangs are weaker, more volatile, more transient entities by far than those in other places.

>>>>>[For your reference, you may care to note the names and locations of the following major inner-city street gangs. These are just a few, and half of them won't exist in three months' time, but here they are:

London (Central)
Brothers in Rhythm, Gold Crescent, Hellhounds, Knives, Red Watch, Rotorheads, Spiderboys, White Rats
London (North)
The Bad, Cutting Corps, Hardcore Nation, Panzer Boys, Society's Victims, Ultra Seven, World of Storms
London (South)
Eagle Star Renegades, The Key and the Gate, New Cross Surfers, Rabid Black Boys, Third World Babies, Walking Wounded
London (East)
Blacklight Massive, Flaming Vandals, Harry Hooks, The JCF, Madballs, Twin City Wrecking Crew, The Underworld
London (West)
Cutters, Howling Carrion, Lions of Judah, Nightwraiths, Uhuru Commandos, Warthogs, Westway Stranglers, White Dynamite
Manchester
Ambulance Chasers, Brain Machine, Moors Maniacs, Ravers, Raindogs, Rusholme Ruffians, Simon Said Kill
Liverpool
Black Eagles, Blue Mondays, Honey Monster Posse, Kings of Pain, Shrouded Moon, Sun Kings
Birmingham
Angry Gang, Infra-red Crew, Killing Crew, Motor City Angels, White Lightning
Scotsprawl
Clan, Diamond White, Falcons, Masters of Reality, Orange Blood, Ravens

The names vary, but you can be sure they all feel the same way about life, love, and the pursuit of violence.]<<<<<
—X-Plod (05:27:14/17-FEB-52)

L O N D O N

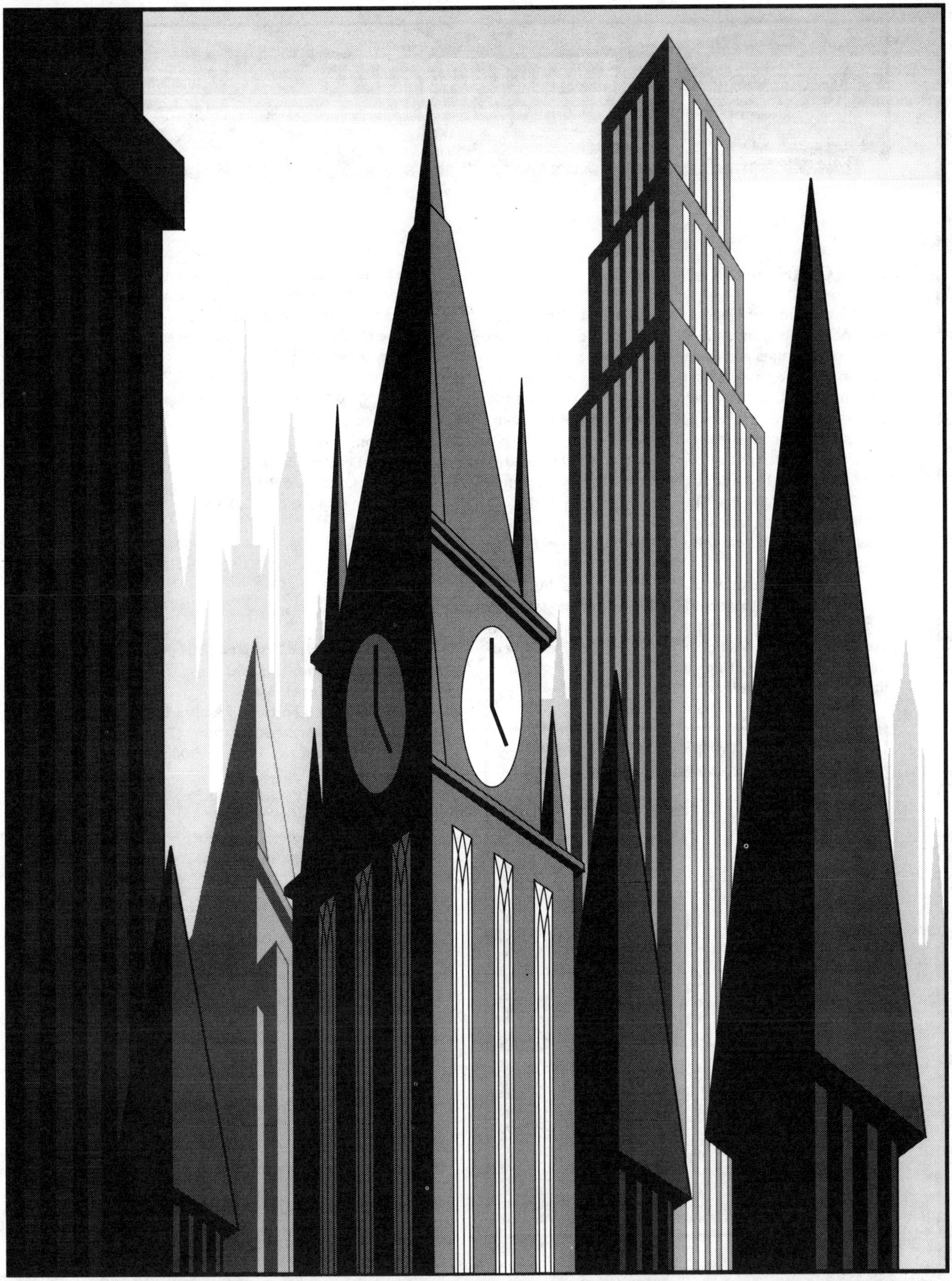

THE SMOKE

THE LONDON SPRAWL

In the time of Queen Victoria, the British Empire dominated the world, and the heart of the Empire was London. Treasures and trade flooded to the city from all over the globe, making it rich in money and culture. Grown beyond all imagining, the city is now among the largest in the world, offering visitors a range of entertainments beyond compare.

Historians tell us that London was first established as a town way back in the Roman era, when the River Thames was bridged for the first time. Today the site of the old settlement covers just a tiny proportion of the great city's total area, which has grown to the size of any other English county.

A city this size has thousands of attractions, but those of most interest to tourists and other visitors are gathered together in the Inner London area. From the hustle and bustle of the Stock Market in the City to the Changing of the Guard outside Buckingham Palace, where His Majesty the King is often in residence, from the antiquities arrayed in the British Museum to the bright young things dancing until dawn in the night clubs of the West End, London offers a range of experiences beyond compare.

The locals call it the Smoke, because it has been old and gray for so long.

VITAL STATISTICS

Population: 9,700,000+
  Inner London: 3,500,000
  Outer London: 6,200,000+
  Annual visitors: 6,800,000+
  Human: 74%
  Elf: 10%
  Dwarf: 2%
  Ork: 11%
  Troll: 2%
  Other: 1%
Density in Populated Districts: 530+ per square kilometer
Per Capita Income: £58,000
Below Poverty Level: 34%
Persons Rated on Fortune's Active Traders List: 1%
Persons of Corporate Affiliation: 47%
Felonious Crime Rate: 11 per 1,000 per annum
Education:
  High School Equivalency: 53%
  College Equivalency: 28%
  Advanced Studies Certificates: 9%
Hospitals: 217 (including national specialists)

GOVERNMENT

London in the 2050s is a vast, sprawling metropolis covering many hundreds of square miles. For administrative purposes, it is divided into five main areas. Inner London lies at the centre, surrounded by a ring of large, mostly featureless commuter districts: Orbital North, Orbital West, Orbital South, and the SX Overspill.

Governing the city is a bewildering array of assemblies and councils. At the top of the pile, central government and the Lord Protector's office are responsible for policy decisions and their implementation, major budgeting, and so on. The Administrative Bureau of the Lord Protector's office appoints the civil service bureaucrats who liaise with local government officials to arrange funding, and data from the Chancellery Net are used to assist economic and demographic forecasting in London.

THE LONDON ASSEMBLY

This group of five assemblymen, one from Inner London and one from each of the four outer districts, is elected (theoretically) by a one-person, one-vote process. One assemblyman comes up for election every year. The Assembly is, in principle, the prime body for liaising with central government in the form of the Lord Protector's Office and the Home Office. Government ministers regularly attend meetings between the assemblymen and civil servants.

>>>>>[They're just media stunts. These people don't have any real influence. They make their case, the government pretends to listen, then they give 50 reasons why, administratively, they can't do anything about London's problems just at the moment. Perhaps a Royal Commission should be appointed to study the problem? The Assembly's as much use as a medpatch on a paraviral lesion.]<<<<<
—MesoStim (14:32:27/27-FEB-52)

The current members of the London Assembly are:

Inner London: Agatha Halpern, Chair
Orbital North: Philip Mainwaring
Orbital West: James Andrew Laurie
Orbital South: Philippa Knight
SX Overspill: Robert Stanford

The Assembly meets once per week in their offices at Alexandra Palace, in the north part of the village. Their research staff process requests from metropolitan councils, corporate interests, and pressure groups about the needs of London at the "strategic" level. The Assembly then debates these, in open or closed session, before its monthly meetings with the Administrative Bureau officials.

>>>>>[It's really just an exercise in self-deception. The Assembly gives a handful of people the chance to feel they're important. And has anyone else noted that hunky little number in the charcoal-grey suit from the LPO making up to Agatha Halpern? She certainly seems to get home rather late from the meetings.]<<<<<
—Anonymous (18:35:29/1-MAR-52)

METROPOLITAN COUNCILS

Metropolitan Councils are also elected on a one-person, one-vote principle, with councillors coming up for re-election every four years. There are 14 London Metropolitan Councils, corresponding to the districts of Inner and Outer London; this confuses many people, because other cities have only one for the whole city (but do not have anything like the London Assembly). Each council has some 25 to 40 local councillors. The Councils are charged with a wide range of legal responsibilities for administering local standards in education and health

provision, street cleansing, sanitation, health inspection, and the like. They are responsible for expenditures and for administering the allocation of funds from the budget they are allowed by government.

>>>>>[But they have no discretion in that; government regulations compel them to pay such-and-such a minimum for different types of expenditure. Although the councils are elected bodies, they are really only administrators of expenditure. The council officers are the people who do that, not the councillors, and they're just rubber-stampers. One consequence is that few people care much about the councils. Only 13 percent of the electorate voted in the last round of elections.]<<<<<
—Stamper (19:26:52/1-MAR-52)

Metropolitan councils cannot influence the taxes levied on businesses and business properties, because these are determined by national government. But they can fix a poll-tax level, within limits. The poll tax is a flat-rate tax levied on all adults over the age of 16 who live in London. The tax rate is partly dependent on level of income, but the government has enforced the principle that everyone should pay something, and councils have a minimum level below which the tax cannot drop.

>>>>>[It's a long-established principle of social mobility among the lower classes in London that you keep on the move in April when the poll-tax inspectors head out of the council departments with that weary "Oh God, here we go again" look on their resigned faces. The poll tax is also a good instrument for keeping people who don't like the government off the electoral register, of course.]<<<<<
—Stamper (23:54:17/1-MAR-52)

There are two areas of operation in which the Metropolitan Councils have an especial influence. The first is transport. In consultation with the London Assembly and the Ministry of Transport, they construct traffic plans, city transport plans, and ergonomic studies of London mobility. The second is in the area of planning. Metropolitan councils are in charge of giving, or denying, permission for the construction of planned buildings within their areas.

>>>>>[No, they're not. If some corporate comes along and says we want to put up this 100-storey monstrosity and the Metropolitan Council has the guts to say, no, we're not going to bulldoze those orks out of their homes just because you want to stick up this hideous-looking thing, the corporate boys will simply appeal to the Ministry of Transport and the Ministry of the Environment. They can always overrule the decisions of local government, and they usually do.]<<<<<
—Stamper (03:14:42/1-MAR-52)

>>>>>[This is true. Michael Hazeldean at Environment has overruled local and metropolitan councils on 75 percent of the appeals he's received in the last two years, and 68 percent of these decisions have gone in favour of inner-city development. The stated reason is that this helps protect land beyond the cities, but that sounds dubious to me. I mean, is relocating out to the Stinkfens some kind of alternative to whacking up a skyscraper habitat in some orbital site?]<<<<<
—Carol K. (07:17:42/1-MAR-52)

LOCAL COUNCILS

Local councils cover some 70 administrative districts within Inner and Outer London. They are funded entirely by central government, save for funds they receive from their own "street level" operations; revenue from parking meters, fines for littering, and similar on-the-spot offences. They are elected, as are the Metropolitan Councils. Their councillors meet once per week on average. They are responsible for much of the day-to-day regulation of London life. Examples of their activities are the maintenance and operation of public car parks, the examination and licensing of taxi drivers, the funding and operation of London's Race Relations Councils, and the operation of Rodent Operative Departments, which deal with the occasional problem of vermin in London.

>>>>>[Occasional? What's this idiot on about? Lambeth's got devil rats big enough to kill grown men one-to-one, and that's occasional?]<<<<<
—Rosie Posie (19:16:00/2-MAR-52)

>>>>>[For people from beyond the Smoke, the local councils can be quite a hoot. The thing is, nobody can be bothered to vote, since they're really such a waste of time. The councils are the bottom rung of the ladder for aspiring politicians, that's about all. But now and then a bunch of local activists can manage to seize control of a council with only a thousand votes or so. With a 3 percent turnout, who needs more? So some weird things happen occasionally. I remember the troll RadFems who ran Croydon for a crazy, wonderful year in 2044. It was mayhem. Couldn't last, of course, and they got voted out the next year, but seeing the council financial administrator made to run a creche was a sight to behold.]<<<<<
—Carol K. (09:11:48/3-MAR-52)

Finally, there is a handful of specialist bodies concerned with very specific duties and issues. These are rarely elected, and are simply statutory bodies. Examples include the three-man Security Committee appointed by the Lord Protector and the Home Office to oversee policing of the Lambeth Containment Zone, the City Company (of which the Lord Mayor is the elected head), and the Zoological and Botanical Board, which oversees the safety and security of the (few) paranormal animals kept at Regent's Park Zoo.

GETTING AROUND LONDON

As in all major cities, those with jobs spend a good portion of their time travelling to and from work. The London rush hours are from seven-thirty to ten in the morning and four-thirty to seven in the evening. Travel information is posted on electronic signs situated alongside many major roads heading into Inner London, and may also be had by tuning into any of the dozens of local radio stations. On those roads where the grid is in operation, information can also be received by all standard-make onboard navigation assistance units.

>>>>>[One of the favorite pastimes of the Dastardly Deckers is to slide in and alter the data that feeds the traffic-information signs. They get a great chuckle from it. Me, I'm gonna smash their fingers if I ever find them.]<<<<<
—Traveller (21:13:52/3-MAR-52)

AIR

Many corporate buildings in the City and the Docklands Districts and a few others such as the British Industrial Angel Towers arcology feature heliports for use by helicopters and tilt-rotor aircraft. London City Airport is situated in the heart of the Docklands District and caters to small fixed-wing aircraft as well as helicopters. These provide short hops to the three main London airports or longer journeys to other parts of the U.K. and a handful of short European hauls.

Air space over London is strictly controlled by the Civil Aviation Authority, who issue licenses very sparingly. A typical journey, say, from the HBK building in the City to Heathrow Airport, takes under an hour (including check-in time) and costs £138.

BUS

London Transport and Capital Cruise continue to run the famous large red double-decker buses for tourists and residents alike, but these museum pieces are rapidly falling into disrepair. Far more common are the small minibuses run like oversized taxi-cabs by dozens of small operators. These buses, similar in style to those that teem in the streets of all Third World capitals, tend to run on short, circular routes, with fares set at a standard £2.50. In Outer London, similar buses connect nearby towns and neighbourhoods. Large, single-deck passenger coaches run to most parts of Britain from Victoria coach station; these are only for the relatively desperate.

CAR

London's roads are one of the greatest sources of irritation for any visitor. The grid system is patchy except on main roads, due to years of arguments over its funding and the U.K.'s continued reliance on its large petroleum reserves. Travelling across London is best achieved by going around the centre using the Inner or Outer Orbital

Motorways (M825 and M25 respectively), though these are almost impassable during the rush hours and at weekends. There is little danger on the main highways, even at night, except on the elevated sections of the M4 in Westway and the M313 in the East End.

In Inner London, the side roads are only passable using internal power or non-electric cars. In the West End Overground, the Lambeth Containment Zone, and parts of the East End and Westway, drivers are warned to stay in their vehicles during the day and not to park at all at night. The presence of parking meters does not guarantee that it is safe to park. The vast underground car parks serving the West End Underplex and the habitats have room for thousands of vehicles, but require the purchase of all-day tickets (typical cost £30 per day). Parking spaces are often miles from one's destination, requiring extensive use of the West End Underplex shuttles.

Car rental agencies operate throughout the capital and beyond. In Inner London there are more than 30 branches of the "big three" international agencies, as well as another 20 smaller and specialist operators that provide limousines and chauffeurs, trucks, and so on. A valid driver's license and insurance are required; the big agencies accept the licenses of most countries, but smaller operators may not. To drive legally, however, one needs a British or international driving license.

Baldini's
magical goods
713 (680-2281)

FERRY

Despite the River Thames' prominent presence in the life of the city, the waterway has never been an important method of travel for most people. A half-dozen small companies do run river buses up and down the river during the rush hours, from as far east as the East London Bridge to Wandsworth Bridge, but most journeys are much shorter. The cost for a trip is £1 for every bridge the boat goes under. The boats have a bad accident record.

During the day and evening, tourist boats and hydrofoils run pleasure trips up and down the river. These can be picked up at several points along the north bank. A typical trip takes 90 minutes and costs £15 per adult. There are also boats that serve as floating residences, clubs, and pleasure vessels.

LONDON UNDERGROUND

The Deep Tube network of vacuum-assisted trains is slowly replacing the old (in some parts, Victorian) London Underground network in Inner London, but both systems are currently running alongside each other on all routes.

The Underground, or Tube, connects just about every part of Inner London, using antiquated electrically powered trains. For the most part, the lines run a hundred feet or so beneath the city streets, but they rise to run on the surface on the outskirts. Underground stations are located every few blocks in the centre, every mile or so in the outskirts. In the West End Overground District, only certain stations are now open at ground level, though all stations serve and may be reached from the West End Underplex. Fares are typically £1 for one district crossed, plus 50 percent extra for every additional district.

Safety on the Tube is a major problem, even during the day. Attacks and muggings by other passengers are common, as are assaults on trains by bored gangs in the outskirts. The dilapidated state of the trains and tunnels has led to a spate of disastrous fires; on a day-to-day basis, delays and breakdowns are commonplace. In several places in the East End, the trains run through the Undercity, with obvious dangers. Travel south of the river into the Lambeth Containment Zone is now only possible after submitting to security and ID checks at Waterloo and London Bridge stations by armed police officers. Despite all of this, nearly a million people make their weary way to and from work each day via the Tube.

>>>>>[My-o my-o my, tube's a bit dodgy these days? Me and mine'll see you and yours there soon.]<<<<<
—Alex (03:29:47/13-FEB-52)

The new Deep Tube links to the main London stations, the West End Underplex, and the City. Work is also currently going on to reach Heathrow and Gatwick Airports. The Deep Tube trains are powered by electrical linear superconductor motors running on ceramic tracks, assisted by a partial vacuum in the tunnels, achieved using pressure seals. Trains are linked to their stations by twin sets of doors more common to spacecraft airlocks. To travel, passengers must buy cards holding units of 5, 10, 20, or 100 journeys; fares work out at £1 per journey, with small reductions for buying larger amounts. This is cheaper than the ordinary Tube, but the Deep Tube doesn't reach many destinations, severely curtailing its usefulness for most travellers.

RAILWAY AND MONORAIL

The only alternative to driving in from Outer London is to use the good old-fashioned BritRail train service. As a result, the government has spent the last decade pumping it full of money in a drastic attempt to pretty it up so it can get rid of it, but with little success.

In London, as in many other parts of the country, the combination of old and overcrowded trains, high prices, and interminable delays continues to frustrate rush-hour travellers. In outlying districts, especially at night, the threat of sabotage, attack, and even armed hijackings is a real possibility. Nearer to the centre, the sheer number of passengers often causes the whole system to blow a chip and collapse. Only in the centre of London has any real degree of modernization touched the system, with trains running down under Inner London to reach the main termini, now buried far beneath the surface around the edges of the West End Underplex. Typical fares are £12.50 for a journey within Inner London, doubling and trebling for longer journeys within Outer London. Travelling further afield is more expensive again.

The updated DLR (Docklands Light Railway as was) is now a state-of-the-art monorail system, which runs from the edge of the Temple District through the City of London, the Dogs and Docklands districts, as far as the East London Bridge. Work has also started on a further extension that will reach the Renraku Complex at Dagenham within two years; this is being funded almost exclusively by Renraku itself. In the Dogs and the City, branches loop around to follow the riverside. Trains are regular, clean, silent, and efficient, and fares are set at a £5 rate.

CABS

Driven by "cabbies," the distinctive large black London taxis are licensed by the appropriate Area Council, which requires the driver to pass grueling examinations before obtaining permission to operate one. There are, however, thousands of unlicensed "mini-cabs," generally private cars operated by chancers, who have a reputation for swindling passengers and getting lost.

In the street, black cabs show their availability by lighting the yellow light on their roof. A cab hailed in the street is supposed to be obliged to pick up passengers if their journey is within six miles, though this does not always work late at night, especially south of the river.

Fares currently run at £2 (initial charge), plus £1 for every half-mile travelled, plus a near-obligatory 20 percent tip. There are extra charges at weekends, after dark, and for large amounts of luggage (up to 25 percent extra in total). Public holiday fares are higher by up to 100 percent extra (at Christmas). If in doubt, negotiate before getting into the cab.

>>>>>[Just maybe you should also hear about the taxi-cab killer(s). Still not apprehended after two years, last I heard, the total deaths, including copycats, were in the low twenties. Remember, kids, if your driver is wearing a hockey mask, just ask to be taken to the nearest police station.]<<<<<
—Jimmy the Mover (07:18:58/12-JAN-52)

MAJOR BUSINESS CHAINS

Prices in the Smoke are higher than in the rest of the country, often extortionately so. On average, however, prices are 10 percent higher than in the rest of the U.K. Because London is used to catering to the needs of the fantastically wealthy as well as the ordinary citizen, everything a consumer could want is available in qualities ranging from standard to astonishingly opulent, with a dramatic increase in prices to match.

Visitors buying items in the street should note that any hint that the customer is a foreigner is a signal for the vendor to increase prices dramatically, especially in noted tourist haunts. The British Tourist Board recommends that visitors always establish the price of an item before deciding to buy it.

The following is a partial list of reliable business chains operating in London. Those chains listed in the Family Style and No Frills categories are located throughout Greater London. Those in the better categories are more likely to be in Inner London areas only. Individual businesses of note are dealt with in the relevant district sections.

Opening hours are a subject of great frustration to overseas visitors used to 24-hour service. Standard opening hours are nine in the morning to six in the evening, although many shops are now extending their closing hours by one or two hours (and most stay open until eight in the evening on Thursday or Friday nights). In London it is still practically impossible to find any large store open after nine at night, with the exception of a very few supermarkets and chemists.

DEPARTMENT STORES

Luxury: Bainbridge's, Fayed's, Jones & Jones
First Class: John Brown's, Elders, Saint Michael's, Steele's, Today Tomorrow
Family Style: BIS, House & Home, Smallwood's, W. H. Johnson, Wordsworth
No Frills: Catalogue City, CitySave, Ford's, Spendwise

GROCERIES AND CONVENIENCE STORES

Luxury: Francome and Moulin's, Swithin's
First Class: Saint Michael's Food Stores, Stamford's
Family Style: Bisco's, Freenaway's, LCS, Safebury's, Westing's
No Frills: Round-the-Clock Minimarts, Troy, 24-24

RESTAURANTS AND FAST FOOD PLACES

Luxury: The Doyle-Cart, Galliano, Le Gamin, Masako, The Place, The Rochester, La Tante Elise, World of India
First Class: Ajimura, Cafe Grace, Dragon Gate, Moghul Brasserie, One Two Three, Tao, Zaporelli's
Family Style: Assam Garden, Bingham's, Farmer's, Jenny Jones, Nidoli, Shanghai Spice, Taste of Honey, You Know Who's
No Frills: The Captain's Galley, The Golden Archers, Non-Stop One-Stop, Pastarelli's, Pizza Slam, Regal Burgers, Soy Joy, Sushi Machine

HOTELS

Luxury: Hilton Hotels, Lucas Hotels, Sheraton Hotels, Winchester Hotels
First Class: Ariel Hotels, Bonnington Hotels, Coralbroke Hotels, European Regal Hotels, Western Hotels
Family Style: Standard Hotels, Ten Counties Hotels, Thistledown Hotels, White Lion Hotels
No Frills: BLT's, Howards, Traveller's Rest, Waysiders Hotels

COMPUTERS AND ELECTRONICS

Luxury: Da Vinci Netware, Stirling Systems, Transys Ultra
First Class: Business Download, Hard & Soft, Silicon Valley, Transys General
Family Style: Chips With Everything, Polasky's, Watts' Electronics, Zappit Software
No Frills: Hack Attack, Ratchett & Sprockett, Technomatic, Zen

>>>>>[While I'm on, don't forget the white and black markets. Best for cheap everyday stuff are in Portobello Road (Westway), Berwick Street (West End Overground), Chapel Market, Islington (Village), Ridley Road, Dalston (East End), and Petticoat Lane, Aldgate (The City/East End). The best for the other stuff are in Chinatown (WEO), Electric Avenue (LCZ), and Brick Lane, Aldgate (East End). For the other places, you have to ask the right people.]<<<<<
—Slow Mo (23:11:18/7-JAN-52)

VISITOR INFORMATION

Tourism in London, as elsewhere in the country, is overseen by the British Tourist Board. The BTB's immense London Visitors' Centre is located on Level C of the West End Underplex (4 Piccadilly West), where visitors will find maps, information on booking guided tours, and personal assistance. There are also smaller visitor information centres at all mainline BritRail stations. A freephone Visitor's Helpline (008-4211) may be dialed anywhere in London, putting one instantly in touch with a knowledgeable operator.

In London, the "listings magazines", *Going Out* and *CityScape,* are invaluable. Published every Thursday and costing a mere £4 each, they manage to cover all events, clubs, films, concerts, sports events, public demonstrations, street markets, and everything else a visitor could possibly want to know about.

In certain districts of the city, visitors can have a portable telecom unit tuned to transmit a PANICBUTTON signal. This may be done at any police station in the City, Temple, Palaces and Estates, and Village Districts. Within those areas, the Metropolitan Police guarantees that at least one officer will arrive on the scene to render assistance within five minutes after someone presses the PANICBUTTON (this is doubly certain after the McFadden case of 2048). The signal cannot penetrate heavy concrete or steel, but many of the larger corporate buildings have PANICBUTTON receivers that will alert security personnel. A PANICBUTTON does not work in the London Underground or in the Underplex, though emergency alarms dot both places. The cost of adjusting the PANICBUTTON signal to the local frequency is usually covered in travel insurance (but not always, so check your policy).

THE WEATHER

Even by British standards, London's weather is diabolical. Two decades ago, in a bravura display of what was to be the best in British experimental technology, the government dug deep into its pocket and funded the building of a vast system of domes, stretching six miles north and south of the Thames. Because of their design and the use of "breathing" biofabric that blocked and absorbed pollutants but passed air, these were heralded as the wonder of the age, but major problems occurred even before the domes were fully operational. Several sections collapsed due to stress miscalculations, while others were rendered useless by failed weather-processing machinery. In 2039, the Pan-Europa virus attacked the biofabric covering of the dome, creating large holes in many areas.

These days, the dome malfunctions so badly that in winter it is not uncommon to witness snow falling inside it! Malfunctioning condensation units keep most of the capital shrouded in a light drizzle of metallic-tasting rain. That is, except for the area over the City and the western neighbourhoods of the East End District, where residents enjoy the return of thick, Victorian "pea-souper" fogs.

>>>>>[And just remember, if it falls from the sky and hits the pavement and fizzes, get indoors bloody quick.]<<<<<
—Malcy (07:42:37/2-JAN-52)

>>>>>[And if it goes splat. It might just be one of those Cage Boys deciding to save himself some time on the way down.]<<<<<
—Yorks (11:28:55/3-JAN-52)

>>>>>[Cage Boys?]<<<<<
—Inquisitive Smoker (11:31:08/3-JAN-52)

>>>>>[Band of punks and urchins who climb the dome framework and then slide and swing around it. Their name comes from the fact that in places where the biofabric is gone, or nearly so, the framework looks like a rib cage.]<<<<<
—Answer Man! (11:45:59/3-JAN-52)

ENTERTAINMENT

The difficulty with describing what to do and see in London is in deciding what to leave out, rather than what to include. The capital is stuffed to the gills with concert halls, theatres, museums, art galleries, night clubs, and sports stadia. In a lifetime of exploring, most Londoners do not manage to get around all of it, so what hope for the casual visitor?

Well, the best way to see London, at least initially, is on a guided tour. These can be arranged at any visitor centre, and may take in a particular site or a larger area. Visits to some parts of London require special escorts, but such trips usually offer no danger to the tourist.

Those interested in history will, of course, go to the major tourist sites, including the Tower of London and Buckingham Palace. A more considered study is possible at any one of London's 500 museums, but the most popular are undoubtedly the British Museum in Bloomsbury (West End District, world history), the Museum of London at London Wall (City District, U.K. history), and the various Kensington museums: Victoria and Albert (design and daily life), Natural History and Science Museums (all in Palaces and Estates District).

Visitors with an eye for the arts should take in the National Gallery in Trafalgar Square (West End Overground/Underplex, world art) and the Tate Gallery on Millbank (Palaces and Estates, British and modern art). The many hundreds of smaller galleries scattered around the capital offer further entertainment for lovers of all types of modern and ethnic art.

Theatre-goers and music-lovers will be bewildered for choice in London. Enthusiasts of the theatre should head for the new National Theatre complex and the rebuilt Shaftesbury Avenue in the West End Underplex. Classical music fans will find much to delight them at the Festival Hall (Underplex) and the Royal Albert Hall in Kensington (Palaces and Estates District).

Younger music enthusiasts need not look far in the West End to find clubs catering to their own particular interest, jazz, electroslam, or deathcore. The enormous arenas at Wembley and Docklands are the venues for the most popular acts. Hundreds of world entertainment-superstars have come from London, and there are thousands more eager hopefuls trying their hardest to join them!

Sports fans can see a wide range of entertainments in London at a number of venues. Britain's national game, cricket, is still played at two major London venues, Lords Cricket Ground (Village District) and the Oval (recently relocated to Richmond). Test Matches (international games) are played during the summer months, last for up to five days, with six hours play per day, and frequently end in ties. Americans generally find the rules of this game impossible to comprehend.

More attractive to many visitors is football (sometimes known as soccer), played at a wide range of levels and many grounds throughout the capital. Wembley Stadium, where the English national football team plays, holds up to 115,000 spectators and is often nearly full for major games. In the English First Division (comparable to the NFL of American football), the major London teams are Arsenal (playing at Highbury Stadium), Westway (at White City Stadium), and Tottenham (at the White Hart Lane Stadium). Visitors are warned that rambunctious behaviour and occasional violence are not uncommon among British football fans and that policing styles are robust at these matches.

Lawn tennis is played at the famous Wimbledon Courts, the last grass courts in the world at which a Grand Slam title is decided. The grass is now synthetic, however, because of toxic corrosion during the last two decades. Dog racing, a traditional sport of Londoners, takes place at a number of smaller stadia in the evenings, under floodlights.

>>>>>[More physical entertainment is easy enough to come by, providing one knows where to go and how to be discreet, since the whole subject is a legal minefield. The best areas are around the main-line stations. We don't recommend that you take advantage of any offers made in the Westway or Squeeze areas, no matter how good the bargain.]<<<<<
—Norm (21:11:37/19-JAN-52)

>>>>>[The Undercity has been a magnet for prospective tour operators since its existence was first revealed to the surface world a few years ago. Due to the dangerous nature of most of its inhabitants and structure, however, only a few select sections are available for guided tours, none of which are recommended by the BTB. Members of just about every race spend their time eking out a desperate living in the Undercity, some coexisting warily but peacefully, others at permanent war. Many of the ancient tunnels run for mile after uncharted mile under all parts of the city, linking up with secret government works, the Tube network, and power maintenance tunnels.

Visitors should be aware of the tremendous risks involved in even the most heavily escorted trips. In other words, don't go there unless you absolutely have to.]<<<<<
—Dapper D (09:15:30/11-JAN-52)

TRIDEO

As for trideo, it offers a plethora of channels, if satellite and cable channels are included, but only a few of these attract more than a tiny minority of British viewers. The most important trid channels are described below.

BBC (British Broadcasting Corporation)

The BBC is partly funded by government, but mostly by direct sales of rights to its programs for overseas broadcasts, sales of spin-off books and media products, and the like. This is a public-service channel that is mostly devoted to news, current affairs, and a small number of "quality" programs (documentaries, drama, wildlife programs, educational programs). It has a reputation for accuracy and impartiality, but its funding does not permit it to cover major news stories with the speed and broad coverage of rival channels. The BBC runs two main channels, a news channel and BBC London.

ITV

This is the Independent Television network, which has 16 regional channels throughout the U.K., which share most of their programming. This is mostly a fairly cheap entertainment service with a high percentage of imported programs of mediocre quality. ITV runs Channels 3, 4, and 5, and ITV London.

OzNet

Owned by an Australian cartel, this network specializes in low-quality entertainment, cheap programming, public-access programs, and titillation. In London, it runs two regular light entertainment channels, together with subscription movie and music channels.

StyleNet

Established in 2046, StyleNet is a high-quality channel specializing in children's programs, coverage of minority sports, arts and drama programs, and upmarket discussion, analysis, and current affairs programs. Because it attracts a high percentage of high-income viewers, it earns advertising revenue in excess of what its market share might appear to justify, and has been clearly successful despite adverse initial predictions.

Specialist Channels

There are also many dozen satellite and cable channels, legal and not, originating in Europe, which households with the appropriate equipment can receive. The specialist channels provide a wide range of entertainment, some of it in English.

RADIO

Unlike other countries, Britain has a long tradition of top-class radio. London is served by nine national stations (produced by either the BBC or the independent network) and over two dozen city-based stations. Pirate radio stations, serving a particular community or filling a musical need, operate sporadically from many tall tower blocks.

NEWSPAPERS

Britain has many national newspapers. The local ones are often evening publications, with morning papers being the nationals. Britain's relative cultural homogeneity and small size makes distribution and sales of national newspapers much easier than in many other countries. Following are capsule descriptions of the leading newspapers.

News UK

The leading mid-market newspaper, *News UK* is informative but weak on foreign news. It is very good for gossip, Royal stories, and sports coverage.

The Times

The Times is a venerable quality newspaper. Its print and format are archaic, but it offers good news coverage in all departments. Also excellent are the listings of official functions, museums and galleries, and all entertainments.

The Standard

Low-brow and rather right-wing, *The Standard* takes a nationalistic slant on news coverage.

The Democrat

The only major liberal/left-wing newspaper, *The Democrat* is noted for long articles on social issues and foreign stories not adequately treated elsewhere.

The Truth

A rather ironically named slander-sheet and borderline soft-core porn tabloid, *The Truth*—for all the trash—offers the occasional gem.

WEST END UNDERPLEX

LONDON UNDER LONDON

Tourists visiting the Smoke for the first time are often bewildered by the choice of attractions laid out before them. Guided tours to all the major tourist sites are an obvious way to start, but many find that the real highlight of any trip to London is the amazing new West End Underplex. London has always been the country's best and biggest shopping centre, but the last few decades have seen a dramatic change in style—because the shops have all gone underground!

At the turn of the century, several West End developments already linked the Underground station complexes with the street level. Construction of small shopping malls began at Marble Arch, Bond Street, and Piccadilly. Compared to the street-level shops, accessible only by braving the typically awful British weather, these new developments were paradise. Soon the pressure of businesses wishing to expand their lower floors to join the underground malls forced planners to drastically expand them. Construction of new malls began around some of the other major West End Underground stations, at Oxford Circus, Tottenham Court Road, and Charing Cross.

Meanwhile, as better-class department stores abandoned the streets of the West End, property values plummeted, allowing all manner of ephemeral businesses to

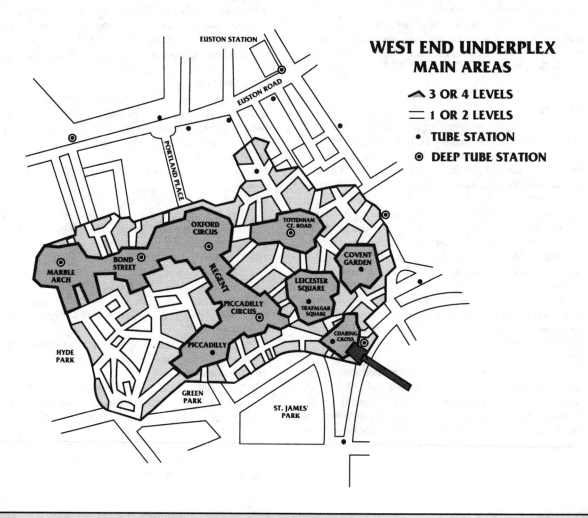

WEST END UNDERPLEX
MAIN AREAS

- ⌃ **3 OR 4 LEVELS**
- ≡ **1 OR 2 LEVELS**
- • **TUBE STATION**
- ⊚ **DEEP TUBE STATION**

move in. This created a huge boom in the West End's already large collection of young fashion shops, along with a steady influx of stores selling the latest high-tech gear, music, and the like, plus cafes, restaurants, and clubs. By their very nature, these businesses were here today, gone tomorrow, and the economic stability of the entire West End was soon teetering on the edge of collapse.

Underneath the streets, though, it was a different story. The first shop-lined tunnels connecting the major Underground station malls were completed in the early 2040s, and some of the malls themselves were sunk deeper. The presence of the larger retailers, together with the controlled, secure, futuristic environment, meant that empty sites were filled as rapidly as they were advertised.

In 2042 the Underplex Corporation was established to oversee the project into its final stages. New tunnels were run to join up with the burgeoning underground development at Covent Garden, and the mainline BritRail stations at Euston and King's Cross added a second underground level. The already immense car parking area beneath Hyde Park was expanded, and many more were dug. Development work is still going on along some of the outlying tunnels, but most of it is complete. The malls are lined with shops, restaurants and cafes, pubs and clubs, and many special attractions, too, all combining to provide a thriving underground city staffed by many thousands of people and visited every year by millions.

>>>>>[People, this is not our sort of place. There are no shadows under the city, just miles and miles of pastel chrome and metallic glass, staffed by security guards and zombies and patronized by the terminally easily pleased. You know how vile most shopping malls are; now string ten of them together, and to make them really interesting, throw in a couple of Cakes From Around the World pavement cafes. Oh yeah, and get a gang of tranced-out dweebheads to trill Murder Muzak over the PA all day and all night. Ugh! The whole plex makes me want to vomit on the floor, which is cool because even that would make the place twenty times more interesting.]<<<<<
—Spider (06:15:46/16-JAN-52)

>>>>>[The West End Underplex is a hall of machines, not a home of man or elf. It is as if the individual has been excluded and everything natural been processed until the spirit has been wrung from it. It is no place for me.]<<<<<
—Sarahana (01:14:36/19-JAN-52)

>>>>>[Wait a minute! I suppose you're going to tell me where else in the city you can get 50 different types of restaurants in a row, or shop in the world's biggest shoe store without getting red-flecked skin from the acid rain? What's so bad about a place being clean, warm, and so well-policed you never get hassled by street trash? I love the plex. It's plainly way too cool for you pixie-headed mellows. This is the future, man, so use it!]<<<<<
—Jimbo (15:38:34/20-JAN-52)

ACCESS TO THE UNDERPLEX

There is now an entrance to the Underplex at every major road junction in the West End area. Most of them are similar to, and sometimes combined with, an Underground station, with escalators, lifts, and moving slopeways to take passengers down. Over the main deep malls, and especially at Piccadilly, Marble Arch, and Trafalgar Square/Charing Cross, more elaborate domes have been constructed to allow floods of light to fall into the cavernous interiors.

>>>>>[Yeah, you look up the centre of Piccadilly D, and you get to experience the wonderful sight of 50 tranced punks making ultradumb faces at you against the glass all day.]<<<<<
—Norm (03:17:18/21-JAN-52)

At every entrance, visitors will find that barriers have been fitted to ease the congestion that sometimes builds up, but they may rest assured that no ticket or other charge is required to enter the Underplex. The Underplex's friendly security staff, instantly recognizable in their neat brown and orange uniforms, are always on hand to assist visitors.

>>>>>[I love these guys. Security in the Underplex is so lax you could hold a rave party in the middle of Oxford West and they'd never notice. Hop over the barriers, just like the tube, and run like crazy. Drives 'em mad, especially 'cuz they can't shoot you. If they do give chase, all you gotta do is make for any of the central wells and jump the escalators or dive into a fountain like Tarzan. No problem.]<<<<<
—Jimmy the Mover (05:07:33/18-JAN-52)

>>>>>[Where you been, Jimmy? Things have changed since the mass occupation by those striking shop workers over last Christmas. The security guys aren't allowed to be armed, but the new Underplex police division sure as hell are! You keep treating the malls like your own personal playground and you'll get a baggie's bullet in your back. Play it cool, term, play it cool.]<<<<<
—Malcy (04:11:56/4-FEB-52)

Most of those who work in the Underplex arrive here via the various stations. The Tube network joins the complex at Level A, the Deep Tube at Level C (at a selected number of stations, see the Underplex map for details). There are also access tunnels from the railway stations at Euston, King's Cross, and Charing Cross, which are fitted with moving pavements and regular shuttles.

The West End Underplex's shuttle system was introduced as soon as the malls extended to sizes beyond which it was really feasible for the public to walk or ride on a moving pavement. The shuttles are squat, driverless

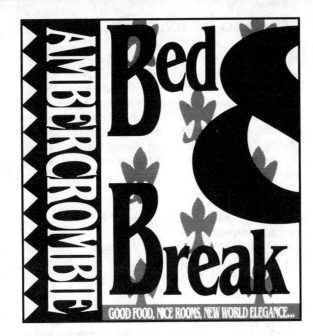

AMBERCROMBIE

Bed & Break

GOOD FOOD, NICE ROOMS, NEW WORLD ELEGANCE...

vehicles that resemble buses with their sides removed. They run in loops throughout the complex, guided by a grid system controlled by the Underplex's vast administrative computer, CANDY. Their paths are marked by yellow stripes on the floor, and on the Smart Maps dotted around the complex. Every so often, a post running from floor to ceiling marks a designated stopping point. Press the large yellow button once, at which point a display provides information on when the next shuttle will be along. (These posts also carry security alarms for use in an emergency and directories of the nearby shops.) The shuttle senses when all passengers are aboard. To stop the shuttle while riding, simply press one of the buttons set beside each seat.

The shuttles can travel surprisingly fast, but safety is assured by their powerful sensors. These sensors will gently stop the vehicle if someone is in its path, sounding a horn if the individual is still there after five seconds.

>>>>>[In the early days, they just couldn't get the sensors on these things to work properly. It was brilliant! The papers were always full of stories of some poor old grannie or other being splattered and then dragged all over the mall floor by one of these things, though I was never lucky to see one, worse luck.]<<<<<
    —Jimbo (16:05:36/20-DEC-51)

>>>>>[Oh gross!]<<<<<
    —Rosie Posie (11:48:05/21-DEC-51)

>>>>>[You know, I shouldn't be telling you this, but when I was having a peer up CANDY's skirts one time, I couldn't help noticing how easy it would be to, shall we say, rearrange the shuttle guidance systems. Not that anything would be gained from doing such a thing, of course.]<<<<<
    —Slow Mo (12:15:02/9-JAN-52)

UNDERPLEX ADMINISTRATION

The Underplex Corporation oversees every aspect of operating the complex. The Underplex Administrator is Sir Steven Conran, and he heads a board of directors composed of senior retail managers, two security experts, and a pair of legal advisors. They work in the Underplex Corporation's huge administration centre located to the east of Regent North. The centre and the four smaller satellite centres located at the extremities of the Underplex include workshops and repair bays, apartments and rest rooms for the staff of the various divisions, cafeterias, a gym and swimming pool, and (at the administration centre) a small clinic.

CANDY, the complex's dedicated computer construct, handles the sophisticated day-to-day operation of the Underplex. It monitors and maintains the constant environment, guides the shuttles and the remote cleaning shuttles, controls the power supply, lighting, and security doors, runs the Smart Maps, and regulates just about every other aspect of the Underplex. CANDY is backed up by a maintenance staff of more than 6,000 people, from highly skilled technicians to simple cleaners. Also among the staff are specialist emergency teams for dealing with fires and other disasters, though they have never been called out to deal with a single major incident since the Underplex Corporation was founded.

There are 1,420 security officers working in the Underplex, recently supplemented by 300 police officers of the new Metropolitan Police Underplex Division. Security is a prime concern in the centre of any modern city, of course, but visitors will find it light and unobtrusive. In the Underplex, nothing must stand in the way of the visitors' enjoyment!

>>>>>[Lined up behind the malls and tunnel is an immense spider web of service tunnels, cable pipes, and climate-control ducts. It would take decades of hard work to map them all from scratch—unless someone can hack a map out of CANDY. Any takers? The main routes, however, are easy to follow. There are some vid cameras and motion sensor alarms, but when have they ever stopped anyone? On the outer eastern edge, the power lines link into parts of the Undercity through the old Holborn tram tunnels. These all make great entry points or escape routes; you could hide out down here for months with no problem. If you know how to handle the Undercity, that is.]<<<<<
    —Truman (04:11:52/15-DEC-51)

>>>>>[You said it, normo.]<<<<<
    —Grishnak (14:03:26/26-DEC-51)

The Underplex opens at 6:00 A.M., and the smaller concourses are cut off by large security doors at 9:00 P.M. Most of the larger malls remain open until 2:30 A.M., allowing access to the many clubs, theatres, and concert halls that dot the complex.

>>>>>[The general security of the Underplex is rated by the Metropolitan Police computer at Hendon as A, though the Corporation's administration centre comes in slightly higher at AA.

Recently, there has been a dramatic increase in the number of Plexrats, the gangs of young homeless kids who hang out in the Underplex full-time, scavenging scraps from the restaurants and sleeping in ventilation ducts to avoid security. It is actually a criminal offense to trespass in certain parts of the Underplex without authorization, but these kids plainly have nowhere else to go.]<<<<<
—X-Plod (22:02:45/2-JAN-52)

>>>>>[These kids really make me fill up, y'know? They hear about the bright lights, all the shops and the burger places, and they come from all over the country to see the heavenly new Shopper's Paradise where everyone has fun fun fun. They get here starving, penniless, and homeless, and if they're lucky, get adopted by the Plexrats. You get them making their crazy dashes through Jones & Jones or Elder's like streams of lemmings, hoping to create enough confusion to grab loads of stuff and all get clean away. Still, I guess it beats being shoved up chimneys.]<<<<<
—Malcy (04:16:11/22-FEB-52)

UNDERPLEX STRUCTURE

A tourist's first glance down the four-floor marvel that stretches down Regent North as far south as Piccadilly is likely to put him in serious danger of dislocating his jaw. The shops stretch away for almost a mile, stacked up four floors high along both sides of the central well. High in the arched roof, lights and a variety of hanging figures and plants vie with the daylight streaming in through the regularly placed domes. On the floor of the well, cafes and restaurants mingle with open plazas, children's miniplaygrounds, and all manner of exhibitions and displays.

New visitors to the Underplex are often completely overwhelmed by its sheer size, until they learn to treat its various halls and malls like normal streets (albeit streets that rise several levels up into the air!). Those who get lost are quickly directed to the Smart Maps distributed through the complex. These can be fingertip- or voice-activated, and even respond to queries as complex as "Where can a guy get a decent umbrella round here?"

Around the edges of the Underplex, and running between the main malls, the halls are usually on only one or two levels. Within the main sections, though, three or four levels are far more likely. Escalators and lifts are everywhere, both on the concourses and inside the many shops that stretch over more than one level.

The main concourses follow their above-ground equivalents and carry their names (Oxford East or West, Regent North or South, and so on). The designers have often tried to recreate the feel of the original neighbourhoods that existed at the time when work first

began on the the Underplex. Thus, the area of the Underplex beneath Mayfair is home to a number of fine restaurants and clubs, casinos, and hotels. The area around the new Leicester Square development is being decorated to a Chinese theme to match Chinatown just a few dozen feet above. There is even a new, underground Carnaby Street, featuring the wildest clothing stores and its famous fully lifelike automatons of the Beatles, Rolling Stones, and other stars of the Swingin' Sixties!

Along with the shops, restaurants, bars, and such, a great number of special attractions are scattered throughout the Underplex. These include the brand-new National Theatre complex on Haymarket (alongside Regent South), the Theatreland development and the two new cinemas between the Leicester Square and Covent Garden Malls, and the new underground extension to the National Gallery and National Portrait Gallery at the junction of Trafalgar Square and St. Martin's (Level A). All told, the Underplex is home to over 5,700 shops and other businesses, places to eat, and entertainment centres and provides a shopping experience that is unparalleled anywhere in the world.

>>>>>[Lies, all lies. I worked in a fashion shop on Regent South for four years. It was quite banging, really, but what got me was how ill working down in this hole makes everyone. Over the years my skin turned green-white, deathly pale, and I lost a lot of hair and body weight. Even now I sometimes get a taste in my mouth that reminds of me of all those mornings when the air conditioning was screwed again, and I still have nightmares about the time we had that small fire and the sprinklers failed to start up. This place is hell, and that ain't where I want to go.]<<<<<
—Kaz (10:14:36/17-DEC-51)

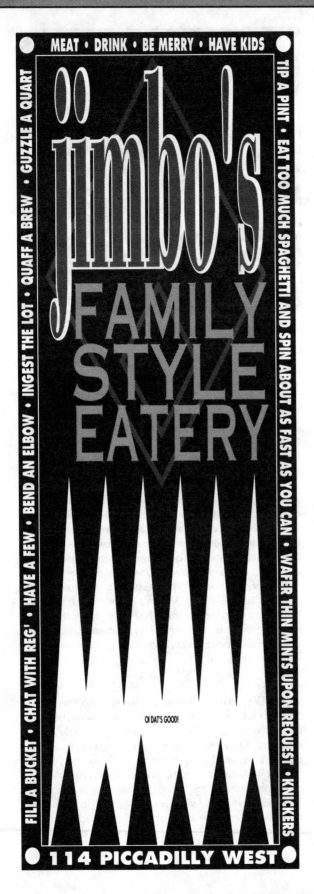

USEFUL ADDRESSES

>>>>>[If you like glass, chrome, and ridiculous plastic mobiles, miles and miles of shops all looking exactly the same and selling the same, used by dourly grimacing zombies driven half-mad by half-baked muzak and expensive croissants, this is the place for you. Like Spider said at the beginning, the Underplex hasn't got shadows, but even here, amid the most controlled environment around, there is stuff you should know about.]<<<<<
—Egon (05:17:33/24-APR-52)

RESTAURANTS AND BARS

Jimbo's (below 17W)

Large Restaurant Archetype/Unit 114 Piccadilly West (B)/Ravi Gavaskar, Manager/BTG# 719 (442-1616).

>>>>>[Huge family-style restaurant, decorated with trid soap opera memorabilia, where the food is awful and the service terrible. Why mention it? Because if you want to talk without being overheard, it's the best place in the Underplex. Honest.]<<<<<
—John (03:14:33/31-DEC-51)

>>>>>[Sounds like a wind-up to me, Johnny boy.]<<<<<
—Malcy (07:38:04/3-JAN-52)

Ragazzo (15W)

Small Restaurant and Bar Archetype/Unit 416 Oxford East (C)/Art Silvestri, Manager/BTG# 719 (606-4286).

>>>>>[Unassuming little place hidden away behind W. H. Johnson's, but this is where most of the Underplex security guys hang out.]<<<<<
—Dapper D (21:11:07/19-DEC-51)

Slide (15V)

Mid-Size Restaurant Archetype/Unit 4 Marble Arch (D)/V. Urbanus, Owner/Bias Against Elves/BTG# 719 (108-8638).

>>>>>[That rare item, a restaurant run by a troll. Actually, it's pretty good, and Big V does lay on human portions as well as his usual monstrous meat platters. This is a good place to relax and rub warts, er, shoulders with orks and trolls. By the way, why does Big V never tell anyone his name? People have been trying to guess for months.]<<<<<
—Rosie Posie (00:28:15/13-JAN-52)

>>>>>[I heard it was Vera, 'cos the Registrar of Births and Deaths wrote it down wrong. No wonder he doesn't tell anyone.]<<<<<
—Malcy (06:04:21/12-FEB-52)

Zowie's (16Z)

Large Restaurant and Bar Archetype/Unit 406 Covent Garden (A)/Cally Delphinus, Manager/BTG# 719 (483-6792).

>>>>>[Slick and modern place. Very popular with the kens and kylies, y'know, the young corporate set. And boy, do these kids like to gossip. The only place in the city where "Hey, what's your password?" actually works! Unbelievable!]<<<<<
—Farron (03:12:43/4-DEC-51)

NIGHT CLUBS

Diamonds (15S)

Casino Archetype/Unit 23 Gloucester (B)/Alec Brandwin, Manager/BTG# 719 (272-4150).

>>>>>[Way too classy gambling club aimed squarely at your traditional Mayfair punters. One of the croupiers, Teresa Fischer, always has plenty of information to sell. Just buy her a drink.]<<<<<
—Lone Sloane (12:17:04/30-DEC-51)

Green Onions (15X)

Night Club Archetype/Unit 1081 Oxford East (D)/ Just Verity, Owner/BTG# 719 (698-9545).

>>>>>[Cool, members-only jazz club, laid-back and expensive. You want to impress someone—a girl, a client— you bring 'em here.]<<<<<
—Lone Sloane (12:27:52/03-JAN-52)

The Snake Pit (15X)

Night Club Archetype/Unit 4 Wardour Plaza (B)/Stu the Fox, Manager/BTG# 719 (484-1242).

>>>>>[Really spaced lowlife den, favoured by 20 types of tranced-up weirdos. Specialty of the house is a real pit, steps down the side and padded with vinyl, where you're meant to writhe to the rhythm of the slam pumped through the floor. Saturday nights in the pit is a great experience, but don't go alone without wearing lockable underwear.]<<<<<
—John (04:04:31/2-FEB-52)

OTHER

Blissful Waters (16Z)

Units 21-11 Covent Garden (C)/Fiona Hamilton-Smythe, Manager/BTG# 719 (174-4218).

>>>>>[Flotation tanks, sensory-pattern isolation, progressive relaxation, all without the poisoning effect of chemicals and burning out your brain with chips, wires, wetware. Just relax and flow with the spirit. Then you will find (4.1 Mp deleted by sysop)]<<<<<
—Janzi Z. (18:43:01/21-FEB-52)

>>>>>[Fiona's never been the same since she did that self-awareness trip in the Salish-Shidhe retreat.]<<<<<
—Samantha (19:32:18/21-FEB-52)

British Heritage (15W)

Small Store Archetype/Unit 1 Bond Street (A)/ Jonathan Carmichael, Manager/Strong Bias Against Metahumans/BTG# 719 (905-2345).

>>>>>[Pleasant, touristy place. Sells jigsaw puzzles of Edwardian paintings, Olde Englande Herbal Pot-Pourri, Victorian recipe books, medieval facsimile maps, harmless stuff. Unfortunately, Jonathan is also a member of the Conservationist Party and the Genealogy Society. We tried entrapping him last year, but he got the weapons out the back of the shop just in time before the baggies came along.]<<<<<
—Sarahana (23:18:44/6-MAR-52)

WEST END OVERGROUND

SHADOWTOWN

Way back at the turn of the century, the streets of the West End resounded to the sound—during the day—of happy Londoners shopping to their heart's content. By night the streets resounded to the sounds of those same happy Londoners being resoundingly entertained. The West End was the place of department stores and specialty shops, selling everything from socks to satellite dishes, where money changed hands so fast it glowed red-hot. Come evening, the restaurants and bars opened up, providing an evening's entertainment for some or just a brief stopover for those going on to the theatre or a swinging club.

Today, many things have changed, but others have stayed exactly the same. The bright lights and the big stores have all but gone, fleeing underground to plush new sites in the West End Underplex. The glitzy theatres and cinemas, the better restaurants and bars, they've gone too. What's left are the tiny specialty shops, the street-corner cafes, the dodgy clubs and the roughest pubs. Money has fled from the West End, and the area has slipped into the shadows.

Of course, some parts of the West End are perfectly acceptable, if a little scruffy. Although the big stores are gone from Oxford Street and Regent Street, indoor markets, virtual bazaars, have taken their places, selling all manner of up-to-the-minute merchandise. At the weekends, the police manage to keep the main roads open and the shoppers safe, providing the latter stay out of the back streets and away from trouble.

At other times, though, it is unadvisable to walk in the West End Overground without an experienced escort. It is all too easy to stroll ten paces from one of the main streets and suddenly find oneself in the midst of a very dangerous situation indeed. At night, it is not recommended that anyone venture into any part of the district without escort, no matter how truly "on" younger tourists may feel the clubs and bars are. Be aware of the dangers, and stay safe.

>>>>>[Heh heh. I don't care what you heard. This ain't the Overground. This is Shadowtown, the place we call our own. Sure, you can have the main streets at weekends; we don't mind selling you trinkets while we pick your pockets. After all, we gotta eat. But the back streets, the alleys and the walkways, they're ours, and ours alone. If you like life at the furthest edge, come on down and bring a friend. After all, the more the merrier. This is our town, we make the rules.]<<<<<
—Jimmy the Mover (04:11:46/12-DEC-51)

GEOGRAPHY AND DEMOGRAPHICS

The West End of London is a flat area covered almost entirely with old and derelict buildings. Most are four or five stories high, with some much higher; away from the main street, the buildings are tightly packed into terraces. Because of the Underplex development, there has been no major new construction in the Overground District for more than 30 years. The main shopping streets that carve up the district are wide and well-kept, but the back streets and alleys are in a poor state of repair.

The one bright spot amid the unremitting greyness of the West End is Hyde Park, which the district shares with the Estates. The park is surrounded by tall railings and may be entered only through gates at its corners. At this end, the park is flat and featureless; only past the central lake, The Serpentine, are there trees and hills. At the top corner of Hyde Park is a spot known as Speaker's Corner. Until recently, one could stand here on a box and declaim freely about any subject under the sun; nowadays, sad to say, it is generally too dangerous.

The thousands of people who crowd into the West End Overground are a wide mixture of races and ethnic backgrounds. Orks are fairly common, the other metahuman races less so. In an area of south Soho is a sizable Chinese community known as Chinatown. West Indians, Asians from the subcontinent, Italians, Greeks, Poles, and a smattering of other Europeans also live in the area. Some of these groups keep themselves to themselves, building their own communities within the greater one, while others are more integrated.

The people of the Overground are a wide mixture of social classes and educational backgrounds. In Mayfair, the remnants of the prestigious old apartment developments and the fine hotels still cater to a select few wealthy residents. On the far side, the once fashionable area around Covent Garden still plays host to artists and musicians, although these days they tend to be of the undiscovered and poverty-stricken variety.

>>>>>[As you can imagine, policing the West End Overground is a logistical nightmare, and the Metropolitan Police seem to have washed their hands of the problem, virtually giving rule of the back streets over to the residents. Of course, every weekend they make a great show of keeping the main streets open for business, but this rarely involves much more than speeding up and down Regent Street and Charing Cross Road with their sirens blaring, making tourists faint and young girls giggle.

Organized crime has got the West End business community just about entirely sewn up. Paying protection has become a way of life, just like paying taxes. But the problem can only get worse. Criminal gangs own many shops and other businesses, using them as fronts for all manner of shadowy dealings.

The gangs operating in the West End area are from a range of backgrounds, but the most sinister are the Chinese. The Tongs rule Chinatown and much of the rest of Soho with ruthless and bloodthirsty efficiency. Don't cross them or meddle in their business affairs; they are not of your concern.]<<<<<
—X-Plod (22:14:06/2-MAR-52)

ECONOMY

Much of the West End's economy revolves around the retail businesses that valiantly cling to their ramshackle sites throughout the area between Wigmore Street and the Strand. Away from the main streets, almost all of the shops are individual units rather than parts of a national chain. This means the area is full of myriad unique shops selling everything from avant garde fashion to ultratech household equipment, from modern jewelry to licensed magical artifacts.

Away from the shopping centre, the offices of many small concerns add another facet to the area's economy. There are few large businesses based in the district, with the exception of the new corporate office developments creeping their way up Roseberry Avenue and Goswell Road, linking the overspill from the City of London and the very fashionable Village District.

In these troubled times, it is somewhat sad to also report that at the heart of Europe's largest city there are many unemployed, squatters, vagrants, and worse. The West End has always attracted them in droves, but now they seem intent on building an entire community.

>>>>>[Nah, that's crap. We only look like we haven't got jobs. Those who know us know us for what we do. Rak it, we aren't going to take out adverts in *CityScape*, are we?]<<<<<
—Malcy (03:12:42/1-FEB-52)

>>>>>[Don't forget that very important economy, the soft one. Years ago Soho was crammed with adult cinemas, book clubs, and more fleshy delights. When they somehow got the idea that Soho could turn into the next Covent Garden—you know, all designer cafes and extortionate clothes emporia, ad nauseam—they kicked everybody out. Now a lot of them have come back, or at least started advertising again, because if the truth be known, most of them never really went away. The tatty residential streets north of Oxford Street are another great place to go if you are on the lookout for some alternative entertainment.]<<<<<
—Norm (14:06:24/18-MAR-52)

NEIGHBOURHOODS

Moving from west to east, the following are the main neighbourhoods of the Overground District.

MAYFAIR

Like a faded dowager slowly wilting into senility, most of Mayfair is well past its prime. Until fairly recently, it was regarded as the most exclusive address in Inner London, an address only the very wealthy could afford. In its streets, chauffeur-driven limousines waited outside the swankiest hotels, clubs, and casinos; all night the flashbulbs popped, snapping away at London society's prime movers.

Since the removal of the West End's most fashionable shops to the Underplex, and more important, the breakdown of law in the Overground area, the rich have all but abandoned Mayfair, leaving only the old and the willful hiding in their crumbling apartments. Only on Park Lane has any sort of last stand been made. The eastern lanes of the wide highway have been sealed at top and bottom and fitted with security booths that allow only authorized vehicles to approach the Dorchester, the Hyde Park Hilton, and the other super-luxury hotels.

>>>>>[Security around the hotels is supposed to be tight, and I hear those security guys are allowed to carry automatic weapons. Anyway, the Metropolitan Police computer gives Mayfair as a whole a security rating A, dropping to B and then C as one approaches Regent Street.]<<<<<
—X-Plod (23:00:09/2-MAR-52)

SOUTH MARYLEBONE

North of Oxford Street, Marylebone's endless rows of large old houses stretch north along wide, badly kept streets as far as Regent's Park. The area has not been truly fashionable for several centuries, and the decline of the West End shopping area has dragged it further down. On the south side of the neighbourhood, many of the buildings are home to squatters. In comparison, those west of the Edgware Road, bordering Paddington, are much better-maintained and provide homes for a community of middle-class professionals.

Along the Marylebone Road, the centre of which marks the boundary with the Village District, Madame Tussaud's Waxworks and the Sherlock Holmes Museum at 221B Baker Street are popular tourist attractions, though strictly speaking, these are in the Village District.

>>>>>[At the moment, South Marylebone has several fairly nasty gangs of street kids hacking chunks out of each other every night; the worst are the Blue Watch and the Hawkeyes. Other than that, the area is a hotbed of political activity, though generally of the more liberal sort. The police computer gives the neighbourhood a security rating of C.]<<<<<
—X-Plod (23:19:20/2-MAR-52)

SOHO

The heart of the West End takes its name from a hunting cry, presumably dating back to when the entire area was covered in nothing but fields and trees. Nowadays it is more a cross between a slum and a bazaar. Tiny alleys and lanes snake between wider streets packed with market stalls; pokey little shops crammed with curios are squeezed into every last corner. There are restaurants and many cafes and food stalls, with clusters of seats set up right there in the street.

South of Shaftesbury Avenue, the delightful Chinatown neighbourhood adds a bright dash of colour. Here the more intrepid explorer may sample the best of every aspect of Chinese culture. Be warned, however. The Chinese are a proud race, and it is not wise to insult them. Nearby Leicester Square provides less traditional entertainment, in the form of its many cinemas, clubs, and ultratech arcades.

>>>>>[You have to be real careful when dealing with the Chinatown cowboys, doubly so if you're on their own patch. The back alleys around Lisle Street are a maze that can be fatal if a clutch of cleaver-wielding orientals are chasing you. Me, I have a special code. I don't work for them, but they can always buy me dinner and ask anyway.]<<<<<
—Jimmy the Mover (04:39:59/28-FEB-52)

>>>>>[You want to be careful, matey. You go to their house and eat their food, you owe them. And they don't forget that kinda stuff in a hurry.]<<<<<
—Malcy (03:17:44/2-MAR-52)

Across Charing Cross Road, now almost entirely abandoned by the bookshops that once made it famous, the fashionable area around Covent Garden tries to cling to some semblance of style and order. The Royal Opera House is still located by the piazza, but, sad to say, audiences and performers often have to be bussed in and out.

>>>>>[You want organized crime, you got it. You want unorganized crime, you got that, too. You've also got trancers, runners, deckers, rogue mages, street samurai by the dozen, and many other unusual types. Hem this rabble in between the Regent Street police vans and Chinatown, and you've got trouble in spades. It's still a wonder that more people don't get splashed on both sides, but I guess there's a kind of grudging respect between the two. Sometimes they need each other, and may well do so again.]<<<<<
—X-Plod (23:47:17/2-MAR-52)

>>>>>[Hey! Round eyes, I don't like the way you speak of my people. You better watch out or someone's gonna cut a forgiveness mantra on your face.]<<<<<
—Hark (23:51:02/2-MAR-52)

>>>>>[Kids! If that's who I think it is, he's eight years old, but I still don't want to meet him in a dark alley on a moonless night.

Soho rates a conclusive E security rating on the Metropolitan Police computer, though a side entry records a solitary exclamation mark for Chinatown. As it implies, the people there take care of themselves.]<<<<<
—X-Plod (00:02:51/3-MAR-52)

BLOOMSBURY, ST. PANCRAS, CLERKENWELL, AND FINSBURY

The grand old British Museum still stands at the heart of this district, and makes for a very rewarding day out for all lovers of history. A little way further north, scattered along several streets, the several dozen buildings of London University help give Bloomsbury a studious air. The rest of Bloomsbury and the other districts consist mostly of low-quality housing, hotels, and seedy office buildings, though there is a thriving Italian community near the mainline BritRail stations on the boundary with the Village District.

>>>>>[The British Museum has a new department devoted to the Awakened cultures. It is not yet open to the public, though a great deal of research is apparently being done here, with experts visiting the museum from all corners of the world.]<<<<<
—ARC (07:30:10/27-JAN-52)

>>>>>[These four neighbourhoods are all rated as C for security purposes; the British Museum and the University rate A. Look out for the Stallions street gang; they're vicious and racist.]<<<<<
—X-Plod (00:21:38/3-MAR-52)

THE BRITISH MUSEUM

AWAKENINGS!

"I NEVER METAHUMAN I DIDN'T LIKE."

USEFUL ADDRESSES

>>>>>[If you're looking for something, if you're looking for anything, come on down to Shadowtown. This is our part of town, you know, the place where what we say goes and no one says no. Of course, you got to have manners and play by the rules that go down here, but they aren't hard to pick up if you're careful. When in doubt, keep your mouth shut and smile.]<<<<<
—Egon (04:59:28/13-JAN-52)

HOTELS

The Crescent Hotel (15Q)

Average Hotel Archetype/81 Edgware Road/Christine Taylor, Owner/BTG# 713 (446-9247).

>>>>>[Quiet and secluded. The cuisine is British with some flair; the seafood's good. A few dweebs come in to talk hot money, but they're not too upfront. If you're seeking affiliation, the barman in the Sunset Grill has a kinsman who knows of unlicensed magical groups.]<<<<<
—Callistra (09:00:00/1-MAR-52)

Hotel Thursday (13Y)

Cheap Hotel Archetype/22 Bedford Way/Thursday Lambert, Owner/BTG# 713 (241-1769).

>>>>>[Great cheap doss-house with secure rooms. Why, you might even find me kipping there some nights. Nuff said.]<<<<<
—Malcy (05:18:38/2-MAR-52)

Julian Hotel (16X)

Average Hotel Archetype/8 Broadwick Street/Toni Dunbar, Manager/BTG# 713 (272-1420).

>>>>>[Fair place to stay, but recommended because Toni's brother, Arturo, is a rogue mage who's always on the lookout for jobs.]<<<<<
—John (20:04:17/2-DEC-52)

Nightingale Hotel (14V)

Cheap Hotel Archetype/11 Devonshire Street/Jim and Joolz, Owners/BTG# 713 (818-4227).

>>>>>[Fair-quality hotel with a lively atmosphere. Jim and Joolz used to be shadowrunners before they retired, though they don't talk much about their past.]<<<<<
—Rosie Posie (04:17:54/15-JAN-52)

The Standard (13U)

Luxury Hotel Archetype/181-2 Gloucester Place/ Rupert Williamson, Owner/BTG# 713 (872-1115).

>>>>>[This hasn't changed much in 30 years, and the name's very accurate. The plumbing doesn't work properly, it feels like Moscow out of summer in the rooms, the room service is slow, the food is stodgy. But it's got charm. Old money finds its way to the Fountain Bar and the grill rooms here on quiet evenings. There's usually a ball or two for debutantes during The Season. If you've got some etiquette and a presentable suit or ball gown, try your luck with the people here.]<<<<<
    —Samantha (18:24:52/22-FEB-52)

Status Quo (17W)

Average Hotel Archetype/188 Charles Street/James Samuelson, Manager/BTG# 713 (315-2948).

>>>>>[Horrible. Fake traditional with Gothic restoration work and plazzy imitation marble. The "mock antique" furniture in the hotel lounge is really disgusting. The Retreat is a good cocktail bar, though. Some people close to street muscle find their way here. You want employment or you need some capable unofficial help, no questions asked, bring your notes along. No time-wasters.]<<<<<
    —Dapper D (17:45:18/19-FEB-52)

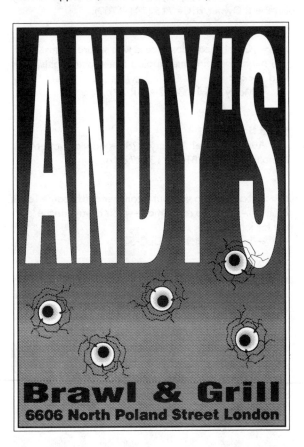

The Wiltshire Hotel (16V)

Luxury Hotel Archetype/2 Upper Brook Street/Lady Diana Malmesbury, Owner/BTG# 713 (614-6440).

>>>>>[Distinctly superior. Where the visiting aristocracy stay if their domestic staff in London didn't manage to get everything aired in time. You can't seriously expect to stay here unless you have a change of ball gown. Discreet, elegant, it costs nuyen just to look at the perfumerie.]<<<<<
    —Samantha (17:52:17/21-FEB-52)

>>>>>[Do I need a change of ball gown to get in?]<<<<<
    —Kendrick (18:01:42/21-FEB-52)

>>>>>[Didn't know that was your thing, Kendrick. But no, try the Wigmore Club for that sort of thing.]<<<<<
    —Samantha (18:07:17/21-FEB-52)

RESTAURANTS AND BARS

Andy's (15X)

Bar Archetype/4 Poland Street/Andy Grimaldi, Owner/BTG# 713 (884-1725).

>>>>>[Go down the metal steps beside the Italian deli, and be prepared for bedlam. This is a favourite street samurai haunt, and things can get pretty rough down here. Watch out for Telly, the gigantic troll doorman; he's a cutie and very shy with the ladies, but don't cross him if you like to use your legs for walking.]<<<<<
    —Janie (03:08:15/12-FEB-52)

The Archipelago (15X)

Mid-Size Restaurant Archetype/130 Great Marlborough Street/Sang Lok, Owner/BTG# 713 (884-5323).

>>>>>[Very expensive but extra-special Thai and Indonesian restaurant. Each table is in an individual booth and is practically sound-proof. Sang and his waiters (mostly members of his family) are very discreet, and they remember courteous customers.]<<<<<
    —Lone Sloane (22:04:15/12-JAN-52)

King William (15X)

Bar Archetype/17 Kingly Street/Arlo Carroll, Manager/BTG# 713 (602-1109).

>>>>>[Dingy pub with good beer. At the weekends, it's a favourite pre-club drinking place with runners, but it's much quieter during the week.]<<<<<
    —Gav (07:53:50/10-DEC-51)

Temple of the East (16Y)

Large Restaurant Archetype/2 Panton Street/Kung Soo, Owner/BTG# [unknown].

>>>>>[Ordinarily you won't ever see the inside of this place, because it's invitation only. The invitations are the sort you don't refuse, though, because they come from Grandfather Soo, and he, well, he runs things 'round here. The food is astonishing and those with invitations are never asked to pay, but it is unlikely you will notice this until long after you leave, if you are allowed to.]<<<<<
—Sister Ray (00:37:38/18-FEB-52)

Tribal (15X)

Small Restaurant and Bar Archetype/161 Oxford Street/Arnie Webster, Manager/Bias Against Orks and Trolls/BTG# 713 (828-1456).

>>>>>[Noisy and cheap, usually live music in the lower level. Upstairs at the back—where you can see both the band and the door—is where the deckers hang out. They're all weasel-faced kids, but they're hot.]<<<<<
—Rosie Posie (08:32:01/4-MAR-52)

The Unicorn (15Y)

Bar Archetype/46 Soho Square/Arven Morn, Manager/BTG# 713 (202-4481).

>>>>>[New pub with very modern interior, usually full of media types. The manager's an elf and he has some good contacts.]<<<<<
—Rosie Posie (08:38:04/4-MAR-52)

The Zen Arch (16Y)

Mid-Size Restaurant Archetype/4 Orange Street/Gary and Ling-Wei 'Lily' Kim, Owners/BTG# 713 (668-3256).

>>>>>[Not the best Chinese in the city by any means, the Zen Arch's reputation comes from the automatic weapons Gary and Lily's friends are able to supply. Of course, you have to be friends with Gary and Lily before you meet their friends, but ain't that always the way?]<<<<<
—John (12:25:00/03-JAN-52)

NIGHT CLUBS

Buddha (14W)

Night Club Archetype/16 Langham Street/"Dez," Manager/BTG# 713 (202-1119).

>>>>>[Kickin' club, mateys. Cheap, too. Pity it's only open Thursday to Sunday and the drinks are so dear, but the music's terminally on. Great decor, too. Did I mention the ultra magic light show they sometimes put on? Dance inside that and you're still cracking when the cocks are crowing.]<<<<<
—Jazzy Jaswinder (06:38:03/29-DEC-51)

Club Hate (15X)

Night Club Archetype/46B Wardour Street/Dalkit Singh, Manager/BTG# 713 (969-0362).

>>>>>[This groovy place used to be Club Love until the police raid last month. Now there's a strict door policy, bouncer pat-downs, and metal detectors. All the prices have gone up and the music's z-grade electroslam. In fact, why the hell do we keep going here?]<<<<<
—Rosie Posie (09:18:32/4-MAR-52)

>>>>>[Because it's the only place that'll let us in, dear.]<<<<<
—Sarahana (09:32:18/4-MAR-52)

Last Days of Man on Earth (16Y)

Night Club Archetype/3 Litchfield Street/Lisa Cervenko, Manager/No phone.

>>>>>[Pretentious name (we just call it the Last Days), but there's honest, straight-down-the-line deathcore on the dance floor every night. This place gets the best long before the rest, and it's always packed to the gills with the cream of Shadowtown.]<<<<<
—John (02:00:32/03-JAN-52)

Toxic Shock (16X)

Night Club Archetype/18 Clifford Street/Emmy Silvereyes, Manager/BTG# 713 (435-2183).

>>>>>[Great fuzzback club done out like the inside of a human head. Always packed to the gills with cool young Chinese kids clocking the trid games set into every table. Don't go if you're feeling old today.]<<<<<
—Jazzy Jaswinder (06:50:34/29-DEC-51)

White Lion Sunrise (16X)

Night Club Archetype/59 Brewer Street/Steven Louis Sinclair, Manager/Bias Against Orks and Trolls/BTG# 713 (422-6782).

>>>>>[Members-only and secure, but most of the clientele seem to be pixies from way out west slumming it with the rest of us. If you can get in, you'll need a big wallet.]<<<<<
—Lone Sloane (04:31:12/17-FEB-52)

OTHER

The Blood Banque (16W)

Small Store Archetype/13 Brewer Street/Bill Henderson, Manager/BTG# 713 (680-3462).

>>>>>[A fast way to get some money if you're desperate. They nick a thumb, get a drop of blood, put it through the fast tests for the usual muck, and then buy you in at 80¥ a pint. The law says you can only give one pint in a month, but these people turn a blind eye as long as your RBC makes the criterion. Ork, troll, dwarf, elf, human, hell, these guys would bleed a wendigo if they could use it. But at least it's clean and safe and the instruments are all sterilized.]<<<<<
—Kendrick (19:32:55/11-FEB-52)

>>>>>[And you get paid on the button.]<<<<<
—Masterson (05:12:18/12-FEB-52)

Serena's (15Y)

Small Store Archetype/7A Frith Street/Serena, Owner/BTG# 713 (680-2281).

>>>>>[Well, she's sure well-known among the knowledgeable. The Templars have this heavy thing about magic, paperwork all over, but Serena can get around that. Up front you can get your fortune told, the cards dropped, the bones rolled, but when you know the lady well, she's blessed with the wires and talismans. You need magic or Matrix, try a spin. She knows names and places. She got friends in high places. The baggies don't put her down.]<<<<<
—Janzi Z. (03:16:53/11-FEB-52)

>>>>>[Who let this girl in here? Look, I know people, too, and Serena is not as safe as you think. They don't need attention drawn to it. And she keeps no cybertech in the place, so don't drop in hoping to find it.]<<<<<
—Callistra (06:00:00/11-FEB-52)

>>>>>[Just don't mess with the cat. If you can see it, that is. It's one serious entity in the world. I wouldn't back a pair of troll samurai with Bond & Carrington's best against that cat.]<<<<<
—Sarahana (16:05:13/13-FEB-52)

Westwood/Westworld (16Z)

Medium Store Archetype/54 Long Acre/Urdana Brakespeare, Owner/BTG# 713 (354-8015).

>>>>>[This is the leading place for New New Age Fashions. The prices are high, but the people are well-spaced, and the spiritual awareness is high enough not to come down. Earth fabrics and colours, good crystals of the goddess, garments for the body, and raiments for the mind. [2 Mp deleted by sysop]<<<<<
—Janzi Z (15:42:17/21-FEB-52)

>>>>>[It's full of poseurs. Elf wannabees, druid wannabees, hell, there are even people who wannabee trees in here.]<<<<<
—Masterson (19:16:26/22-FEB-52)

>>>>>[The truth is somewhere else. This is a good place. It's better to care naively than not to care at all. It's also a place to meet those who follow gentler paths in life. Shamanic art influences the designs here, and some are very fine. Some have Welsh influence, some Scots, and if your eyes look to those finer lands, you might find a kindred soul or two here from time to time.]<<<<<
—Sarahana (22:18:32/22-FEB-52)

Zimmer's Famous Emporium (15Z)

Medium Store Archetype/3-4 Shorts Gardens/Zimmer, Owner/BTG# 713 (354-1727).

>>>>>[How the hell did he get in here? Old Zimmer, and his father before him, they've been selling authentic souvenirs of historic London for decades. You know, a genuine brick from London Bridge, surplus-issue Beefeater hats, a pane of glass from Crystal Palace in its Victorian heyday, the same spiel. And people still fall for it. Mind you, the shop's great. All plazz and pizazz, fake history, aspidistras, a tapestry or two, real Persian carpets all the way from Sevenoaks, and whatever Zimmer thinks he can sell to the gullible.]<<<<<
—Malcy (09:13:52/12-FEB-52)

>>>>>[Sure, what he sells up front is just for the tourists. But he's no fool. He does have some things in the back room that talismongers would be pleased to handle. He won't handle weaponry, or drugs, or chips because he doesn't understand them. But he deals a little magic, and he knows what information is worth knowing. He's helped out some street people down on hard times, and some of them got up again; they don't forget him. Zimmer knows names. If he likes you, he might know a man who knows an ork who knows a place…Don't be deceived by appearances.]<<<<<
—Callistra (05:00:00/14-FEB-52)

THE CITY

HEART OF THE SMOKE

"Convince the City of London and you can control the world!" runs Herbert N. Aspinall's famous line, and indeed, many have tried. Along with Tokyo and Boston, the London financial district runs the finances of the world, just as it has done for more than a century. As one walks the narrow streets with their peculiarly medieval names—Bishopsgate, Poultry, Paternoster Row, Cheapside—one can almost hear the delicious clinking of sovereigns as the merchants count their money. These days, of course, the money is all theoretical, and the counting is done by the powerful computers that control the Stock Exchange, but it is impossible to rid the City of the hustle and bustle of the financial world.

The City is the heart of London today, but a thousand years ago, it was all of London. Today one can still divine the ancient city boundaries from looking at the streets and stations with names like Aldgate, Moorgate, and London Wall, which ring the area around the Tower of London and the Bank of England. After the Great Fire of London in 1666 (remembered for obliterating most of the city rather more than for killing only six people), the first steps in the development of the modern City of London began with the rebuilding of St. Paul's Cathedral and the construction of numerous other splendid churches, most of which are still around to be visited and enjoyed today.

Signs of the first wave of economic prosperity are even more numerous: the monumental office buildings, banks and exchanges, and the marvelous engineering oddity that is Tower Bridge. The latter, so famous it has virtually become a symbol for London, was completed in 1894, and has remained in operation ever since, except for a hiatus of four months after the terrorist attack of 2038. It is still raised and lowered to allow tall vessels through every few days, and on special ceremonial occasions, too.

The City is administrated, as it has been for centuries, by the City Corporation, which is led by the Lord Mayor of London, currently Sir Archibald Watts. Within the City, he ranks above everyone except the monarch. If you are in London on the second Sunday in November, be sure to catch the Lord Mayor's Parade, which is rivalled in pomp and splendour only by royal state occasions.

Other things to see are the Tower of London and its famous Beefeaters, and the newest London Bridge (the City keeps selling the previous ones to people who think they are getting Tower Bridge; the last one is now in Osaka!). There are also all the exciting new developments, the lofty glass skyscrapers and the bizarre new offices that seem to spring up, as if out of nowhere, in every other corner. Best of all, though, is to simply stand on the corner of Threadneedle Street, and watch the messengers bustling between the banks and exchanges, the talented young whiz kids striding back and forth, lips forever pressed to their portable phones, making deals involving millions of pounds and nuyen as you look on.

GEOGRAPHY AND DEMOGRAPHICS

The City is a modern, congested area of tall buildings built, for the most part, around twisting medieval street patterns. In some ways, it is indistinguishable from the financial centre of any other modern city. But despite the incessant demolition and construction work that constantly chokes the streets, the City still possesses numerous splendid old buildings, including the Bank of England and the Royal Exchange (on opposite sides of Threadneedle Street). In many places, though, these grand old ladies are literally overshadowed by the new skyscrapers, including the NatWest Tower, the HKB Building, the Overmann Tower, and, of course, the brand new Stock Exchange Tower.

The modern City District stretches from Holborn and Blackfriars to the east as far as Limehouse Basin beyond the new corporate developments at Wapping and Shadwell. In the east, the land rises steeply up Ludgate Hill until it reaches St. Paul's Cathedral. From there the land rises further to the north, but the rest of the district is flat, its landscape delineated by the rise and fall of the buildings.

It is only with the advent of the corporate habitats that great numbers of people have begun to live in the City, and even now many areas seem spookily quiet when the trading stops for the weekend. Now, with the building of the habitats at Tobacco Dock, the old Barbican Centre, and Aldgate, close to 75,000 more people now reside in the area. The slow but inevitable expansion of the City into Wapping and then Shadwell allowed the larger companies to develop elegant housing for their executives along Cable Street, the Highway, and a number of smaller developments behind Wapping High Street. All of this housing is in the form of luxurious, low-level apartment blocks and refurbished warehouses sited amid new parkland. Some older housing remains on the very edge of the City District, around St. Luke's and City Road, but even here it faces the inevitable prospect of corporate redevelopment in the near future.

The people who live in the City District are almost exclusively upper middle-class, wealthy, and well-educated. However, such are the specialist skills required by stock market trading that many of these people come from very different social and ethnic backgrounds. It is not unusual to find men and women of West Indian and Asian origin working in the City. Elves, too, are starting to make a major impression in certain areas, their intuitive methods bringing drastic changes in the way brokers approach the market.

>>>>>[The crime rate in the City has remained constant, at an above-average level, for many years. The streets of glitzy stores, so much more accessible than most of the shops in the Underplex, provide a great temptation for both professional and amateur thieves. Add to this the close proximity of the East End families, who have always regarded the City as their own personal crime supermarket, with bullion vans and naked data stacked high for them to pick from.

Of course, when half a million goes missing from the accounts of Overmann, HKB, or Lewis Klein, it does not make it to the evening news; corporate security may not always be good at preventing thefts and infiltrations, but it is superb at keeping news from getting out! Which is just as well, of course, because news of a breakdown in data security could wipe more off a company's market value than the thieves could steal in a lifetime of late-night hacking.]<<<<<
—Dixon (06:01:18/3-JAN-52)

ECONOMY

The City is built around the stock market and the other exchanges, and its foundations are the many services that keep them functioning. Thus, along with the many banks, dealers, and corporate headquarters, other major employers are those of cleaners, caterers, communications and computer experts, and the like. The largest of all the service employers are those involved with corporate security ranging from simple armed guards to experts in Matrix data protection. Almost all the workers commute into the district to work, meaning that its transport links are the best in the city. The huge numbers of workers of all types manage to support the wide range of excellent shops that stretch along Cheapside and Wapping High Street and that crowd the shopping mall inside the Aztechnology Habitat.

>>>>>[So, you want to talk corporate crime? Where do you start? Everyone is doing it. That is everyone. You can't tell me that the young secretary wandering off with computer chips and paper clips is any different to your average corporate data thief, except in terms of scale. Where do you draw the line? People whine on about the corporations this, corporations that, and they're taking their company for everything they can get. Everyone's guilty. Every last rakking one.]<<<<<
—Janie (00:16:38/2-JAN-52)

>>>>>[Too simplistic by half, young lady. It's no use getting angry. You must have a sense of perspective if you are going to make anything of the corporate world. An understanding of the finer points of chess certainly wouldn't go amiss either. Check out the stuff on corporations in the chapter on **Economy** for some eye-openers.]<<<<<
—MesoStim (09:12:17/23-FEB-52)

NEIGHBOURHOODS

There are two main neighbourhoods in the new City of London: the ancient City itself, and the narrow riverside overspill of Wapping and Shadwell.

CITY OF LONDON

The average tourist can find much to see and do in the City of London. Within easy and safe walking distance of the Bank of England are the Stock Exchange, the Overmann Tower, and the HKB Building, all of which offer guided tours throughout the day (weekdays only). Many of the other exchanges allow tours if arranged in advance.

It is those with a keen interest in the history of the capital who will most enjoy a wander through the City of London. Starting in the very far east of the district, there is Ludgate Circus, named after the ancient king; it is now the site of the City of London's Druid Lodge. At the top of the hill sprawls the magnificent Christopher Wren-designed St. Paul's Cathedral; the Whispering Gallery up in the dome is especially popular with tourists. A little further west stands the monument commemorating the Great Fire of London; its tightly spiralling 311 stairs (no lift!) take one to a superb view that has changed a great deal since the tower was constructed in 1677. Also to be seen in this part of the city are several other splendid Wren churches, the Old Bailey and the new City Justice Courts across the road, and the ancient roman temple to Mithras on Queen Victoria Street. Just past St. Botolph's, the splendid Museum of London can tell a visitor the full history of all these buildings, and a great deal more besides. Ever in touch with the pulse of the city, it has recently opened an exhibit devoted to metahuman history.

The major attraction, however, is the Tower of London, lying on the Thames at the southwestern side of the City. The Tower dates back, in part, to at least Norman times, and maybe much earlier. In its time it has served as both a fortress and a prison, but its role today is strictly as London's biggest traditional tourist attraction. A guided tour taking in the Beefeaters (the traditionally dressed guards), the six legendary ravens, the White Tower, the Bloody Tower, and especially the Crown Jewels in Waterloo Barracks, is essential. Be warned, though: the crowds here are ferocious, especially in the summer; come early in the morning to avoid the queuing! By prior appointment, as a really special treat, one can witness the nightly Ceremony of the Keys. As the two Beefeaters, immaculately turned out in their gold-embroidered scarlet uniforms, exchange passwords and the great ring of keys, it is as though the computerized money markets vanish in the distance as one travels back through time to a nobler age.

>>>>>[As you might expect, the whole of the City rates AAA-AA on the police computer. The City Police Force is a separate department to the main Metropolitan Police divisions, and ultimately responsible to the City Company. Incidentally, they have a large and experienced Matrix Protection Department, though it is not as large as their Visitor Protection Department, known as the Tourist Team.]<<<<<
—Dixon (06:01:18/3-JAN-52)

WAPPING AND SHADWELL

As the City grew overcrowded, space became scarce and rents rose. So the City expanded. Seventy years or so ago, Wapping was a quietly fashionable district of select houses and old shipping warehouses converted into art galleries and restaurants. The peace was disturbed when the various national newspapers at Fleet Street, forced to change their approach by the introduction of computer technology, moved virtually en masse to new sites in Wapping and the Isle of Dogs. Their arrival sparked a huge corporate buy-out of the whole area south of Cable Street as far as Limehouse (and now way beyond!). The redevelopment work has only just about finished, and the area is now dotted with pleasant corporate housing in a wide variety of styles.

The biggest single feature of the new Wapping is the Aztechnology Habitat in Tobacco Dock. With a single-storey shopping mall and another 40 or so floors, it is fairly small by comparison to BI's real arcology "Angel Towers" at Battersea and Aztechnology buildings elsewhere in the world. One of the features it does share with the corporation's other buildings is its traditional flat-topped pyramid shape.

Along the river, at either end of the Wapping overspill area, are large man-made marinas, where some of the richer residents of the area dock their vessels. Those interested in water sports will find much to keep them occupied here.

>>>>>[Wapping and Shadwell have an overall security rating of AA. The Aztechnology Habitat at Tobacco Dock has a security rating of AAA, plus an immense dossier concerning the confrontations between the City of London force and the corporate security. Seems they keep shooting people with weapons they aren't supposed to have. Naughty naughty!]<<<<<
—Dixon (06:01:18/3-JAN-52)

>>>>>[Hey, slugs, there's one neighbourhood you are forgetting—or perhaps you still don't know about it. The Undercity, babies. Yeah, down there, right beneath your feet! We're creeping like little mices to steal the cheese out of your fridges. Just you watch us.]<<<<<
—The Man with the Cunning Plan (01:37:51/12-JUN-52)

USEFUL ADDRESSES

>>>>>[People, the City ain't so good for shadows, but sometimes you gotta go to the clients, know what I mean? The following addresses may prove useful.]<<<<<
—Egon (14:11:02/23-FEB-52)

HOTELS

The Tartan Hotel (14Ca)
Average Hotel Archetype/13 Charterhouse Street/ Alasdair McTaggart, Owner/BTG# 711 (165-9011).

>>>>>[Even the carpets are tartan here. It's rather overdone. Most of the staff are about as Scottish as the average Salish-Shidhe, but the Loch Ness Bar has an interesting clientele of mostly ex-company men. The barman, Hamish, has a lot of friends among these guys. He always knows someone who knows someone who's disenchanted with corporate life and wants out, or someone who wants a safe passage back in if he has protection while negotiating. If you need to check street talk on a London corp, try here. There's usually someone talking into his drink if you know how to listen.]<<<<<
—MesoStim (23:12:43/1-MAR-52)

The Wheel Hotel (15Da)

Luxury Hotel Archetype/4 Wood Street/Paul Remington, Manager/BTG# 711 (182-3261).

>>>>>[The accommodations and food are very good, and fairly cheap—if you're here for the house business. This place has eight licensed casinos, and it's the top venue in town for the spin of cards, throw of dice, roll of the wheel. There are the plazzy rooms for the rakkies, and plush, quiet retreats for the real rollers. Not a bad place to find employment, someone down on their luck who might sell information for one last handful of cards, a chica turning tricks who might have heard a thing or two. And of course they're assensing here, so don't try anything stupid. The place only fixes things a little in its favour. I've known a lot worse.]<<<<<
—Callistra (03:00:00/4-MAR-52)

RESTAURANTS AND BARS

Hooley's (14Da)

Mid-Size Restaurant and Bar Archetype/442 London Wall/Niall Maloney, Manager/BTG# 711 (812-4262).

>>>>>[Rather quaint establishment, with an Irish theme. Niall has had several run-ins with the law for selling all manner of dodgy gear out of his office, but has never been charged with anything. The word is that he knows some influential people.]<<<<<
—Betty B. (16:41:37/7-JAN-52)

Queen of Hearts (16Fa)

Small Restaurant Archetype/26A Mincing Lane/Elizabeth Wilkes, Manager/BTG# 711 (405-1764).

>>>>>[Splendid French restaurant, for once offering huge portions instead of that ridiculous nouveau slop. Not many people know it, but Elizabeth is a rogue mage, and a rather good one at that.]<<<<<
—Wattie (12:24:07/27:12:50)

Swithin's (16Fa)

Bar Archetype/Gloucester Court, off Tower Hill/Trevor Williamson, Manager/BTG# 711 (226-2380).

>>>>>[This after-hours drinking den is the place where some of the flashiest of the City's financial whiz kids come to unwind, and where they feel they can talk without having to guard their mouths. Which is rather rash of them, is it not?]<<<<<
—Billy L (06:17:28/11-JAN-52)

>>>>>[And you think nobody reads this sort of stuff in the City?]<<<<<
—Dave (12:48:26/4-FEB-52)

The Twin Oaks (15Da)

Bar Archetype/3 Bread Street/Steven Althorp, Manager/Racial Bias Against Metahumans/BTG# 711 (272-6424).

>>>>>[Dreadful stockbroker's bar, useful only because the manager has an inside source in the Temple and often has sensitive stuff to sell about comings and goings in the Lord Protector's office. Better take advantage of it while it lasts.]<<<<<
—Phantom (01:38:17/6-FEB-52)

OTHER

Forbes Security Transport (15Ga)

Small Store Archetype plus Garage/15 White Kennet Street/William George, Manager/BTG# 711 (664-3489).

>>>>>[This is where the corporates go for bullet-proof limos and a chauffeur who packs some worthwhile heat. It's licensed, if you belong to the right corporation. For runners out there, it's always a question worth asking whether you can meet your corporate contact in one of these limos. If the man agrees, you know a serious proposal is about to come your way.]<<<<<
—MesoStim (11:32:17/11-FEB-52)

United Meat Products (15Da)

41 Gresham Street/Sir James Thomas, Manager/BTG# 711 (364-0559).

>>>>>[The showroom and PR office of the most disgusting business in the country. "If it moves, we'll stuff additives into it and make it into burgers," should be their motto.]<<<<<
—Norm (19:41:43/12-JAN-52)

THE TEMPLE

THE LORD PROTECTOR'S DOMAIN

The Temple District is the centre of official and judicial buildings in London. Connected by overground walkways and subterranean passages, the myriad buildings of the Lord Protector's offices sprawl along both sides of Chancellery Road (formerly Chancery Road). The Law Courts stand at the end of this street, where it joins the wide Strand and Fleet Street. Seemingly guarding the whole area is the Stone Dragon of Temple Bar, a magnificent and threatening statue of a silver-coloured dragon. The whole district is low-rise only; the Metropolitan Council does not grant permission to construct buildings that might block the view of the immediate skyline for the rich and influential people who can afford to live in the luxurious and ultra-expensive penthouse suites atop the buildings here.

Visitors who require the licensing of magical operations or restricted items such as cyberware must apply for licenses and permits to the Lord Protector's Offices. The Administrative and Licensing Bureaux deal with such applications.

There are some businesses in the area, but they tend to be distinctly superior in tone. Personnel agencies for specialist requirements (specialist secretaries, domestic servants, translators, and the like) sit next to small bespoke tailors and shoe shops, exclusive wine shops, and the like.

Down by the Embankment is the splendid Temple Church, from which the district takes its name. It is not currently open to the public.

THE LORD PROTECTOR'S OFFICES

The Lord Protector's offices spread along both sides of Chancellery Lane and down along Holborn Road to the north. There are almost 140 different buildings, with many knocked together behind the front facades and others connected by walkways and tunnels. The five bureaux of this sprawling organization (also known as The Lord Protector's Department and sometimes by its old name of the Ministry of the Interior) do not have entirely separate office complexes. Staff members from the Administrative Bureau, for instance, have offices spread throughout the buildings, and many conduct investigative and ergonomic studies for the other bureaux. Also, different bureaux sometimes cooperate in their work. The Administrative and Educational Bureaux cooperate in training of civil servants, for example.

Although the Chancellery Net is partly located here in the 13 floors of basements below the major complex of buildings (with a further four floors given over to air conditioning), it is also redundantly coded in other locations (which have equally powerful security).

The finest chinese cuisine on the isle. Carry out available.
BTG (668-3256), 4 Orange Street
11 A.M.-12 P.M. daily.

>>>>>[Security is very tight. The policemen all along the road carry Bond & Carrington elite hand weapons. There are hermetic wards within the offices, and the IC protecting the Chancellery Net is as black as you'll see this side of hell. Keep a low profile, do your best with the dumb-foreigner act if you need a license when you're in the U.K., and be polite at all times.]<<<<<
—MesoStim (19:54:02/26-APR-52)

C-NET

The central offices of the public information data network are located on the site of the old Public Records Office in Chancellery Lane. The spacious and modern six-storey building has a series of ever-changing displays on British public life, aspects of British society, British economic and demographic factors, and similar items of interest.

>>>>>[Yeah, it's boring as hell. And don't forget that it's just down the road from the Templars, right? So of course nobody would ever think of running a little node down to keep a log of who asks what type of question and constructing a profile from query categories. Try asking C-net about the weather a lot and pretty soon you're getting junk-faxes and stuff from people trying to sell you umbrellas, suprafabric wetproof jackets, and holidays in the Caribbean. Well, a financially responsible government does know how to pass on the data for best tax savings. Try asking too many questions about government installations on C-net and you get a quite different response.]<<<<<
—Sarahana (23:11:19/23-APR-52)

Blissful Waters

Units 21-11 Covent Garden BTG#719 (174-4218)

A quiet, relaxing spot

THE LAW COURTS

These resplendent buildings still have the superb Victorian mock-Gothic frontage that has survived the unfortunate corrosive effects of the London atmosphere. Major trials are held here; crimes against the state, subversion, computer crime and fraud, and terrorist offences are all subjected to hearings at the Law Courts. Other major offences, such as murders and major assaults, are dealt with at the Old Bailey and the new Criminal Justice Courts in the City. The British jury system of trial does not operate for all categories. A panel of three judges hears the evidence and delivers its verdict on the cases dealt with here. It is sometimes possible for visitors to attend court hearings, but considerations of national security often restrict this public accessibility.

>>>>>[Note that all judges who try cases here are Law Lords or Appeal Court Justices, and in either case, they are automatically ennobled for their pains. Very nice for them. It helps make them terribly grateful to the nice government that so favoured and promoted them and even tolerates their cluckings about judicial independence of the executive. Then when a nice subversion or terrorist case comes along, the judges find for the prosecution—97 percent of the time in the last decade. That's British justice for you.]<<<<<
—Mole Man (23:54:42/24-APR-52)

>>>>>[It's essential to grasp that British law has nothing to do with justice. Judges are concerned with the due majesty of the processes of law. That, after all, is what allows them to dress up like 18th-century transvestites, drink themselves stupid, act like reactionary chauvinists, and get paid a fortune for the privilege. Law has nothing to do with justice.]<<<<<
—Carol K. (02:12:43/25-FEB-52)

THE TEMPLE

The Temple Church is a remarkable site dating from the late 12th century and erected in part by the historic Knights Templar. The Norman porch, restored some 130 years ago, is visible from the roadway, but the Temple is not currently open to the public.

>>>>>[Let me tell you why. It's because the Lord Protector's London druidic circle (not the one at Warwick Castle, where he hangs out for the big festivals) meets in the vaults of the Temple. During the Awakening, something erupted from the guts of the Earth into those vaults. Like the stone circles in Royston, the standing stone at Primrose Hill, or the whole stone circle that demolished the town centre in Brecon, Wales. Try assensing what it's like down there and you get a powerful headache as well as a bunch of watcher spirits on your tail. And you better take precautions against ritual sorcery.]<<<<<
—Callistra (15:43:55/26-APR-52)

>>>>>[Ever hear of the Order of the Fire Lions? They were a hermetic group who really had it in for the Lord Protector and his ilk. They prepped themselves, did what they had to do, and went astrally en masse, via the metaplanes to avoid pursuit should it come, into the lower levels of the Temple.]<<<<<
—Magister (02:31:16/05-MAY-52)

>>>>>[And? And? You bastard.]<<<<<
—Cleo (11:25:46/05-MAY-52)

>>>>>[Found them catatonic. Every one of them. Does anyone out there know what could do that? Anyone? Please?]<<<<<
—Magister (12:06:55/05-MAY-52)

TEMPLE BAR

In Victorian times, the stone dragon here was sculpted and placed on the site of the old Temple Bar, which was one of the ancient gates to the walled inner city of London. Now, this is the site where the Lord Mayor of London ceremonially hands the silver sword of state to the reigning monarch if he comes this way when visiting the City of London, to the east, in state.

>>>>>[Weird thing, that stone dragon. He exists in astral space like some kind of watching, guarding thing, but he doesn't act or react. He's just there. They say that during the Awakening, over Christmas, he changed shape; he used to be closer to a heraldic griffin, but the stone grew and changed. I've seen a salamander hanging around the dragon, too, more than once. Kinda scary.]<<<<<
—Callistra (19:15:15/26-APR-52)

USEFUL ADDRESSES

>>>>>[Security in the Temple is, to put it mildly, absolutely ridiculous. As a result, it is possibly the last place in London that runners will want to go. On the other hand…]<<<<<
—Egon (03:38:12/4-MAR-52)

The Crusting Pipe (15Ba)
Bar Archetype/8 Fetter Lane/Denis Williamson, Manager/Racial Bias Against Metahumans/BTG# 710 (442-6130).

>>>>>[The name comes from the sediment in the pipes of port wine that are laid down and shipped out. The sediment settles in 'em so you can decant the stuff more easily. Vile, if you ask me. But those guys in the frock coats and silly wigs love it. This is where to see the Great British System of Justice at play.]<<<<<
—Malcy (19:19:23/26-FEB-52)

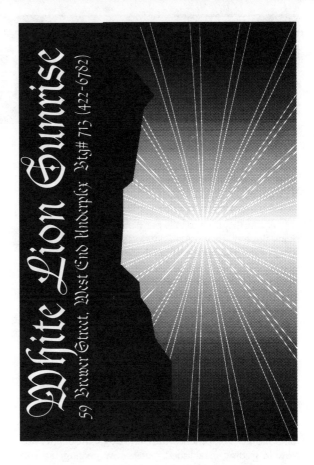

White Lion Sunrise
59 Brewer Street, West End Underplex   Btg# 713 (422-6782)

>>>>>[And without needing a membership for some gentleman's club you couldn't afford and they wouldn't let you into. But, more important, there's the coterie. There are some people from the Lord Protector's Offices here most nights, and there are people from trideo and other media sniffing out stories. Dress very smartly, don't attract attention to yourself, and just listen. On a good night, you might overhear something interesting.]<<<<<
—Callistra (20:00:00/26-FEB-52)

>>>>>[Unfortunately, I have to say that only applies if you're human.]<<<<<
—Hampstead Hi-Jack (18:46:03/27-FEB-52)

Morgans (15Z)
Small Store Archetype/28 High Holborn/Samuel and Casper Morgan, Owners/BTG# 710 (209-2901).

>>>>>[The best wine shop in town. Samuel and Casper are men with a mission. Glorious Gewurtztraminer, beautiful burgundy, ravishing rioja, brilliant beaujolais, stunning saumurs. I could go on and on. Show them you're knowledgeable and they'll talk for hours. Those with a nose rather than a pose buy here.]<<<<<
—Champagne Charlie (19:24:18/21-FEB-52)

RIVERSIDE EXPANSION

As the City started to expand outward into Wapping, many developers were already foreseeing a time when it would expand even further. In those days, the Isle of Dogs was part of a sprawling, seven-mile riverside wasteland of abandoned deep-water dock facilities and failing light industry. It was a simple matter for the new London Docklands Development Consortium (LDDC) to buy up some of the land, and arrange for the rest to be allotted to any corporation prepared to stump up the money. Unfortunately, this was the time of the corporate mergers and full-scale buy-outs. By the time the dust settled, almost half the investors in the LDDC no longer even existed.

Over the last decade, however, the economy's continued growth and resultant pressure on space in the City and the new Wapping developments has finally resulted in the full-scale redevelopment of the Isle of Dogs. The district was slow in getting established, but is now gearing up as a further, fully operational outpost of the City, complete with business centres, office complexes, and well-designed company housing. Many of the more progressive corporations and companies have moved into the new space offered by the riverside developments, often bringing at least some of their personnel with them. Other jobs in the area are involved in providing the basic services that allow the neighbourhoods to function, though most of the workers filling these occupations commute in from somewhere more affordable (i.e., the rest of the East End).

For the future, the planners are now commencing work on the Canary Wharf development in the very centre of the Isle of Dogs. Much delayed, this is planned to be a small commercial city, with several million square feet of office space, two huge, international-quality hotels, a four-floor shopping mall and sports centre and—the *piéce de resistance*—three landmark towers, each a mile and a half high. It seems that the future of the City of London starts here.

>>>>>[Future? That's a joke and a half! They drew up the plans for this monstrosity 40 years ago, and it's taken them this long to raise all the cash for the project. Know why? Because the whole development has been jinxed from day one, and it's lost more money in the last couple of decades than Argentina. Even if the thing does get built someday, it'll be 2100 before it ever starts to pay for itself.]<<<<<
—Jimmy the Mover (13:04:05/17-JAN-52)

>>>>>[Maybe, matey, but all that wet concrete is a great place for hiding things. Just ask the Stepney wide-boys.]<<<<<
—Reggie (10:28:07/26-JAN-52)

NEIGHBOURHOODS

The Dogs and the Docklands divide neatly into those two areas, separated from each other by the mouth of the River Lea. The whole area is served by the new DLR monorail system.

THE DOGS

The Isle of Dogs is made up of three neighbourhoods: Poplar, at the northern end, Millwall in the lower western half, and Cubitt Town in the lower eastern half. All are fairly identical, being a mix of over-designed and very expensive housing and enormous corporate headquarters. Those with an interest in modern architecture or in meeting corporate personnel will relish a day out on the Dogs, though tourists should note that the intensive building work recently begun on Canary Wharf is disrupting the area somewhat. In the middle of the island, alongside Crossharbour DLR station, is a large (two-storey) shopping mall, the Crossharbour Centre. At the far tip of the island, a Victorian foot tunnel leads under the Thames to history-laden Greenwich, a trip well worth making.

Finally, for those who like fresh fish, the place to go is Billingsgate Fish Market, near Poplar Station. Get there by nine o'clock any morning of the week, and a bargain or two is guaranteed. Health and Safety experts stationed at the market will ensure the "catch" is safe to eat.

>>>>>[The Dogs gets a security rating of A on the Metropolitan Police computer. While rooting through the files looking for something else last week, I came across a peculiar file entitled "The Increase in Teenage Suicide in Poplar." Seems the author puts this down to either BTL addiction, a rock music-inspired death cult, or simply the sheer boredom of having to live on a corporate estate. I'm only surprised there isn't a great deal more of this.]<<<<<
—X-Plod (04:17:20/16-FEB-52)

DOCKLANDS

Not only has the development of Docklands taken far longer than planned, it has also resulted in an unbalanced landscape of finished, half-completed, and abandoned developments. Of those that were finished, London City Airport and the enormous Docklands Arena have been a moderate success. Others, though, such as the clearing of much of the southern half of Canning Town and Custom House (the names date from way back when the docks were still operating) to make way for the expected influx of new corporate developments, are verging on a fiasco. The barren areas of half-demolished housing estates have become home to some several thousand members of London's outcast population. The people who live here are homeless, jobless, and often from the ethnic groups most discriminated against by society. The area is extremely hazardous.

123 ASPEN WAY   712 (410-4452)

>>>>>[You're telling me! These maniacs have started attacking the M313 at night with concrete slabs and small arms fire.]<<<<<
—Anonymous (02:14:47/15-FEB-52)

>>>>>[There are several distinct gangs squatting here, plus many more unaffiliated individuals. Of the organised ones, the nastiest are the Iron Horse Sioux, a leather-clad biker crew who borrow their lifestyle wholesale from Native American culture. They must certainly have picked this up in its entirety from old Westerns; these guys make anyone who challenges their authority go through a Sun Dance-type ritual. Looks like another wonderful American export, the go-gang, has finally arrived in the U.K. for us all to share and enjoy.]<<<<<
—Janie (20:28:24/31-JAN-52)

>>>>>[Fraggin' aces, term. Hope we catch ya out there.]<<<<<
—Wilco Wilde (08:22:37/5-FEB-52)

Further east, the neighbourhood around Beckton has managed to retain its belts of poor and middle-class commuter housing for the time being, though using the roads to access the western section has become impossible. One interesting feature of the Docklands District that has attracted tourists for decades is the Thames Flood Barrier, a remarkable line of movable dams that stretch across Woolwich Sound. The barriers can be individually lowered to allow ships to pass or raised to protect London from rising waters. Visitors should note that they cannot be used to cross the river and that the visitors' centre is situated on the South Bank.

>>>>>[Most of the Docklands District rates B for security; Beckton has slipped to a C; Canning Town and Custom House rate an F. As far as I can tell, the Metropolitan Police are waiting until the squatter gangs actually kill someone important enough for the media to notice, and then they'll sit back and call in the army to do their dirty work for them. Can't be long now, I'd guess.]<<<<<
—X-Plod (04:31:14/16-FEB-52)

USEFUL ADDRESSES

>>>>>[Even in a place as sterile as the glop-heap those on the box call "the New Isle of Dogs," there are a few discreet places for the likes of us to do some real business deals. Docklands? Nobody goes to Docklands.]<<<<<
—Egon (14:50:39/23-FEB-51)

Hotel California (16Qa)
Average Hotel Archetype/123 Aspen Way/Robert Anton Leary, Owner/BTG# 712 (410-4452).

>>>>>[It had to happen. The latest psychedelic revival. The decor is, well, imagine you swallowed 40 gallons of dayglo multicolour paint and threw it up for a few hours. It was raided by the baggies last month, but there are still interesting things to smoke if you're inclined that way. Nothing really trancing, though. The wholefood is OK, and the Eagles revivalist band The Desperadoes are OK too, in a dozy, mellow kind of way. Not my scene, but pixies and the handful of Amerinjuns we get here seem to like it.]<<<<<
　　—Egon (11:17:32/16-FEB-52)

The Lounging Lizard (16Qa)

　　Night Club Archetype/16 Poplar High Street/Stephen Blake, Manager/BTG# 712 (358-6614).

>>>>>[It costs you £50 just to get in for a night unless you're a guest, and membership is corporate only, save for some exceptional people from other walks of life. Open until six in the morning, this place is so discreet most people don't even suspect it exists. There's nothing illegal about it, though. It's just that the customers are usually so important their feet hardly touch the ground. Protected by a hermetic ward. And heat. And more. If someone invites you to a meet in one of the private rooms, you're going to be offered something very serious. If you decline the offer, your prospective employer may not like the idea of you leaving here still knowing about the place. So think carefully about attending.]<<<<<
　　—Callistra (02:00:00/27-FEB-52)

>>>>>[The ceramic dragon motifs on the walls are beautiful, though. Lacquered work from Kyoto, ornate but very delicate. I wonder if it says anything about certain associates and interested parties?]<<<<<
　　—Lone Sloane (21:17:43/27-FEB-52)

Wilson's Work-Out (15Na)

　　Gym/60 Three Colt Street/Len Henriksson, Manager/BTG# 712 (358-1440).

>>>>>[Entrance for members and their guests only. An interesting clientele. The membership isn't a fixed sum; it's discretionary. Yet the place does very, very well. They don't buy in their equipment for nothing, and their instructors don't live in poverty, either. The people who train here come from all over. I've seen an elf and a very heavy-duty troll leave here, bow a little to each other from the waist, and walk away as if they'd never seen each other in their lives. Very peculiar.]<<<<<
　　—Dapper D (20:16:17/17-FEB-52)

>>>>>[Let's just say that the people who congregate here are rather unusually talented in the physical specializations they have chosen to follow. I think it's just a club for those who accept a bond with others who follow their path, no more than that.]<<<<<
　　—Callistra (18:00:00/19-FEB-52)

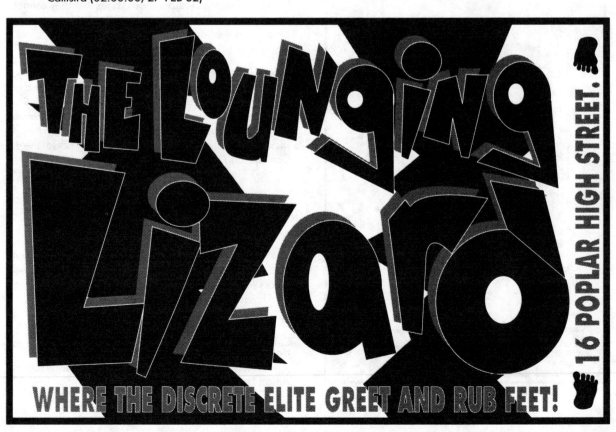

THE LOUNGING LIZARD
16 POPLAR HIGH STREET.
WHERE THE DISCRETE ELITE GREET AND RUB FEET!

PLACE OF MISTS AND SHADOWS

At night, shrouded in the incessant fog that twists its ghostly apparitions through the narrow streets, the East End of London seems to belong to a bygone age, a time of wet cobblestones and the rattling of carriage wheels, of raucous pubs and knives in the shadows. During the day, however, the contrast between the timeless cries of the costers in Petticoat Lane Market and the looming glass-sided monoliths of the nearby City and Wapping reveals the truth. The modern East End is a district caught between past and future, between the dark miseries of poverty and the shining new opportunities offered by the new money. If that all sounds somewhat poetic, well, so be it. There is a wistful and romantic spirit that only just hides behind the cheery smiles of the—genuine!—Cockneys who live there to this day.

For tourists, there is much to see in the western part of the East End district, though little of it is as immediately spectacular as the historic cathedrals and palaces found further west. Instead, visitors come to the East End to meet its people, to join with it in celebrating life.

>>>>>[That's all very well, you know, but a great many tourists come out of the East End having narrowly missed losing their lives when some happy, smiling Cockney suddenly turned nasty. All those years fighting to keep the yuppies out of Docklands has transformed some of them into a right set of headcases. Watch your mouth and your money, or you might be the next wise guy floating down the river.]<<<<<
      Malcy (17:08:55/4-JAN-52)

GEOGRAPHY AND DEMOGRAPHICS

The district now officially referred to as the East End is a conglomeration of the traditional area of that name, plus the areas further east that were added, a piece at the time, as London expanded and the docklands stretched further and further toward the sea. The Cockneys (in its truest sense, the term refers explicitly to those born within the sound of "Bow bells," St. Mary-le-Bow, in the City) delight in keeping their own peculiar version of history alive, and still pour scorn on those who just happen to live in Hackney, Leyton, or East Ham.

The old East End, snuggling close to the walls of the City of London, has long been a melting pot for people of every nationality. In earlier times, people settled where they came off the boats that brought them to this country. In more recent times, families were forced into the area by poverty and peculiarly punitive council housing policies. Nowadays, the new outcasts, the metahumans, have made the area their home, adding to the already bursting mixture of cultures that makes the East End the lively and thrilling place it unquestionably is. The Undercity area reclaimed by the orks and dwarfs has several entrances in Whitechapel, though most of it is strictly beneath the City.

The new East End stretches northward up both sides of the River Lea, and further east as far as the old Essex border, marked by the M825 Inner Orbital motorway. Eighty years ago, the whole area was one immense low-class housing expanse, its interminable streets a mixture of crumbling Victorian houses overshadowed by crumbling tower blocks. As the pressure on housing increased, developers bought up whole sections of the East End and proceeded immediately to gentrify them. Roads were relaid, trees were planted, houses were completely renovated and knocked together, and sold for then-astonishing sums.

When the population suddenly dropped again 35 years ago, the pressure on the undeveloped parts of the East End to drag themselves out of the gutter eased again. Many of the newly refurbished areas were allowed to fall into a sorry state, and those that had never been gentrified slipped inexorably into squatter status. The incessant reorganisations of local government structure and financing meant that no one could afford to knock down the old housing, so it now rivals the worst of Seattle or Calcutta.

The people of the outer East End are as numerous as ever, and belong to a surprisingly wide variety of ethnic and educational groups. Parts of the turn-of-the-century middle-class enclaves around Stoke Newington, Hackney, and Limehouse have walled themselves in to keep their own property values high. Beyond the River Lea and its line of chemical works, sewage plants, and treacherous salt marshes, the houses and low blocks of flats stretch away forever.

ECONOMY

All around the edge of the City of London, parts of the old East End have been transformed into an overspill for the capital's financial district. Old import/export warehouses have been gutted to provide offices for financial consultants and data services, while others have simply been flattened and replaced with lofty glass-sided corporate towers. To the north, the area around Hackney is still littered with struggling manufacturing and clothing factories, though these are rapidly being replaced by more artistic and media-related concerns. The narrow ribbon of wasteland on either side of the River Lea is the site of endless estates of warehouses and storage facilities, plus the two gigantic, festering waste tips at Walthamstow Marshes and Twelvetrees. Beyond the river, the vast commuter belt provides for little except shopping and real estate.

>>>>>[The real economy of the East End is the same as it has always been. You want something stolen for you, you want something illegal, you want someone killed, just ask. And if you know who to ask, you'll know what it costs. Despite all the changes in the old East End, the old families still rule the roost, but now they're incredibly sophisticated, employing the Matrix and modern weaponry with the same ease as the old cutthroat razors and sawed-off shotguns.]<<<<<
—X-Plod (03:00:42/15-DEC-51)

>>>>>[That's not to say they don't still use the old methods when they need to! Other guys you want to watch out for are the Sikh families, seriously close-knit and religious as hell, and the trolls. There ain't all that many, but they're sure throwing their weight around! Some nights down Whitechapel way, you can't hear the sound of old Bow bells for the rattle of automatic fire.]<<<<<
—Slim (22:14:26/21-JAN-52)

>>>>>[You speak the truth, Slim, but you know our code is absolute silence. You know that we know where you live. Be seeing you.]<<<<<
—Anonymous (22:15:50/21-JAN-52)

NEIGHBOURHOODS

The following are the main neighbourhoods of the old East End.

SHOREDITCH

The area directly to the north of the City, stretching from the edge of the far eastern tip of the Village round to Spitalfields and Brick Lane, was originally the site of the very first theatre in England (James Burbage built it in 1576), and later of one of the most famous music halls in the East End. Nowadays the main attraction of the area is the Shoreditch Centre, between Curtain Road and High Street, which is home to a brand-new shopping mall, the City Theatre, and a large part of City University. Hidden under the eaves at the southern end of the centre is the centuries-old flower market, from where fresh blooms are transported to vases on desks and tabletops throughout the Smoke.

Elsewhere, the crumbling 20th-century housing has only partially been updated, leaving many pockets of poor housing. This does not dampen the spirit of the cheerful Cockneys who teem through the area. One aspect that always surprises visitors, even in these cosmopolitan times, is to hear a genuine jaw-grinding Cockney accent coming from a young Londoner who is plainly a member of the Indian or ork community! It just goes to show that, no matter who you are, if you were born within the sound of those old Bow bells, you are accepted as a Cockney through and through, and nothing more need be said!

>>>>>[The Shoreditch Centre, known locally as The Bog because of the peculiar shape of its upper levels, has a police computer security rating of A, but the estates around it can only manage a C. Main guys and gals to watch out for around here are the Harry Hooks, an unpleasant bunch of yobs who model themselves on characters from Dickens novels; their favoured vice is psychotropic drugs and their favourite weapons are cut-throat razors. Very nasty.]<<<<<
—X-Plod (04:07:06/15-DEC-51)

SPITALFIELDS

Once the site of London's ghetto for immigrant Jews, then Jamaicans, then Indians and Pakistanis, Spitalfields has now been swamped by new money. Several large financial concerns have made the area their home, including Taylor Taylor Kleinfeldt, in their award-winning, cone-shaped office development on Buxton Street. Dozens more modest developments also line the main streets, housing all manner of consultants, corporate lawyers, and data services.

Come the weekend, when the financial offices are closed and the suits have all gone to the country for the weekend, the locals come out of the ground, it seems. Brick Lane becomes a bustling street market selling all manner of delightful (and sometimes disreputable!) goods. Visitors to the area should note that the best time for a bargain is very early Sunday morning, when one can round off a few hours of hard shopping with a delicious bagel at Beigel's Bake or perhaps a bowlful of ork delicacies at Grunt's.

>>>>>[If you're looking for chips or add-ons, try some of the stalls hidden away in Sheda Street (just off Brick Lane). All kinds of stuff, from cannibalised parts and secondhand units to experimental prototypes. It's no questions asked and no money back, so check before you buy. Best stuff is dealt by the two Vallance boys, though they ain't there every week. If it's any recommendation, this is where I do all my shopping, but don't mention my name, OK?]<<<<<
—Malcy (23:08:47/17-FEB-52)

No guide to Spitalfields would be complete without mention of its most famous resident, Jack the Ripper. For several months in 1888, the mysterious knife-man stalked the foggy streets, killing and mutilating prostitutes. Nowadays, of course, the streets of Spitalfields are perfectly safe (though, as with anywhere in modern London, we do not recommend unescorted visits after dark). Guided tours of the area, following the path of the infamous murders, may be picked up at Shoreditch Station every day at 12:00 noon and 6:00 P.M.

>>>>>[One of the facts of life about living or working in the Jack the Ripper Land theme park is that you are always the butt of sick jokes. Every other week, some twerp decides that it would be bloody hilarious to leave a dismembered body lying in George Yard or Bucks Row. Of course, the Met have caught on to this now and the whole area is rigged with IR cameras. Despite these intrusions by the mentally disadvantaged, the area now earns itself a security rating of B on the police computer.]<<<<<
—X-Plod (04:19:36/15-DEC-51)

>>>>>[When the fog comes down on Spitalfields, something happens to the streets, you know? It's like the old place, my old place, was still there, hiding behind the glass and steel during the day, but coming back out at night to greet me. Those alleys still twist, the fog still twirls, the gas lights glow so dimly, those dirty, blasphemous women still screech from the street corners. I don't know what's happening to me. I carry my knife wherever I go these days. It's my only friend in the darkest hours.]<<<<<
—Anonymous (06:13:23/12-FEB-52)

>>>>>[Come off it, Clazz! What do think you're trying to do? You think this is funny, do you? It is you, isn't it? Oh yeah, I'm dead scared now.]<<<<<
—Lizzie the K (15:48:01/12-FEB-52)

STEPNEY

Most of the remaining real-life Cockneys, the traditional close-knit families with their Mafia-like intrigues and rituals, live in Stepney, the only part of the old East End that has not been bought up by developers for transformation into yet another copy of Docklands. The area is a strange mixture of old apartment buildings and modern houses, dotted with warehouses and abandoned sweatshops and factories. Few of the city's corporations have built new developments in the area, though it cannot be long before the pressure on the City becomes too great and the area goes the way of those around it.

For the young at heart, the abandoned warehouses provide great venues for a night of wild dancing at an unlicensed warehouse party, though we must point out the twin dangers from drugs and poor safety standards at such events.

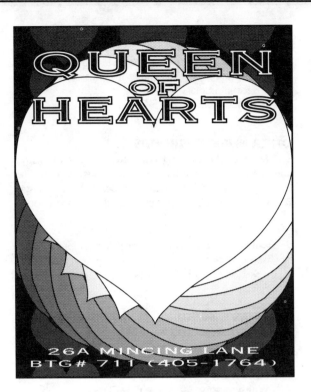

>>>>>[Stepney as a whole rates a D, security wise; however, it must be noted that the old families like to police themselves and their fellow residents. Justice the East End way is swift and violent, and even today often involves the fitting of concrete boots for a swift dip in the river. Just as dangerous are the younger gangsters. Always trying to make an impression on the older members of the families, they are not slow to resort to all manner of outrageous crimes and punishments in pursuit of their roots.]<<<<<
—X-Plod (04:39:24/15-DEC-51)

WHITECHAPEL

As the financial companies slowly crept along Cable Street into Wapping and the Dogs, many of their employees needed a place to live close by. At the turn of the century, vast tracts of Whitechapel were bought up cheaply, levelled, and rebuilt as high-quality apartment buildings. Gentle hills created by the excavation of new foundations were grassed-over and trees planted. The whole area, which stretches between the M313 flyover above Commercial Road and Cable Street, from Leman Street to Limehouse, now looks more like a corporate New Town development than one of the oldest parts of the capital.

One of the most interesting newer developments is Greenleaf Park, close to the Shadwell monorail station. The planting of several thousand trees has turned this area into a small patch of woodland and its innovatively designed houses and apartments are inhabited almost exclusively by elves.

>>>>>[The whole of Whitechapel rates A on the Metropolitan Police computer. The only crime you get around here is the occasional outbreak of PIXIES GO HOME or YUPPIES WILL DIE graffiti, and sometimes the mass arrest of expense-account fiddlers.]<<<<<
 —X-Plod (05:02:27/15-DEC-51)

OTHER NEIGHBOURHOODS

Most of the outlying part of the East End District consists of little more than vast expanses of commuter housing, dotted with the occasional local shopping centre. Following are details of the other residential neighbourhoods.

>>>>>[I've added the Metropolitan Police computer's security ratings.]<<<<<
 —X-Plod (21:53:52/3-JAN-52)

	Security Rating
NORTHERN EAST END	
Forest Gate: Low Class	C
Lea Bridge: Low Class	C
Leyton: Low Class	B–C
Stratford New Town: Low Class	D
Walthamstow Marshes: Low Class	C
SOUTHERN EAST END	
East Ham: Low Class	C
Little Ilford: Middle Class	B
Plaistow: Middle Class	B–C
Plashet: Middle Class	B
Stratford: Middle Class	B–C
Upton: Low Class	D
Wallend: Low Class	C
West Ham: Low Class	C
WESTERN EAST END	
Bethnal Green: Middle Class	A–B
Bow: Low Class	D
Bromley: Low Class	D
Clapton: Low Class	C
Dalston: Middle Class	B–C
De Beauvoir Town: Middle Class	B
Globe Town: Low Class	C
Hackney: Middle Class	A–B
Haggerston: Squatter	E
Homerton: Low Class	C
Limehouse: Upper Class	A–AA
Mile End: Low Class	D
Old Ford: Upper Class	A
Shacklewell: Squatter	E
Stamford Hill: Middle Class	C
Stoke Newington: Middle Class	A–B
South Hackney: Middle Class	B

USEFUL ADDRESSES

>>>>>[Duckin' and divin', wheelin' and dealin', givin' it all that! They have plenty of words for it around the East End. Following are some of the places where they do it.]<<<<<
 —Egon (17:31:05/23-DEC-51)

HOTELS

Calzoni's (14Ga)

Cheap Hotel Archetype/117 Commercial Street/ Gianluca Calzoni, Owner/BTG# 717 (408-1236)

>>>>>[Cheap and cheerful Italian family-owned guest house. Good place to stay if you don't want to be particularly visible. Food's cheap and fair, and plenty of it. Boy, did I put on a few pounds with Maria's lasagna. No great contact place; it's just inexpensive and convenient.]<<<<<
 —Kendrick (18:26:02/2-MAR-52)

Hotel Vera Cruz (14Ha)

Cheap Hotel Archetype/17 Whitechapel Road/Coll Mathurs, Manager/BTG# 717 (645-1550).

>>>>>[Ultra-cheap flophouse, but then it needs to be. Last time I had to stay here, I sat up all night picking off the roaches with a hastily improvised catapult, while weird moans and groans came from the room next door until dawn. Still, the Vera Cruz is open 24 hours, and no one ever asks any questions.]<<<<<
—Slim (18:45:03/3-DEC-51)

Knightsbridge Hotel (12Fa)

Cheap Hotel Archetype/90 Pitfield Street/Sutri Desai, Owner/BTG# 717 (377-8604).

>>>>>[Unofficial overspill of the Brick Lane market. You can come into the hotel bar any night of the week and pick up all manner of useful/useless items. But, make sure the guy you're doing business with gives you what you've paid him for. Some of these chumps are experts at the old switcheroo.]<<<<<
—Malcy (24:28:53/17-FEB-52)

Margate Sands Hotel (12Ga)

Cheap Archetype/278 Hackney Road/Tom Willard, Manager/BTG# 717 (377-2821).

>>>>>[You often see advertising flyers for this place lying around in runners' haunts and other cheap dives. "Luxury at a price you can afford," they say, and "Own room, all facilities." Trouble is, Margate spent all its cash on their advertising and none on the hotel. The rooms are tiny cubicles separated by thin board walls, and the "all facilities" turn out to be two dirty sheets and a basin of cold water. The only reason people ever stay here is because by the time you get here, there's nowhere else to go.]<<<<<
—Slim (19:04:06/3-DEC-51)

RESTAURANTS AND BARS

Dalston Arches (8Ga)

Mid-Size Restaurant Archetype/52 Kingsland High Street/Del Talon, Manager/BTG# 717 (664-3663).

>>>>>[The last genuine Pie & Mash shop in the East End. Now, this really is the proper taste of English cuisine. Steak and kidney pudding, eel pie and heaps of mashed spuds, all fresh made that morning. Lovely jubbly! The food's piled high and the mugs of tea are only 20p. You want to meet some real East Enders, you start here.]<<<<<
—Dapper D (03:26:42/22-JAN-52)

>>>>>[Yeuch! Have you seen this place? They have live eels in a basin of ice outside the shop. You want a piece of eel pie, they grab the nearest one, hack its head off with a cleaver, and toss it in the pot. The smell of 50 panicking eels and the fresh splatters of green blood were enough to have me tossing my breakfast. Avoid unless you like feeling ill, or you're a troll with no sense of taste.]<<<<<
—Malcy (00:21:57/18-FEB-52)

House of Scrumpy

Bar Archetype/84 Stoke Newington High Street/Alf Cutler, Manager/BTG# 717 (845-3164).

>>>>>[Beer's not what you drink here. Scrumpy's a fermented-apple drink from Somerset in the West of England. Six pints, you're completely steaming. They have folk dancing on Friday evenings. It's sort of odd, but after six pints of scrumpy, it's slamming.]<<<<<
—Del (20:43:17/4-MAR-52)

>>>>>[Warning: Del's a troll. I'm an ork, and I say four pints. Humans and pixies, stick to two.]<<<<<
—Garnett Steele (23:16:47/4-MAR-52)

Marquess of Queensbury

Bar Archetype/502 Mile End Road/Del Watts, Manager/BTG# 717 (300-4592).

>>>>>[This is the kind of East End pub that you really want to visit. Once. The beer is great, the food is cheap (if alive)—try the jellied eels or the soup-in-a-basket for the real sophisticated touch. The gopis and snakegirls here make elves look fat. Friday and Saturday nights they have bare-knuckle troll fights in the cellars after they clear away the barrels. Put your money on the troll with the slight hunchback. He's a real bastard.]<<<<<
—Lofty (01:45:16/18-FEB-52)

The Moon & Sixpence (15Ja)

Bar Archetype/10 Bigland Street/Reg Butler, Manager/BTG# 717 (644-3276).

>>>>>[You don't turn down an invite to visit this place in a hurry. The Arnold Brothers operate their whole "organization" out of the back room of this traditional East End spot, and there is always plenty of hired muscle around to ensure nothing gets out of hand without their say-so. The brothers have been running this part of Whitechapel for ages, and have their own little corner of the underworld all sewn up. You want to deal in Whitechapel, you have to talk to these guys first. Be lucky!]<<<<<
—Slim (06:33:10/10-FEB-52)

The Siren (15Ha)

Bar Archetype/53 Commercial Road/John McConnell, Owner/BTG# 717 (628-4371).

>>>>>[This is a fairly ordinary-looking "drink until three if you've nothing better to do" watering hole. The house band is OK if you like saxophones with terminal world-weariness. The girls look as glum as the sax player, and the siren hologram looks as sad as most of the clientele. Oh, hell, this place is just depressing.]<<<<<
—Marco (11:28:54/19-FEB-52)

>>>>>[But keep your eyes on the owner. McConnell was in government employ for some 18 years. He spent a lot of that time in and around Teesprawl, and word is he was involved in the operation to evacuate the Fringe Zone in Yorkshire. Don't know what he did, SAS or intelligence or coordinating, but I do know he's been the subject of a few boxing attempts over the years. Some determined-looking gentlemen in suits show up to talk quietly with him from time to time. Word is, he's hidden what he knows on quadruplicated chips in very secure places. According to one very reliable source of my acquaintance, it could do a lot of people a lot of damage.]<<<<<
—MesoStim (15:32:17/19-FEB-52)

Toadslab (12Ja)

Mid-Size Restaurant and Bar Archetype/458 Bethnal Green Road/Sazz Maroon, Owner/BTG# 717 (311-4865).

>>>>>[The name needs some explanation for visitors. "Toad in the hole" is a traditional British dish of sausages cooked in a huge bath of batter. Very unhealthy and very British. Well, the orks have gone to the top with this. No pretence, just hot, filling food for a low, low price, and better than burgers. I think.]<<<<<
—Dapper D (14:32:18/19-FEB-52)

>>>>>[Look, Dapper, just because half your family works in the joint. It's mayhem here. They serve the stuff by carving out a square foot of this batter with a trowel, then flick it at your table so you get to catch it with your plate. If no one in the way gets to catch it in mid-flight, that is. Sometimes you lose a sausage or two on the way, although I admit the real strong-arm guys can throw your toad a cool fifteen yards and hit you in the face if you keep still. Keep a knife handy in case some of the gravy is still a bit lively. The pickles are good, too.]<<<<<
—Malcy (16:22:19/19-FEB-52)

>>>>>[This is a great place to get friendly with good ork people. If you want their trust, buy a beer or two here. They'll get used to you quick enough.]<<<<<
—Del (19:15:33/19-FEB-52)

>>>>>[Yes, Del, but you are a troll and that helps.]<<<<<
—Janzi Z (22:16:01/19-FEB-52)

NIGHT CLUBS

The Warehouse (13Ga)

Converted Warehouse/Unit 3 Club Row/Billy and Dave, Owners/BTG# 717 (885-2132).

>>>>>[The only place to go if you're in the East End and want to dance. This club is built inside an old shipping warehouse, and it's now fitted out with high-tech trid lighting and sound systems. It runs from midnight till dawn every Saturday and Sunday. Clientele are a wide mixture of East End kids, corporate kylies slumming it, and your usual black-clad lowlife. Bring your dancing pumps, baby, 'cos you're gonna need them.]<<<<<
—Gav (22:31:06/9-JAN-52)

OTHER

Shastri's Old India (8Ga)

Small Store Archetype/3 Kingsland High Street/ Rurani Shastri, Owner/BTG# 717 (567-7121).

>>>>>[Nice shop. Good curries, biryani mixes, lovely Indian sweets. Don't try them if you want to keep your real teeth, because they're all raw sugar with some cochineal and coconut and extra sugar. Lovely ornaments, too, some carved ivory from antique stores, a few really good carpets. Fine place to browse.]<<<<<
—Lone Sloane (17:52:11/11-FEB-52)

>>>>>[And a little more. Sunil Shastri has knowledge of Indian occult matters. When he has your confidence, he may speak of such things. Be respectful.]<<<<<
—Ravindra (22:17:43/11-FEB-52)

>>>>>[You don't have to be quite so coy, Ravi. He has a license for his interests. The food's nice, but the talismongering is of a higher quality.]<<<<<
—Callistra (00:00:00/12-FEB-52)

THE PALACE AND THE ESTATES

ROYAL LONDON

For several centuries, London has been a city with four distinct centres: the City of London, the financial centre; the West End, the entertainment centre; Westminster, the political centre; and Buckingham Palace, the royal centre. The last two come together in this district, the Palaces and the Estates.

The area is laid out like a physical representation of the traditional balance of power. At the head of the district, alongside the river, the ancient Houses of Parliament still hold the two assemblies that govern Britain. In nearby Whitehall, the most prominent members of His Majesty's Government, including the Prime Minister and the Chancellor, have their official residences in Downing Street. Above, and squarely behind Westminster is Buckingham Palace, the London residence of the Royal Family. Behind the palace, moving east, lies the Estates, so-called because it has been divided up into a great many small squares, each the London residence of one of the country's noble families. Travelling further west still, one meets the areas where reside many of the rest of London's wealthiest and most influential.

For those interested in the history of Britain, and especially the king and his family, there is much to see and do in this district, whether it be watching the Changing of the Guard, rubbing shoulders with the rich in the elegant stores in Knightsbridge and Kensington High Street, or perhaps managing to catch a rare glimpse of His Majesty himself.

>>>>>[Oh yeah, the King, right? Didn't I see him on the box last Christmas lunchtime?]<<<<<
   —Dee (14:32:04/12-FEB-52)

>>>>>[No, that was just a very accurate computer simulation. The real thing is even more tedious and looks just like a waxwork that has escaped from Madame Tussaud's and been allowed to run the country.]<<<<<
   —Willie (01:38:53/17-FEB-52)

>>>>>[Now that Whitehall has effectively been moved lock, stock, and barrel to join the Lord Protector at the Temple, Westminster is not the hotbed of intrigue and frantic lobbying that it once was. The move has effectively left the district wide open to the Byzantine machinations of the nobles and lesser royals, be it on the floor of the House of Nobles or in the estates that divide up the district.

In the rest of the district, and especially the upper-class shopping streets (High Street Kensington, Knightsbridge and King's Road, Chelsea), the sole instruments of power are money and influence, no matter how they are gained. At the turn of the century, these were wielded by foreigners, particularly Arabs and Europeans, who were prepared to use whatever methods were available to them—legal or otherwise—to secure their aims, chiefly ownership of everything that would turn a profit. Corruption at local government level was so wide that the Metropolitan Police Fraud Squad eventually had to move against the entire district council. After a public outcry from the residents of the district, who either refused to believe that their elected representatives were a bunch of crooks or who were also implicated, all charges were dropped, but none of the councillors and officials was allowed to practice politics again.

Of course, the only real upshot of all this was that these corrupt politicians were replaced by people even more corrupt. This time, though, the people paying the bribes and exerting their influence were the new nobles. With the return of the monarchy and its attendant trappings, the new traditions upheld by the Lord Protector, and the resurgence of the ancient British traditions and religions, the nobles have regained a tremendous influence, which they exert at all levels. These lords and ladies are now playing for stakes far higher than the control of Harrods or ownership of Cadogan Square, and they are using everything in their power.]<<<<<
   —Mole Man (23:17:06/4-FEB-52)

GEOGRAPHY AND DEMOGRAPHICS

The Palaces and the Estates District (the almost meaningless official division between them runs down Grosvenor Place and Buckingham Palace Road) are edged to north and south by Hyde Park and the new Royal Thamesside Park at Sands End. Both are large, neatly maintained areas of grass and trees, with lakes and riding paths. On Sunday mornings, the centuries-old tradition of the rich and privileged promenading in the parks, on horseback and in carriages, has been revived.

Between the parks, the district is mostly flat and divided up into hundreds of wide, tree-lined avenues, between which lie many smaller squares and crescents. Houses in the district almost all date from the early 19th century, and are large, solid affairs designed for habitation by huge families and many servants. In the narrow streets between the squares, the old stable buildings have long since been turned into mews dwellings, fashionable apartments and houses peopled exclusively by the young and wealthy.

Despite the resurgence in British wealth and the old noble families, the district includes a wide mixture of ethnic backgrounds, though all residents are from the upper and upper middle-class strata of society. It seems that anyone with the money to live in the district and the breeding to act with propriety and manners is accepted. Hence, one will find very traditional English upper-class families living next to Arabs, Swiss, Americans, Indians, or Germans. Many of these wealthy residents are elves, who are accepted alongside their human neighbours.

Several decades ago, the southwestern end of Chelsea, especially around the quaintly named World's End, was London's artists quarter, a centre for all that was radical in art, fashion, and music. Nowadays, the artists are still here, but the radicals have moved on, leaving behind the financially successful ones, now totally integrated into the establishment.

>>>>>[Despite the acceptance for the elven community, there is plenty of hidden racism within the district. In the residential areas away from the shops where orks might legitimately work, these metahumans are often stopped and searched, albeit very discreetly, and escorted away from the wealthiest neighbourhoods. Despite the national success of many entertainers, sports stars, and even politicians from ethnic backgrounds, it is still commonplace for them to be stopped and questioned about stealing if they drive through the Estates in a new car. The racism of the educated and privileged is sometimes the hardest to weed out.]<<<<<
—Phantom (21:56:29/20-DEC-51)

>>>>>[Yeah, term. Soon the black rain will come from the north and sweep the titled scum from the streets. Spoken.]<<<<<
—Ambrose (00:23:11/17-JAN-52)

ECONOMY

Many of the residents of the district are rich from inherited wealth, their lifestyles maintained by ownership and investment dividends. As a result, of course, their lives are spent in a round of little work and a great deal of socializing, down to the country for the weekend, then returning to manage their investments or plan a party. Many of the richest nobles, with endless amounts of free time on their hands, have become fascinated by the twin attractions of politics and business, approaching both with savage grace. The younger members of the wealthy families often find half-hearted employment in the City or in an undemanding profession such as nursery school teaching or nannying.

The district generates a great deal of its own income from its property and from the famous expensive shopping streets. Harrod's (at Knightsbridge) may be the only name familiar to most overseas visitors, but they soon learn to enjoy the delights of the thousands of other fabulous department stores and shops. The latest attraction, the three-storey Phillimore Shopping Hall on Kensington High Street is just one of many ports of call guaranteed to lure the money from any shopper's wallet. Around these areas, many high-class hotels and other businesses, such as publishers and law offices, also provide employment and income.

The area around the Palace earns huge profits from tourism every year. The concentration of so many historic attractions central to the concept of British royal pageantry and tradition pays great dividends, though at the expense of huge crowds during the summer months.

NEIGHBOURHOODS

The Palaces and the Estates divide neatly into those two divisions. Though the latter is almost five times as large as the former, it is mostly residential, and certainly does not have all the tourist attractions of the Palaces.

THE PALACES

Everyone knows Buckingham Palace, the official residence of His Majesty the King at the top of the Mall, but what of the others? Halfway down the Mall, St. James's Palace overlooks the pleasant park that shares its name, and is still the official London royal palace, though no members of the Royal Family presently occupy it. Across the park, the familiar shape of the Houses of Parliament conceals the Palace of Westminster, which is the traditional name for the building, and especially the eleventh-century Westminster Hall that stands at its heart. In earlier times, one would also continue across the river to Lambeth Palace, the traditional seat of the Archbishop of Canterbury, head of Britain's church.

Around the royal palaces, Lancaster House and Clarence House are used by members of the Royal Family as official residences. At the far end of St. James's Park, past the rows of gentlemen's clubs lined up as if for inspection along the Mall and Pall Mall, Horse Guards Parade still houses the King's official escort. The Cavalry Regiments of the Household Division (specifically, the Life Guards and the Blues and Royals) are on duty daily, changing guards every hour to the delight of the flocks of tourists. The parade ground is the site of the annual Trooping of the Colour, on the Saturday nearest to the King's official birthday, when he takes the salute at the head of his guards.

The area around Westminster houses many other tourist attractions, including the immense Westminster Abbey; the country's monarch is always crowned here, amid the graves and memorials to many of Britain's most famous people. Downing Street, lurking behind its immense metal gates and anti-missile screens in the shadow of the monolithic grey Foreign Office building, is remarkably drab in comparison. On Petty France, the sinister-looking ex-Home Office building now houses Scotland Yard, the Metropolitan Police headquarters. From its overhanging upper levels one can almost imagine the Commissioner and his officers keeping a watchful eye on the whole city.

>>>>>[The old New Scotland Yard building in nearby Victoria Street is now used as a headquarters by covert operations and special security units of the police and army, usually known as S-Division to coppers on the force.]<<<<<
—X-Plod (04:01:30/7-FEB-52)

The area behind the Abbey, south and west of the Houses of Parliament, houses many of its MPs, and also Westminster School, one of the oldest in the country (it moved here from another site way back in 1461!). Further

south still, the neighbourhood known as Pimlico provides much more top-class housing. Where it meets the river at Grosvenor House, many of the old corporate showcase buildings vie for space with the Tate Gallery.

>>>>>[This whole neighbourhood rates AA on the Metropolitan Police computer, though His Majesty pulls in a higher rating than that. The embarrassingly frequent break-ins to Buck House and the regular but harmless hacking into the Duke of Edinburgh's personal computer files in the latter part of the last century forced the Royal Family and their advisors to rethink security. They can no longer afford to be instantly available to the general public.

By the way, talking about security leaks, you would be amazed at just how many high-class prostitutes live and work in the area around Westminster. Or perhaps not.]<<<<<
—X-Plod (04:13:28/7-FEB-52)

>>>>>[Be warned also about the level of security, aerial and astral, in this area. Combat drones by the score sitting at the ready, a corp of specialist mages, and, yes, even a couple of patriotic shamans just waiting for somebody, anybody, to try something. And don't think you can catch them napping. The automated defense, SAMs, AVMs, watchers, et al, are hair-triggered.]<<<<<
—Wire Guided (23:26:48/12-FEB-52)

THE ESTATES

The return of the nobles to Belgravia, Chelsea, Brompton, and Kensington has subtly but significantly changed the area, in some ways turning back the calendar several hundred years. At the turn of the century, the neighbourhoods were like many other parts of the Smoke, a mixture of old houses and new roads. More recently, though, the nobles have been returning the old squares to their original forms, as enclosed estates owned by individual families. Cadogan, Chester, Montpelier, Onslow, and Tedworth Squares, and any number of others, have been fitted with railing and gardens, with access permitted only to those with business at the great houses standing at their heart. Other areas have followed suit, with individual streets and mews enclosing them, partly for security but mostly for the status that living on a traditional estate (albeit a fake one) seems to bestow.

Further west, in neighbourhoods like South Kensington, Earls Court, and West Brompton, the housing is of a lesser quality, and often much newer. The older parts of Earls Court, once the first home of immigrant Australians, New Zealanders, and South Africans, have been replaced by modern, high-class housing developments that, for the most part, blend well with the surrounding areas. The large and venerable exhibition halls at Olympia and Earls Court still stand, though there are plans to replace the latter with a more modern centre and classy shopping mall.

South, alongside the river, Sands End Royal Park stands on what used to be a ramshackle collection of industrial units and poor housing. Today the entire area either side of Wandsworth Bridge Road, from King's Road to the river, is a semi-wild parkland of rolling hills and many trees, complete with birds and even a few deer, in which it is possible to wander for hours without meeting another soul. In the centre of the main part of the park, a small druidic grove has been formed around a neolithic standing stone.

>>>>>[You know, I could have sworn that standing stone wasn't there when that part of Sands End was the Elswick Street flats. Did they conjure it out of the land or deliver it in a truck, that's what I want to know!]<<<<<
—Rosie Posie (23:11:07/22-DEC-51)

>>>>>[The park is dangerous at night, but only because it is crowded with dozens of young Sloane Square debs making out with their boyfriends in the backs of their limos while their security men mill about at a discreet distance having a quiet cigarette.]<<<<<
—Lone Sloane (15:17:31/28-JAN-52)

>>>>>[Hey, what's the penalty for killing the king's deer?]<<<<<
—Robin (14:08:19/12-FEB-52)

>>>>>[You get to marry Princess Caroline, but not to sleep with her.]<<<<<
—Anonymous (05:11:37/15-FEB-52)

>>>>>[These neighbourhoods are rated A for security purposes by the Metropolitan Police computer.]<<<<<
—X-Plod (05:48:34/7-FEB-52)

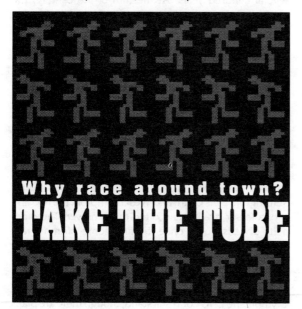

Why race around town? TAKE THE TUBE

USEFUL ADDRESSES

>>>>>[This whole area drips serious money, ladies and gentlemen. Make sure you dress the part or you won't get in the front door—and we all know how demeaning the tradesman's entrance is, don't we?]<<<<<
—Egon (17:09:45/23-FEB-51)

HOTELS

The Orchid Hotel (19T)
Luxury Hotel Archetype/4-5 Ennismore Gardens/ Kuang Kwan Lee, Owner/BTG# 715 (091-0671).

>>>>>[Fabulous. Operated in Singapore style, beautiful fabrics, orchids in every room, food is incredible. Try the Passion's Wings and Dragon Flutter hors d'oeuvres. Far-eastern visitors usually stay here; top Japanese corporates when they have to visit. Lots of muscular gentlemen sitting quietly in the lounge reading the newspapers, keeping their eyes on their charges. Money drips along the carpets here. Look very cool and rich if you want to try anything.]<<<<<
—Samantha (18:44:17/22-FEB-52)

The Waterloo Hotel (19V)
Luxury Hotel Archetype/9 Belgrave Square/Sir Nigel Hamilton, Owner/BTG# 715 (132-4514).

>>>>>[This is where visiting politicos stay when they're in the Smoke. Sure, the ambassadors stay in their embassies, top diplomats, too, but the whole second echelon and the top guys from second-level countries, they stay here. Service is very fast, very discreet, with bills to match. If you can afford to stay here, you can hear worthwhile things. And if you can take the risk of augmenting your surveillance, you can hear a great deal. Obviously, there's IC, anti-surveillance electronics, and precautions against snooping users of power. Take care.]<<<<<
—Callistra (01:00:00/3-MAR-52)

RESTAURANTS AND BARS

Alfalfa (23Q)
Small Restaurant Archetype/16 King's Road/Nicol Trueheart, Owner/BTG# 715 (816-3994).

>>>>>[Great vegan food, cheap, and service is quick. Tahini tofuburgers are a dream, food of the gods. Hang around if you need contacts who have enterprising approaches to world problems.]<<<<<
—Deep Green (19:14:32/16-FEB-52)

>>>>>[Trouble is, enterprise takes different forms. Shamanic people, fine. Some genuinely concerned people, harmless drifters, kindly souls. But watch the ones with the harder eyes and the more determined arguments. Direct Action people look out for recruits here.]<<<<<
—Ravindra (22:15:22/16-FEB-52)

>>>>>[Yes, but this is a good way into enlightenment of many forms. One rash person does not spoil the company of a dozen kinder souls.]<<<<<
—Sarahana (00:32:17/17-FEB-52)

Gofers (18P)
    Fast Food Restaurant Archetype/188 Hornton Street/ Joy Bramwell, Manager/BTG# 715 (337-1272).

>>>>>[Tucked away behind Kensington High Street, this is a sandwich place and cafe used by most of the local secretaries and other staff. Keep your ears open and you'll hear exactly what Lady X is doing and with whom, and why Company Y has just been raided again. You know how those girls gossip.]<<<<<
—Rosie Posie (03:14:52/28-FEB-52)

The Peppermint Twist (18U)
    Bar Archetype/114 Knightsbridge/Tiffany Rodgers, Manager/Racial Bias Against Orks and Trolls/BTG# 715 (909-3890).

>>>>>[The most expensive cocktail bar in town. You don't get let in here unless you're wearing something that looks like it costs six months' salary, and it has to be up-to-the-second fashion. The people inside are so beautiful they faint with self-appreciation. Even the mirrors check out their own reflections. Lots of silver and black, pale complexions, enhanced cheekbones, cybereyes with variable hue control, dangerous dependencies, people in serious need of ego-reduction surgery.]<<<<<
—Spacer (23:23:17/25-FEB-52)

The Winter Garden (19U)
    Large Restaurant Archetype/82 Brompton Road/ Valentina Owzianowki, Manager/BTG# 715 (355-2173).

>>>>>[Ultra-sumptuous restaurant serving a mixture of French and more esoteric special dishes, all set in a three-level area decorated with fountains, waterfalls, and pools. The faint splashing of the water mingles with the gentle murmur of conversation and the jingling of cutlery and jewelry. My favourite restaurant, and if I see any one of you rabble here, there will be trouble.]<<<<<
—Egon (02:21:08/26-FEB-52)

>>>>>[Sounds like the perfect place for a good old-fashioned troll party!]<<<<<
—Del (04:11:21/2-MAR-52)

OTHER

Glendower Export Associates (19U)
    36 Sloane Street/Sukirissi Clearwater, Director/BTG# 715 (582-3578).

>>>>>[This office building houses the export agency for the orichalcum and magical goods that the Countess of Snowdown lets out from her lands. Export only; and you need a licence from the Lord Protector's Office, which is easy to get because it earns Britain export funds and hard currency. Getting it into your own country will require an import license, of course—most of the time. Depends on your own home laws. Suki, who runs the place, drives a hard bargain. She's sassy, no fool, not to be haggled with. If she's smart enough to mask her own aura, she knows one end of a credstick from another. Don't waste her time.]<<<<<
—Callistra (06:00:00/14-FEB-52)

>>>>>[She's cute, too. Terminally cute. She usually takes cocktails at the Peppermint Twist after work, if you want to try your luck. But you'd better have a BIG credstick.]<<<<<
—Sarahana (14:42:19/15-FEB-52)

>>>>>[I still say there's no way the Countess could be mining orichalcum. It simply cannot occur naturally. It can't. No question.]<<<<<
—Magister (00:15:51/21-FEB-52)

>>>>>[Then explain it.]<<<<<
—Turo (05:29:50/21-FEB-52)

>>>>>[I can't.]<<<<<
—Magister (21:06:52/21-FEB-52)

High Roller (17P)
    Casino Archetype/23 Kensington Church Street/ George Stock, Manager/BTG# 715 (717-9195).

>>>>>[Very discreet casino, very plush. If you have the credstick clout, champagne and hostesses at your beck and call. Some interesting people get into debt here. Word is out on Michael Hazeldean's eldest son, Jeremy. If you owe George, you'll pay. You don't have the nuyen, check the prices for body tissues. They'll get what they can, and they won't care whose son you are.]<<<<<
—MesoStim (02:16:42/19-FEB-52)

>>>>>[Be careful here. I hear that the yakuza are behind this place, putting up the money for George. Not everyone in debt gets boxed; Jeremy won't be. The yakuza will love a contact like this. Be very, very careful.]<<<<<
Phantom (05:11:15/19-FEB-52)

Sun Spot Solarium (19N)

Above 84 Kensington High Street/Amanda Ferguson, Manager/BTG# 715 (732-9073).

>>>>>[Let's face it, there isn't much sunshine in London. This is the most popular solarium for that healthy, tanned, bronze look.]<<<<<
—Samantha (19:14:45/5-MAR-52)

>>>>>[Mmmmm, that really good pre-melanoma look.]<<<<<
—Kendrick (19:17:12/5-MAR-52)

Universal Brotherhood Meeting Hall (19V)

1 Belgrave Square/Luther Cartwright, Administrator/BTG# 715 (909-4253).

>>>>>[The official blurb says that this organization is dedicated to teaching people to fulfil their own inner potential. Truth at the Core of Your Being and all that stuff. They put some emphasis on the unity of all sentient races, which sounds fine by me, but there's something rather hollow about it all, this talk of people being "agents" with total responsibility for their own actions. It's all a bit too mellow, and I'm not sure I like the feel of it.]<<<<<
—Sarahana (18:52:42/16-FEB-52)

>>>>>[You're too stale, Sarahana. I've attended my first two meetings and it's very beautiful and uplifting. Belonging is a first path to the unity of all people. You should try and open (1.7 Mp deleted by sysop)]<<<<<
—Janzi Z (19:44:17/16-FEB-52)

>>>>>[Be wary of these people. I heard some very strange stories from friends in Tir Tairngire. People trying to recover kidnapped children who'd gotten too heavily into the Brotherhood. Journalists investigating the Brotherhood who found themselves most definitely warned away. One case, maybe just coincidence, of death, but a couple of disappearances. Not enough to point the finger, certainly not enough evidence for anything substantive, but I wouldn't enter the Octagon they have in the Estates any more than I'd enter the one in Seattle or Washington or anywhere else. If you're thinking about trying it, think again.]<<<<<
—Frazier Cloudline (21:17:22/17-FEB-52)

>>>>>[I've heard tell of a file dump circulating some of the American shadownet boards about the Brotherhood. Truly horror-show stuff, from what they say. Am trying to get a copy.]<<<<<
—X-Plod (06:54:52/19-FEB-52)

LIFE UNDER THE TRAFFIC

For half a century, those travelling between the prosperous mid-west of England (Oxford, Swindon, and beyond) and the capital have travelled on the M40 motorway. As it reaches the densely populated edge of central London, the highway rises onto stilts and runs, 75 feet above the ground, for almost three miles. This road is known as the Westway. In contrast to more modern cities, there was no room to carve a channel for the road, so it was simply raised off the ground to pass over houses and alongside tower blocks.

The estates lying in the shadow of the Westway are some of the worst in Britain. On many of them, law and order has broken down entirely, and the gangs rule with a savage and cruel hand. What makes the anarchy seem that much worse is its close proximity to the luxurious Estates district only a couple of miles to the south and the rapidly gentrifying eastern area around Paddington.

The sole attraction of the section of the Westway District lying under the motorway is the glorious Portobello Road street market, where one can buy almost anything for the most surprising prices. It is very strongly recommended that any visitors to the market be professionally escorted.

>>>>>[I read somewhere that some travel insurance companies are now refusing to honour claims for incidents occurring during visits to Westway, even with an armed escort.]<<<<<
—Janie (08:41:09/11-JAN-52)

>>>>>[The insurance you need to go to Westway these days is the sort that comes in exchange for five hundred sovs in a plain brown envelope to a man called Jerry in the bogs of a pub in Kilburn.]<<<<<
—Anonymous (13:12:04/31-JAN-52)

Further west, stretching as far as the M825 Inner Orbital motorway, the neighbourhoods show the very obvious results of years of neglect and economic recession, with old industrial parks lying derelict and aban-doned between the huddling commuter enclaves. Not entirely coincidentally, it would seem, the area is home to London's largest prison, Wormwood Scrubs. British Industrial PLC maintains a huge, sprawling storage and assembly facility at Gunnersbury. It is surely only a matter of time before the Smoke's large corporations redevelop this land, taking advantage of plummeting land prices. To the south, following the gentle curves of the river, the old-world charm of Chiswick and Fulham seems a lifetime away from the despair of the northern zone.

>>>>>[Westway is Inner London's forgotten zone. At first glance, one might think that The Squeeze is the absolute pits, but at least people pay attention to every last little protest riot there. Without wishing to sound like a bigot, a stretch only has to stub his toe in Brixton Road and he's lead story on the nine o'clock news. You could splash the whole of Notting Hill with a small nuke and—providing the fallout blew west—no one would bat an eye.

In such an area, you can imagine what the residents do for fun. All manner of illicit substances abound, controlled by the stretch gangs with the help of what gets called the Westway slice, a home-made, razor-sharp sickle knife more like a whale flenser than a hand-to-hand weapon. Each gang cooperates with all of the others to control its patch, with boundaries usually marked with colours and graffiti. In times of great need, the gangs work together as a syndicate under an elected committee. It was just such a committee that carved up all the land west of the West Cross flyover into individual patches, and allotted them to each gang to do with as it liked.

Many of the gangs are extremely racist, with humans from ethnic backgrounds banding together against metahumans. My intelligence is that one or more of the more extreme anti-metahuman policlubs are gradually manipulating themselves into a position of great power behind the Westway gangs. Eventually they will be able to goad one of the crazier gang leaders—Ambrose Forde of the Nightwraiths, maybe, or Mick Sloane of the Cutters—into using the "metahuman threat" to suggest that the Westway crew join together for a combined assault on the "elven" Estates. And then there will be a war in West London.]<<<<<
—Phantom (02:29:04/18-JUL-52)

>>>>>[In the last two months, a major crackdown (almost certainly instigated by the Oversight Board) has reputedly taken the Westway gangs down a peg or two. Certainly, there have been a great many police on the streets of Notting Hill and Westbourne Green, and hundreds of arrests. As usual, this caused an immense riot that lasted three days but was largely ignored by the media. A bit more of the Orwell and Huxley estates got burned down and half a dozen people got killed, so I guess the news people thought it was business as usual.]<<<<<
        —X-Plod (02:10:36/20-DEC-51)

GEOGRAPHY AND DEMOGRAPHICS

Almost the whole of the Westway District is low-lying and virtually featureless, carved up by roads and swarming with decaying industry and sprawling housing estates. Only in the far eastern tip, where it meets the West End around Paddington, is the area indistinguishable from the districts around it. This neighbourhood is rapidly increasing in popularity, now that even some wealthy individuals are still not rich enough to afford a residence in the Estates District. Most of Paddington's residents are well-educated professionals, many of whom keep an in-town apartment here to save them commuting back and forth from the country every weekday.

To the north of the Westway motorway, the land rises through an area of tightly packed middle-class housing up to the border of the Village District. Many elves have settled in leafy Maida Vale, to the extent that they are the dominant ethnic group in certain streets.

The people of the desolate central Westway Districts, centered on Notting Hill, Westbourne Green, and North Kensington, are a jumbled mix of English, West Indians and Africans, together with some more isolationist Indians and Pakistanis. Mixed-race children are very common. The people of these sections are uniformly ill-educated and scrape out a living way below the poverty line.

>>>>>[If it wasn't for the struggling saints and angels in the National Health hospitals, the infant mortality rate in central Westway would rival that of many African countries. Grim.]<<<<<
        —Phantom (03:28:00/18-JUL-52)

The residents of the western half of the district are principally middle and working class, of a variety of ethnic groups that include Irish and Italians as well as West Indians and Asians from the subcontinent. There is a small ork community, though it is struggling against violent racism. Many commute into the centre of the city to work, though a small minority still find employment in the factories and warehouses that have not yet succumbed to the area's smothering economic malaise.

Along the edge of the Thames, the residents of Chiswick and Fulham have clung to their riverside parkland, at least partially fending off the threat of development. The people who live here are principally white, middle- and upper-middle class, and well-educated. There is a small druidic temple in the grounds of Chiswick Park.

Prospective visitors to the area should note that, in addition to the hazards mentioned earlier, the protective dome above Westway is holed in so many places as to be rendered entirely useless. Protective clothing is therefore required at all times.

ECONOMY

The Westway District is very poor. Few businesses are located in the area, and most of those that remain operate purely on a local level. Those of the residents who do have jobs tend to commute into the West End or the City to work. Most are ancillary workers or shop assistants, rather than managers and consultants.

The British Industrial PLC complex at Gunnersbury is a major employer, drawing most of its workers from nearby Acton and Turnham Green. Most of the work is in warehousing goods, supplies, and equipment destined for the "Angel Towers" Arcology. The area's other major employer is London Transport. Their largest Underground train depot is at Shepherd's Bush, and many of its drivers and guards live nearby. (Union rules still insist that the fully automated trains carry a fully trained driver and guard in the event of computer or mechanical failure.)

JACKSON HEIGHTS HOTEL

461 LADBROKE

>>>>>[It has to be said, though, that most of the income generated in the shadow of the Westway comes from the dark side. Some of it, of course, comes from the grey market, from dealing in goods that are only borderline dodgy—knock-off stuff, no questions asked. Keep your cool in Portobello Road any day of the week and you'll always get a bargain and a half. Much more is on the black market, which is where you start dealing with the gangs. There is a big trade in old-fashioned hardware: vehicles, weapons, BTLs, bodies. The "softer" services have taken longer to become established, but there are now plenty of whiz kids around who can jury-rig chips or hack data or dollars with the best of them. Just don't ask for a money-back guarantee.

Finally, a few words of advice: don't try selling your own goods in someone else's shop, know what I mean?]<<<<<
—Malcy (04:02:28/14-FEB-52)

NEIGHBOURHOODS

The following are the most important neighbourhoods in the Westway District.

NOTTING HILL

Believe it or not, Notting Hill was first the name of a farm on the site, bought to be covered with houses by a James Ladbroke way back in 1823. The vast, curving roads of huge Victorian houses built over the next 50 years are still standing (for the most part), but they have long since lost any trace of their grandeur. Over the years, increasingly large sections of the area have been bulldozed and covered with high- and low-rise apartment blocks, often long after the designs involved had been discredited. The increasingly ethnic nature of the community made it a lively and vibrant area, famous throughout the land for the annual Mardi Gras-style carnival that runs during the last weekend in August.

>>>>>[Now the carnival is fun. You simply must check this one out. Especially if you like being deafened by the loudest reggae in the world, mugged by smiling children, and stabbed when you complain. Party till you puke.]<<<<<
—Rosie Posie (02:17:28/8-JAN-52)

>>>>>[Had a bad experience, did we? I must say, every carnival I've ever been to seemed very sedate. Perhaps you just don't like those of us who happen to have the wrong complexion?]<<<<<
—Malcy (05:14:27/14-FEB-52)

>>>>>[I think she is simply aware that gang activity is always at a record high over Bank Holiday weekend. When I was in the force, we all hated that weekend. You know all those telly news shots of jacketless coppers dancing arm in arm with delirious Jamaican mamas? Faked, every last one of them.]<<<<<
—X-Plod (02:17:21/20-FEB-52)

For a time, Notting Hill joined Chelsea as the most fashionable area in swinging London. Writers and artists moved in to take advantage of the multicultural society. Political visionaries of all persuasions, too, have long been a feature of the neighbourhood. In the early part of the century, however, the extreme politics of the area so alienated London's leaders that Notting Hill and its surrounding neighbourhoods were effectively starved of all investment and attention. As the area became poorer, its people began to fight harder for a rapidly diminishing share of the pie. It is to be hoped that the City will soon see clear to investing some of their millions in what must surely be the most perfect development area in the capital.

On a happier note, the market at Portobello Road dates back to late Victorian times. It is one of the country's longest street markets, and it would take several weeks to examine everything that is for sale at the hundreds of stalls. Different days see different goods on sale on some of the stalls (antiques on Saturdays, clothes on Fridays, electrical and electronic goods on Sundays, for example), but many of the stalls are the same day in and day out. The cheap prices are the main constant of the market, however, and anyone with a keen eye and the nerve to haggle with the sharp market vendors is guaranteed a bargain. Visitors must be aware of the high standard of good manners the market traders insist upon. They should also take care to avoid the many pickpockets.

>>>>>[The market lies on the territory of the Howling Carrion (north of the Westway) and the Nightwraiths, who jointly police it. For the most part, the groups are discreet and deadly in their dealings. Mellow-heads who are stupid enough to cause trouble generally end up trying to swim the Grand Union Canal without the benefit of their arms and legs.]<<<<<
—Malcy (07:18:37/14-FEB-52)

>>>>>[With unerring accuracy, the Metropolitan Police computer notes that Notting Hill has a security rating of E. There is also reference to a supplementary data file the size of an average town's tax record. When I have a spare month or two, I guess I ought to find out exactly what's in it.]<<<<<
—X-Plod (03:32:41/20-DEC-51)

PADDINGTON

The neighbourhood around the station used to have a bad reputation as a centre for pleasures of the flesh eminently suitable for the relief of tired businessmen on their way home. With the decline in the West End Overground, and the complementary rise in scarcity of available and affordable property in the Estates District, redevelopers have pressed Paddington's unfussy rows of solid Victorian housing into service once more. The area is particularly popular with those who need city apartments during the work week, but who return to their larger country dwellings at the weekends.

North of the Westway lies an area long known as Little Venice because of the preponderance of houseboats moored on the Grand Union Canal, which flows through the district on its way to the Thames, on the other side of the City of London, at Limehouse Basin. The locale is a favourite place for wealthier locals to relax on those rare balmy August evenings.

>>>>>[Paddington as a whole is rated A on the Metropolitan Police computer, though certain individual establishments have security far in excess of that.]<<<<<
　　—X-Plod (03:56:50/20-DEC-51)

>>>>>[My data tells me that notable residents of Paddington Model Village, as we cynics call it, include two junior cabinet ministers, five MPs including Michael Hazeldean, our beloved squeaky-Green Environment Minister, and a couple of gen-u-ine trid celebrities, in the shape of chat-show host Larry Legion and breakfast telly's Jane-Marie St. Clair. If you ask me, having any of that little lot move in next door to you would be far more likely to lower house prices than raise them, but what do I know about real estate?]<<<<<
　　—Slugger (21:12:12/14-JAN-52)

>>>>>[Along with the political and showbiz celebs, other famous residents of nouveau Paddington include East End extortionist Charlie Horse and a certain Tong boss. I'd love to know what would happen to property values if that leaked out. Not that I'm telling, of course.]<<<<<
　　—Anonymous (04:11:48/2-FEB-52)

WESTBOURNE GREEN AND BAYSWATER

Cast adrift on either side of the Westway, these two neighbourhoods are currently at the same stage; one is declining, however, and the other is rising. Westbourne Green, basically one immense estate of lofty tower blocks, is slowly sliding into the same state as Notting Hill. The area gained a certain level of notoriety a few years ago when a free concert by Slam-Abuse, local boys-turned-superstars, ended in a riot that left drummer Malkit Singh shot and killed. Since then the area has been virtually a no-go zone.

>>>>>[If someone wants to arrange to meet you in one of the Westbourne tower blocks after dark, don't go. Leave the country instead. You want excitement? Go to Malaya, Beirut, the moon.]<<<<<
　　—Malcy (07:48:56/14-FEB-52)

>>>>>[The nastiest guys around here are the Warthogs, so-called for their initiation ceremonies, which involve the presentation of an ork's head to gang leader Dermot Hammer.]<<<<<
　　—Anonymous (18:04:39/17-FEB-52)

>>>>>[If that's a joke, it's not funny.]<<<<<
　　—Garnett Steele (07:09:50/19-FEB-52)

Bayswater, on the other hand, looks set to be a much happier place. With the recent demolition of the notorious Hallfield Estate to make way for corporate housing for Tarbuck McClintock Financial, the area is plainly on the rise. Paddington will soon become so full and expensive that people's only option will be to look further west. It just goes to show that not all the news from the Westway is bad news.

>>>>>[Westbourne Park has a police computer security rating of D, while Bayswater is rated as C and rising.]<<<<<
　　—X-Plod (04:06:47/20-DEC-51)

OTHER NEIGHBOURHOODS

Most of the Westway area is little more than a vast expanse of poor and fair quality housing collected into communities. Only where the district meets the river does the status of the neighbourhood rise. Following are the main remaining residential neighbourhoods.

>>>>>[Once again I have added the security ratings from the Metropolitan Police computer.]<<<<<
　　—X-Plod (04:12:17/20-DEC-51)

	Security Rating
Acton: Low Class	C
Acton Green: Middle Class	B
Bedford Park: Middle Class	B–C
Chiswick: Middle Class	B
East Acton: Middle Class	C
Fulham: Middle Class	A-B
Grove Park: Upper Class	AA–A
Gunnersbury: Low Class	B–C
Hammersmith: Middle Class	B
Kensal Town: Low Class	B-C
Kilburn: Low Class	C
Maida Hill: Low Class	C
Maida Vale: Middle Class	A–B
North Kensington: Low Class	D
Old Oak Common: Low Class	C
Parsons Green: Upper Class	A
Shepherd's Bush: Low Class	D
South Acton: Low Class	C
Turnham Green: Middle Class	B
West Kilburn: Low Class	C

USEFUL ADDRESSES

>>>>>[Once again, terms, we've extracted a few places that may prove useful to you. Be lucky!]<<<<<
— Egon (18:17:31/23-FEB-51)

HOTELS

Blue Ribbon Hotel (16P)
Average Hotel Archetype/177 Bayswater Road/James FitzAlan, Owner/BTG# 715 (175-8113).

>>>>>[A living example of the Old Boy Network. Graduates from Oxford and Cambridge get a 15 percent discount on all accommodation here. So the clientele has plenty of brains, but the level of social skills on offer is distinctly baboon-like.]<<<<<
— Kendrick (16:02:13/20-FEB-52)

>>>>>[That's a little extreme. Anyway, don't forget that Cambridge has one of the best hermetic studies programs in Europe. You want to touch the Power, then this isn't a bad start. Hide any accents, though.]<<<<<
— Callistra (19:19:46/20-FEB-52)

Hotel Antonioni (16Q)
Average Hotel Archetype/56 Porchester Gardens/Vivo and Enrico Antonioni, Owners/BTG# 715 (274-3650).

>>>>>[Fair quality hotel. The Italian brothers who own it represent several street samurai, hiring them out as bodyguards for special jobs.]<<<<<
— Spider (17:01:51/23-JAN-52)

Jackson Heights Hotel (13L)
Cheap Hotel Archetype/461 Ladbroke Grove/Steve O'Donnell, Manager/BTG# 715 (535-2286).

>>>>>[Large place, always plenty of rooms. Sad Steve, the manager, is high up in the Nightwraiths gang; other gang members often use rooms for unknown purposes.]<<<<<
— Malcy (02:18:34/4-FEB-52)

Old Willow Hotel (12R)
Average Hotel Archetype/85 Lanark Road/Sir Brian Johnston, Owner/BTG# 715 (831-8851).

>>>>>[This is bizarre, but it's kinda terminal. The manager is a cricket freak and the halls are full of framed ancient pictures of famous cricketers. The carpets are all green, and cut in multiples of cricket-pitch length. They even have pitch markings on them. The soaps are in the shape of those red cricket ball things, and about as hard, too. The towels are marked with the shape of those sticks they put in the ground to play the game. You get Australians and guys from the Caribbean League states staying here, and people who come just to visit the country for the test matches. Weird or what?]<<<<<
— Kendrick (15:29:17/28-FEB-52)

>>>>>[You also get people who use that as a cover staying here. So when the test matches are on, check the incoming flights list on a suitable datanet. Check out who checks in. It can be rewarding. Some people may need a little help.]<<<<<
— Callistra (01:00:00/1-MAR-52)

Weatherby House (15N)
Cheap Hotel Archetype/102 Talbot Road/Emeline Cornelius, Owner/BTG# 715 (448-1202).

>>>>>[Small and lively guest house-cum-drinking club much beloved of several Westway shadowrunners, including yours truly.]<<<<<
— Malcy (03:37:59/11-FEB-52)

RESTAURANTS AND BARS

The Elgin (16M)
Bar Archetype/1 Elgin Street/Una Thorssen, Manager/BTG# 715 (101-4650).

>>>>>[Now this is the place, the legendary, the ultimate, the unique. OK, it's just a really great runners' pub. But the stories I could tell you about it and all its regulars. Perhaps I should write a book.]<<<<<
— Spider (17:48:51/23-JAN-52)

>>>>>[Don't keep us in suspense, Spiderboy. Tell us! Tell us!]<<<<<
— Rosie Posie (18:32:17/23-JAN-52)

Govinda's (14M)
Mid-Size Restaurant Archetype/14 Portobello Road, Notting Hill/Anand Gavashta, Manager/BTG# 715 (448-7724).

>>>>>[This place gets my vote for the best Tandoori place in West London, and half my fellow runners say likewise. Service is fast, management discreet, and Anand's gorgeous wife Usha is a thousand words by herself.]<<<<<
— Malcy (19:22:34/11-FEB-52)

The Sutra Palace (14M)

Small Restaurant Archetype/138 Portobello Road/ Tiny Krishnamurti, Manager/BTG# 715 (448-0212).

>>>>>[No, forget what I said above. This is the best Tandoori in West London, and all my other friends say likewise. The service is slow, but the atmosphere is so great, you don't mind. The management are friendly, and Tiny tells the wickedest elf jokes around.

Yeah, yeah, I know. Sometimes I love one place, sometimes I love the other, and some nights I stand in the Portobello Road caught in the crushing grip of indecision. So sue me. Oh, almost forgot: the Sutra Palace hasn't got a drink's licence, so you'll have to bring your own.]<<<<<
—Malcy (19:37:09/11-FEB-52)

NIGHT CLUBS

Niagara (17P)

Night Club Archetype/771 Notting Hill Gate/Amber Delors, Manager/BTG# 715 (667-5583).

>>>>>[Very fashionable weekend-only club, especially popular with deckers because of the new dance floor set-up. The guy who designed Niagara wired up the entire floor, so to get the full benefit, dancers need to be physically chipped into the system! I only tried it once; it felt like being on the point of ecstasy and the point of death at one and the same time. Me, I'm too old for this stuff.]<<<<<
—Malcy (20:16:00/11-FEB-52)

the CRUSTING PIPE
8 Fetter Lane, in the Temple
BTG# 710 (442-6130)

The Railroad Club (14N)

Night Club Archetype/200 Great Western Road/ Delroy Adams, Manager/BTG# 715 (412-7862).

>>>>>[Heavy-heavy place slap bang under the Westway, but the only spot to meet all kinds of eminently useful people. Most of the clientele are stretches from the local gangs, who seem to use it like a clubhouse. The music is mindscraping dub, gut-wrenchingly loud, and if you ain't dancing, you've got to stand in the back yard. Word of warning: don't stare too long at someone unless you intend to kill him.]<<<<<
—Spider (04:27:49/2-FEB-52)

OTHER

Phillips Personal Protectors (15S)

Small Office Archetype/37 Praed Street/Dave Phillips, Owner/BTG# 715 (972-4156).

>>>>>[This is the best place in town to get bodyguards if you need to. Corporate hiring usually keeps the very best on permanent retainer, but for a payment over and above the odds, you can do well here. I don't know where old man Phillips finds his trolls and orks, but, by god, they're big. They're not licensed to carry firepower, but one smack across the head from one of them is enough to put someone out for the count. They've got dermal plating, plus every defensive and protective cyber-advantage you've heard of. And one or two you haven't—if you pay top rates.]<<<<<
—Phantom (02:17:43/15-FEB-52)

>>>>>[I hear they're not so hot. And you've got to admit they look silly in those light blue suits they issue as regulation. Not to say uncomfortable. I mean, it's all just sitting around in plazzy clubs minding nervous little rakkies who's scared of their own shadows.]<<<<<
—Sarahana (09:24:25/15-FEB-52)

>>>>>[You say that to my cousin Albert. He works for them, has done for two years, and he has the scars to prove it. And the take-home pay. Look, Pixie, you've got 32 teeth and Albert can redistribute all of them throughout your body with one enhanced swipe. Right?]<<<<<
—Del (18:44:17/15-FEB-52)

>>>>>[**Westway Hang-Gliding Club (15N)**
Flat 14-38 Julian Cope Tower, Colville Terrace/Selwyn Pierce, Founder/ BTG# 716 (312-3351).
Great! These crazy stretches go hang-gliding off the tallest Westway towers. Terminally banging! Almost for free, good people. Plenty of fringe business with the people if you want. They know most of the good places and people around. If you've shown you're no rakkie. Take the jump. The wind rush is truly slamming.]<<<<<
—Malcy (19:14:52/2-MAR-52)

HILLS AND HAPPINESS, TOWERS AND TROUBLE

Pointing at the heart of the Smoke like a giant triangular wedge is the Village District, an island of sedate greenery poking slyly from the crumbling ruins of the previous century's planning disasters. At its heart, the vast expanse of Hampstead Heath, still suitably wild and windswept for the most part, continues to persuade those who live at its edge that they are deep in the countryside and not just a few miles from the busiest city in western Europe. The area is a bizarre conglomeration of old world charm and ultra high-tech, reflecting the style and aspirations of some of the capital's wealthiest residents.

Like the super-hard tip of a drill, the headquarters of the London lodge of the druids sits at the southern end of the wedge. From the lodge's lofty perch on Primrose Hill, it is possible on clearer days to gaze out across the whole of central London, which from here looks more like a full-scale and infinitely detailed model rather than a teeming metropolis.

>>>>>[A great big "spin it!" to the snobbery and pretensions of those Hampstead Village no-hopers. The only real style these media jack-outs ever had was bought in Fayed's. Just like everyone, their time will come. And as for the silver-haired sandals skulking in their gothic toilet, prancing around in their dresses and waving their sticks around—ha! It won't take more than a few inches of cold, hard steel to cut through all their mumbo-jumbo.]<<<<<
—Rosie Posie (02:11:23/21-JAN-52)

>>>>>[Oh puh-lease! What does this girl want, a trid series of her own? Well, she'll just have to work her way up from teaboy like the rest of us!]<<<<<
—Terry C. (14:05:40/29-JAN-52)

GEOGRAPHY AND DEMOGRAPHICS

The landscape of the Village District is dominated by the enormous wild parkland at its heart and by the sharply rolling hills that run through three quarters of its area. Many of the roads, especially in the more exclusive and inaccessible parts of Hampstead and Highgate, are very steep, indeed, though luckily for car drivers, most of the area has been joined to the grid system. The areas circling the heath are home to some of London's wealthiest, often from the more glamorous sections of the media, entertainment, and business worlds. More discreet are the nobility, whose high-walled estates have been hereabouts for centuries. By economic necessity, most of the residents of this sparsely populated area are human or elf. It is rare to see an ork or troll in Hampstead Village in anything other than a menial position.

Away to the north and west, the land continues to rise and fall until it reaches the great gash that holds the teeming M825 Inner Orbital motorway that marks the district's northern edge. Between the heath and the road are great swaths of sedate upper- and middle-class suburbs, from traditionally Jewish Golders Green in the west as far as Muswell Hill further east, neatly laid out in vast tree-lined rows around central shopping centres, just as they were a century ago. The people who live here are middle- and upper-management types or small business-owners and entrepreneurs.

As one rounds toward the east, past Highgate and Archway, the land drops away suddenly, sweeping gently through Tottenham toward the River Lea. The landscape is one of endless middle- and low-class housing, often collected into immense sprawling estates. This is the start of the vast commuter land that stretches outward from here for drab mile after mile.

As the district drops down toward the south and the West End, it begins to resemble an inner-city area once more. The sprawling areas around Islington and Camden Town are dotted with closely watched pockets of extreme poverty and overcrowding. But intermingled with these are some of the most modern private developments in the Smoke, home to the well-educated and the monied, closed to the deprived and dangerous. As one reaches Regent's Park and St. John's Wood, the money seems to pop right out onto the streets in blatant and often fool-hardy displays of wealth. These neighbourhoods seem to be populated by people who need to be close to the very centre of the capital, but who aren't prepared to venture into the full-scale battleground that is the Overground today.

>>>>>[You want crime? We got it. Behind the walls of those huge houses up in Hampstead, every last one looking like it's got its own resident ghost, the real criminals are ripping off millions from the stock market, doing data transfers, and all those other delightful white-collar crimes. S'funny, but you would have thought that someone's gonna ask where all that money is coming from. I mean, it can't all come from legit sources, can it?

Elsewhere in the Village, just walk the streets, you know? Sooner or later some little kid with his big brother's gun in his pocket is gonna try to flip you. You want to live to grow up in those endless blocks of flats that drop from the hills to the river, you got to be like that. Ain't nowhere else to go, ain't nothing else to do.]<<<<<
—Johnny Nowhere (17:14:21/11-JAN-52)

>>>>>[They breed them tough in the East Village, no question about it. Life is right at the bottom of the glop pile if you're stuck in one of those blocks with nothing to see but other blocks stretching down through Tottenham and away east into the distance. One day they're all going to go down like dominoes, one after the other. It never ceases to amaze me that they don't all band together and go partying in the houses of the rich and careful on that big old heath. Guess most of 'em are too busy just trying to stay alive.]<<<<<
—Phantom (21:03:04/14-JAN-52)

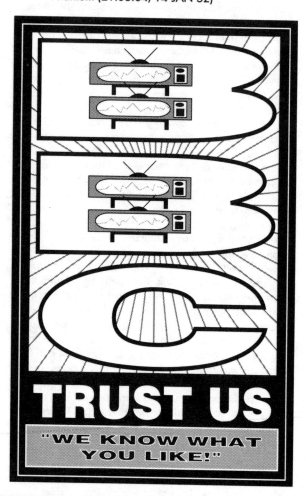

BBC
TRUST US
"WE KNOW WHAT YOU LIKE!"

ECONOMY

The vast sweeping neighbourhoods around the outer edge of the Village District are home to some of the millions of commuters who crowd into the City and the Underplex every morning. Local industry in this area is confined to the immense electronics and manufacturing companies that line the M313 and stretch out northward along the M1 into Hendon and the furthest reaches of Orbital North. Eastward one finds more traditional factories and warehouses, sweatshops and offices.

Venturing further south, into Islington and Camden, one encounters more corporate presence, especially in the large office complexes of data companies such as InfoGen and Halcyon Systems. The north of Camden is crammed with the offices of several large media concerns, including several trid production companies, film studios, and a major publishing house. The most modern development is the immense BBC complex at Agar Grove, opened just last year and employing more than 15,000 people. Of course, most of the profits from such enterprises tend to disappear up the hill into Hampstead or down the hill into the City, leaving nothing for use in revitalizing the surrounding slums.

NEIGHBOURHOODS

Much of the Village District consists of miles and miles of residential sections housing the capital's commuters. At the heart of the district, though, are the neighbourhoods that give the village its very individual character.

CAMDEN TOWN

At the end of the previous century, Camden and Brixton were the twin centres for entertainment for the young and fashionable. While the southern neighbourhood has been allowed to dwindle and rot inside the Lambeth Containment Zone, its northern counterpart has risen to a whole new category. The young pleasure-seekers who used to frequent Camden's clubs and markets have stayed as they grew into slightly less-young professionals, turning the area into a centre for all branches of the entertainment industry. The roofs of the sparkling new buildings squatting off the Chalk Farm Road bristle with dishes and aerials, and every lunch-time the area's bijou wine bars and restaurants are crammed full to bursting with young producers and executives chewing through the latest viewing figures and production budgets.

At night and at weekends, the new young generation take over the street markets, shops, and clubs for a round of spend spend spend and party party party. Those of a nervous disposition are advised to stay well clear of the area, but if careful, everyone else can come and join the fun.

>>>>>[North of central Camden, especially along the corridor leading to Gospel Oak and Hampstead, is rated by the police computer as AA-A for security. Elsewhere, the neighbourhood only garners a C. Note the presence in west

Camden of the Ultra Seven, a discreet and deadly gang of mixed ethnic background that has some unspecified ties with the Knights of Rage of the Squeeze.]<<<<<
   —X-Plod (22:25:18/14-DEC-51)

HAMPSTEAD

With its narrow, winding streets and steep alleys dotted with quaint pubs and gift shops, much of Hampstead looks more like a theme park than a thriving community. What it actually means, of course, is that the residents of this small piece of old England have a great respect for their community, and have kept outside influences from changing it for the worse if they could prevent it.

>>>>>[That's a bit gentle, chaps. Some of these people are violently militant! Mind you, they have to be; Golden Archers have been trying to build one of their dogburger dispensaries on High Street for 60 years, and are rumoured to have tried all manner of dodgy tactics to get in there.]<<<<<
   —Egon (13:32:39/18-JAN-52)

On the picturesque lanes that wind up around the edge of the Heath, the immense hideaway homes of the rich and famous lurk behind imposing walls and fences. Among the many famous residents of the area are computer magnate R. J. Crawford, the actor Paul Anderson, novelist Stevenson McBride, and no less than four members of rock giants Mutator! Note that visitors are free to visit the main streets of the village, but that it is inadvisable to wander around the back lanes.

Hampstead Heath is a massive (789 acres) expanse of rolling woodland and meadows, the last genuinely natural place within greater London. It is dotted with ponds and lakes, and despite all of the city's environmental hazards, still provides a home for many types of bird. The druids have adopted parts of the heath around the barrow on Parliament Hill (reputed to be the burial place of Queen Boudicca) as the site of regular rituals. Other nearby sites have, unfortunately, been the scene of murders and muggings in recent times, and visitors walking the Heath after dark do so strictly at their own risk.

>>>>>[All of Hampstead rates A or more on the police computer, with individual homes and estates clocking in much higher. There are some seriously well-guarded houses up here, with cyberdogs, land mines, laser mesh, the works. Of course, some of these places have a lot to hide.]<<<<<
   —X-Plod (22:48:41/14-DEC-51)

PRIMROSE HILL

The imposing Regency-period buildings that curve along the upper edge of the grassy mound known as Primrose Hill used to be home to London's foremost literary figures. In 2034, however, the government gave ownership of Primrose Hill and the row of curving terrace

A Nice **Quiet** Place To Dine. Live Bands Mondays and Fridays

buildings overlooking it to the New Druidic Movement to house their new headquarters.

The terrace frontage has been left intact, but behind it, the buildings have been joined together and refitted to create a sumptuous and palatial headquarters. At the rear of the building is the Druidic School and apartments for resident initiates. Directly across the hill, atop the ancient barrow, a single standing stone marks the spot where, four times a year, the druids celebrate the mysteries of their art.

Since the arrival of the druids, the community around Primrose Hill has become more contemplative and cloistered. One regular event that has not changed, however, is the Primrose Hill Festival, which starts in Chalcot Square behind the druids' headquarters on Midsummer's Eve and lasts through the final week of June.

>>>>>[I know it's blasphemous and dangerous and all that, but I just can't help laughing when I think about all those poor repressed little boys in their dresses dancing around their maypoles on top of the hill at midnight as if it were the most natural thing in the world. Guess the lunatics really have taken over the asylum.]<<<<<
   —Rosie Posie (23:15:22/4-DEC-51)

>>>>>[Yeah, and kicked out anyone who doesn't look exactly like them. It's a pity they've got that rule; I could swear old Marchment's ears are going pointy.]<<<<<
   —Anonymous (01:18:55/5-DEC-51)

>>>>>[One more thing—why ain't there no primroses on Primrose Hill anymore?]<<<<<
   —Rosie Posie (01:22:03/5-DEC-51)

>>>>>[Because our beloved Lord Protector sold them all to the Japanese.]<<<<<
   —MesoStim (23:21:09/9-DEC-51)

>>>>>[Primrose Hill rates AAA in security. There are armed police everywhere, but not so you'd notice. That is, not until you cough just a little too loudly and suddenly you feel a dozen barrels jammed into your neck.]<<<<<
   —X-Plod (23:11:53/14-DEC-51)

OTHER NEIGHBOURHOODS

Not all of the Village District is as cosy as Hampstead or as dynamic and shiny as Camden. Following is a list of other residential areas within the district.

>>>>>[I've added the Metropolitan Police computer's security ratings for those who need them.]<<<<<
—X-Plod (00:17:24/15-DEC-51)

	Security Rating
NORTH VILLAGE	
Crouch End: Middle Class	B
East Finchley: Middle Class	A
Fortis Green: Luxury Class	AAA
Harringay: Low Class	D
Highbury: Middle Class	B
Highgate: Upper Class	AA
Hornsey: Middle Class	B
Hornsey Vale: Low Class	B–C
Muswell Hill: Upper Class	A
Noel Park: Middle Class	A
Stroud Green: Middle Class	B
South Tottenham: Low Class	B–C
Tottenham: Middle Class	B
Wood Green: Middle Class	A
WEST VILLAGE	
Dartmouth Park: Upper Class	AA
Golders Green: Upper Class	A
Vale of Health: Luxury	AAA–AA
South Hampstead: Upper Class	A
West Hampstead: Luxury	AA
EAST VILLAGE	
Brownswood Park: Middle Class	B
Canonbury: Upper Class	A
Finsbury Park: Middle Class	B
Holloway: Squatter	E
Tufnell Park: Low Class	D
Upper Holloway: Middle Class	C
SOUTH VILLAGE	
Barnsbury: Upper Class	A
Gospel Oak: Upper Class	AAA
Islington: Middle Class	AA–B
Kentish Town: Low Class	B–D
Marylebone: Middle Class	B
Pentonville: Low Class	C
Regent's Park: Upper Class	A
St. John's Wood: Upper Class	AA–A
Somers Town: Low Class	D

USEFUL ADDRESSES

>>>>>[Here are some especially useful addresses for your diaries, matey. Use wisely.]<<<<<
—Egon (20:07:16/23-DEC-51)

HOTELS

Conway Castle (4U)
Luxury Hotel Archetype/10 Merton Lane/Branwyn Griffiths, Owner/BTG# 716 (311-3122).

>>>>>[This place is amazing. It's actually a replica of Conway Castle in North Wales. At the front, anyway. Inside, the facade is fairly well-maintained. Suits of armour, Welsh heraldics, a good stone dragon by some Welsh sculptress or other, maps of riding tours in the Wild Lands of Wales. Four-poster beds, too, but they're too soft for my liking. Good trivid introductions to Welsh culture and places to visit.]<<<<<
—Samantha (18:16:25/3-MAR-52)

The Stretford Hotel (9W)
Cheap Hotel Archetype/74 Kentish Town Road/Clive Coppell, Owner/BTG# 716 (613-4481).

>>>>>[This is a weird one. Although it's a hotel, half the space is taken up by night clubs and bars. It has a direct line to the Manchester scene; they had Identity Zero playing their new album, *Blazing Paranormal Ambulance*, before Manchester had heard half of it. Excellent contacts to the whole Manchester and Merseysprawl scene. Dwarf barmen, troll bouncers, ork slammers—not for sensitive souls. Weekends are no good. You get corporate type hangers-on who think they're cool, and the night ladies pick 'em up when they've filled their skins with drink. Unedifying. Keep to weekdays. Enjoy the downtime.]<<<<<
—MesoStim (11:13:13/2-MAR-52)

White Lawns Hotel (9X)
Average Hotel Archetype/71 Camden Street/Joe Longfield, Manager/Racial Bias Against Elves/BTG# 716 (508-3378).

>>>>>[This is a typical middle-class guest house, but check out the basement. Joe's a real techno freak, jerry-builds the stuff almost from scratch.]<<<<<
—Anonymous (22:06:28/12-DEC-51)

RESTAURANTS AND BARS

Apples (9X)

Small Restaurant Archetype/12 St.Pancras Way/Elise Barry, Manager/BTG# 716 (185-5628).

>>>>>[Old Elise runs an expensive little vegetarian bistro during the week, but at weekends she can often be seen wandering Hampstead Heath, consulting charts, and prodding the ground with a stick as she walks. She's never found anything, as far as I know, and so everyone thinks she's a bit batty. Still, anyone who can make such great flapjacks must have something up there.]<<<<<
—Gav (21:14:38/11-JAN-52)

Le Petit Canard (6R)

Mid-Size Restaurant Archetype/11 Hampstead High Street/Jean-Paul Truffaut, Manager/BTG# 716 (337-8140).

>>>>>[Best French restaurant in town. The cuisine's even better since Jean-Paul repaired the firebomb-damage last spring. Try the duck, the glazed lamb, or the noisettes of veal in champagne sauce. Paradise. A high class of company, too, people from theatre and the arts. Delightful, dears, just delightful.]<<<<<
—Egon (11:27:31/18-FEB-52)

>>>>>[This restaurant won't be open much longer. We don't want this kind of food. Roast beef, carrots, and boiled potatoes! Death to the French!]<<<<<
—Patriot (17:32:32/18-FEB-52)

>>>>>[Rosie, I know that's you. Cut it out!]<<<<<
—Sarahana (17:38:16/18-FEB-52)

>>>>>[Sorry, Sarahana. How could you tell?]<<<<<
—Rosie Posie (17:43:46/18-FEB-52)

NIGHT CLUBS

The Beast (10W)

Night Club Archetype/14 Parkway/Attila X, Manager/BTG# 716 (447-3275).

>>>>>[Thursday night, this is the only place to be for seven hours of brutal heavy-bass brain massage. This is a favourite deckers haunt; you can see them all sitting near the DJ console, taking notes. Personally, I'm too busy slammin'!]<<<<<
—Jazzy Jaswinder (02:37:42/30-JAN-52)

Romans (9W)

Night Club Archetype/5 Hawley Road/Peter Ullrich, Manager/BTG# 716 (223-4165).

>>>>>[Lively club but with plenty of dark corners, so a favourite with the local runners. Decorated according to a crazy Germanic theme, with leather and horned helmets everywhere, so hell knows why it's called Romans.]<<<<<
—Gav (12:57:43/29-FEB-52)

the Beast
14 PARKWAY/ATTILA

OTHER

Body And Soul (10W)

Small Store Archetype/318 Camden High Street/ Jasmine Lawson, Owner/BTG# 716 (422-3196).

>>>>>[This one actually is a real, organic, safe-ingredient beauty shop. No tissue or animal testing, no chemicals. It's so natural, like belladonna and aconite. But frankly, my grandmother smelt of patchouli oil, my mother smelt of patchouli oil, and if I have to smell any more of it, I'm going to throw up all over whoever's wearing it.]<<<<<
—Hampstead Hi-Jack (18:24:16/23-FEB-52)

Gaeatronics U.K. (9V)

38 Chalk Farm Road/Graeme Deforest, Manager/ BTG# 716 (302-2204).

>>>>>[This is a small subdivision of the company owned by the Salish-Shidhe. It's really only a kind of publicity office to give the corp some presence in Britain, although they do have a stake in the Cornish windmill estates. I hear they're trying to get up a scheme combining protection from coastal erosion with the use of barrages to harness wave power along the east coast of England.]<<<<<
—Sarahana (17:32:18/26-FEB-52)

>>>>>[There's no production capacity here, but I gather they have a small-scale macro-fusion testing laboratory in Cambridge. Clean energy, it's claimed, but we've heard that one before.]<<<<<
—Kendrick (19:16:34/26-FEB-52)

Guises/Disguises (5R)

Medium Store Archetype/1 Heath Street/Philippa Rawlinson, Owner/BTG# 716 (624-7813).

>>>>>[The best theatrical costumier in the country. They can do anything. When I wanted to hit the Swanage New Year celebrations dressed as the pope, they did it right down to the holy-water sprinkler in 15 minutes. They can dress a score of elves as harlequins at the drop of a credstick.]<<<<<
—Hampstead Hi-Jack (19:22:22/9-MAR-52)

>>>>>[Or vice-versa?]<<<<<
—Minstral (00:02:32/15-MAR-52)

Natural Beauty (5S)

Medium Store Archetype/91 Hampstead High Street/ Muriel Sanderson, Owner/BTG# 716 (414-4852).

>>>>>[Essential oils, incense, fragrances from around the world, where there are good ones left. This company buys only certified natural products for its cosmetics. No animal or tissue-testing is involved and (1.8Mp deleted by sysop)]<<<<<
—Janzi Z (19:42:44/4-MAR-52)

>>>>>[Not true. There are additives in these preparations. Some customers keep coming back for more. Some find certain side effects that neurologists would recognize without a quarkspin axial tomographic brain scan. Look for the pharmaceutical company behind this.]<<<<<
—MesoStim (21:14:37/4-MAR-52)

Sanders Investigations (12X)

Small Office Archetype/49 Cardington Street/ Reginald Sanders, Owner/BTG# 716 (107-4223).

>>>>>[Contrary to the name, which suggests a private investigation bureau, this firm deals in security and surveillance equipment—providing the surveillance is non-intrusive. That is, you can buy a remote-controlled video camera here, but not a nice little bugging device. There are, of course, some items on the borderline, where the law is, well, not entirely clear-cut, such as for restrainers and certain forms of communicators. Mr. Sanders and his staff take a sympathetic view of such matters. Negotiate carefully, but pay well. Don't haggle first time around.]<<<<<
—Malcy (15:15:27/12-FEB-52)

>>>>>[And don't ever push your luck. Mr. Sanders has a pair of LARGE troll assistants out the back.]<<<<<
—Dapper D (17:32:54/12-FEB-52)

Stanton's All-Nite Druggerie (9W)

Medium Store Archetype/282 Camden High Street/ Harold Stanton, Owner/BTG# 716 (142-9888).

>>>>>[Imagine an ork who has seen too many old American trideos and has a slightly deranged imagination. Now give him plenty of nuyen after a distant relative with a big stash happens to expire in his home. Harold buys a store. He sees a market opportunity for an all-night chemist. He opens one and indulges his old movie fixation. You end up with this. Strange, indeed.]<<<<<
—MesoStim (19:16:48/2-MAR-52)

>>>>>[Stanton's is a good place to find some extra medical service if you need it. Harry can hide you out with friends. Treatment isn't exactly high-tech, but the conditions will be clean and safe. If your bone marrow matches the tissue register, you can get patched up at a discount. If desperate, send your best friend to plead here.]<<<<<
—Kendrick (23:05:17/2-MAR-52)

ANGEL TOWERS

BRITISH INDUSTRIAL ARCOLOGY

This small district of London is named after, and dominated by, the arcology of British Industrial PLC (Public Limited Company, a technical commercial term in U.K. law). It is on the site of the old Battersea Power Station, which was demolished and reclaimed in the first decade of this century. To the south and east of this huge structure, which houses the headquarters of one of Britain's largest home-grown corporations, lie the markets of Covent Garden. Wholesale fruit and vegetable markets dominate the centre of the sprawling warehouses and stalls, but fortunate visitors can find the odd bargain or two at the periphery if they visit at the right time. The BritRail maintenance facilities in the southwestern Angel Towers district are not exactly a tourist site, but they help serve the BritRail southern network to Kent, Sussex, and Surrey.

>>>>>[The worst in the known world. These rail carriages actually have shock amplifiers. I have evidence that BritRail are paid by an orthopaedic surgery agency to design their carriages this way.]<<<<<
—Ravindra (15:14:32/16-FEB-52)

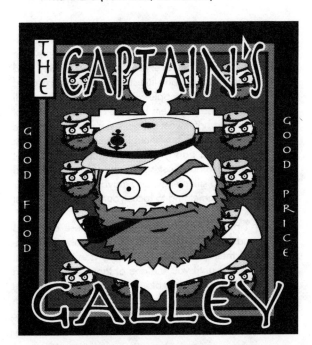

INSIDE ANGEL TOWERS

The arcology is split into two separate sections, a low-rise section to the northwest and the larger 78-storey executive arcology across Battersea Park Road.

The 30-storey main polygon has two levels of underground car parks, then three floors of shopping malls featuring British Industrial's consumer and electrical products, plus products made by other companies under license from British Industrial. The exhibitions installed on the ground floor plaza emphasize British regional achievements and manufactures. In the same area, the Captain's Galley and Regal Burgers fast-food chains do a roaring trade among the many millions of curious visitors to the arcology every year.

>>>>>[God, don't remind me. Glum-looking buggers in kilts swinging haggises around to the tune of a dismal set of bagpipes while the loudspeaker roars out stuff about, "Och aye the noo, real Scottish produce in our shop today, Scotch whisky and real Scotch haggis!" It's so plazzy, it's unbelievable. But the wilmas seem to love it.]<<<<<
—Kendrick (19:43:43/17-FEB-52)

The next floor showcases the very best of British Industrial's goods, which incorporate traditional qualities of British workmanship.

>>>>>[Like, it might last weeks instead of just days before falling apart.]<<<<<
—Kendrick (19:53:19/17-FEB-52)

>>>>>[No, that's unfair. Their good stuff is worth having, just keep away from the mass-produced material. Like everything else in this life, you get what you pay for.]<<<<<
—Samantha (20:01:12/17-FEB-52)

>>>>>[Oh, come on. What about the rakking Panda?]<<<<<
—Kendrick (20:04:16/17-FEB-52)

The top floors are devoted to administrative, maintenance, environmental, agricultural, and warehousing facilities, although the company handles most of its product storage at their large complex of warehouses at Gunnersbury.

The main executive arcology across the road is linked by numerous enclosed walkways. This section consists of working space and offices for the firm's clerical personnel, with a few floors given over to research and development. The familiar sight, to South Londoners, of Peter the Panda stands atop the tower.

>>>>>[Great, a 50-foot tall purple-neon panda with a digital clock in its head that runs around waving its arms up and down. This logo infests quite a few of BI's products, which people apparently buy because they subconsciously feel that something with a panda logo must be vaguely cuddly and eco-friendly. Unbelievable.]<<<<<
—Kendrick (21:14:53/17-FEB-52)

>>>>>[What a pile of plazz this is. It's lucky for BI that they built the tall tower just far enough from the river to keep it from sinking. Yet. If you can get at the records of the construction group that built this thing, check out their actual component costs. This tower was built for a lot less than it should have been. And those greedhead rollers in the top penthouses still haven't paid for the damage to those middle floors on the west side done by that missile strike that went astray from the LCZ ten years ago. Still got the scaffolding up. Are these guys mean or what?]<<<<<
—MesoStim (22:52:13/19-FEB-52)

ARCOLOGY SECURITY

Security around the arcology is not especially strict. Razor wire and aggressive, neurally chipped dogs on patrol are enough to deter the ordinary desperadoes of the LCZ, who usually confine themselves to throwing the odd rock or chunk of pavement at the armoured buses that ferry workers from and to Lambeth every morning and evening. More seriously organized criminals would not likely bother with British Industrial, because most of what's kept here is of poor quality and/or hard to move. As for BI's few industrial secrets, a decker can ferret them out in the Matrix without ever having to enter the arcology. The security measures are mostly to reassure a staff still nervous ten years after the missile strike that killed 217 of them. It's hard to see how razor wire will keep out a misguided, homemade surface-to-surface missile anyway.

Security around the whole area is really a second skin of razor wire. With the national and local government, British Industrial, BritRail, and the traders of Covent Garden sharing the costs, it's never been possible to agree on funding for anything much better. Armed police do regularly patrol this side of the LCZ at the perimeter, however, and they can call up chopper and heavy weapon support within a matter of minutes.

COVENT GARDEN MARKET

The centre of this area, which looks like a string of huge market stalls strung out inside a series of loosely interconnected airplane hangars, is a wholesale fruit and vegetable market where London shop owners, street traders, and restaurateurs buy their requirements. Visitors may be more interested in rummaging through the fringes of the market, however.

>>>>>[This is where the Indian Orks do their thing. The Narindras and Bhaterjees are the best-known families. The whole family comes in every day from Wembley and Harrow, from grannie to the littlest kids, all running around and helping out. These people will do you a fair deal on all kinds of stuff if you pay them fair and don't try and cheat them. Drink their hot, sweet coffee, see if you can manage to eat their spicy biscuits without first treating your mouth with asbestos, and parlay gently. You can get excellent carpets from the Middle East, spices and ornaments and old carved ivory and silk pieces, and maybe the odd book or two and a little something to focus your interest, if you get my meaning.

Don't push. Don't be over-hungry. These are good people, and they have many friends in the Smoke. Take time to befriend them. And hell, you really don't know what culture shock is until you see one of those lady orks in a typically gorgeous technicolour sari, complete with the traditional spot of colour in the centre of her forehead. Then wait for her husband to turn up with his turban. Wild.]<<<<<
—Kendrick (16:32:18/22-MAR-52)

THE SQUEEZE

LAMBETH CONTAINMENT ZONE

"Going south of the river?" is a long-standing Londoner's joke, usually delivered in the early hours of the morning by an inebriated club-goer to a cabbie desperate to finish for the night. The traditional cabbie's answer, of course, cannot be printed in a polite publication. It just goes to show that London is really two cities, divided by a common river. On the north bank are the financial, shopping, and entertainment centres, the tourist attractions, and the best of everything. South of the River Thames, there is only the Squeeze.

At the turn of the century, the neighbourhoods south of the River Thames were a mixture of low-class commuter housing and ailing light industry, gathered haphazardly around a number of central shopping areas. The random nature by which the areas developed gave the landscape an unfinished look. The commuter roads crossing the area thundered with traffic, leaving it dirty and polluted. Decades of poor urban planning had created vast low-class estates, onto which families were dumped by local councils starved of cash by central government.

Faced with such conditions, it is perhaps understandable that many of the locals were disgruntled. In the eyes of many other Britons, however, it did not excuse the taking up of arms against the forces of law and order. After a number of shocking terrorist outrages, the government used the medical emergency following the failure of the Adams-Hoffmann "Project 42-20" to set up the Lambeth Containment Zone (popularly known as "The Squeeze") to bring the rule of law back to the south London area. These attempts have only been partially successful, however, and a state of emergency still exists in the area.

Tourists and general visitors are advised not to visit the Lambeth Containment Zone. Those who must visit should be accompanied by the appropriate security personnel at all times. Note that most travel and medical insurance is invalidated if one's passport shows an LCZ stamp.

>>>>>[What? Who is this guy trying to kid? Conditions in south London became so bad that major riots broke out in different neighbourhoods in 1979, '82, '92, '98, 2004, '05, '17, and '21, not to mention hundreds more minor disturbances. Over the years, as the local councils col-

lapsed into bankruptcy and businesses fled from the area in droves, the Metropolitan Police created a special task force to deal with the area's problems. Does that sound like a few "disgruntled" locals?

But that's not all; there's something much bigger behind this. In 2038, the revelations by Channel 7's "Medicine Bag" program about the Adams-Hoffmann "Project 42-20" brought the huge company crashing to its knees and unprecedented numbers of rioters onto the streets. Many people, including myself, continue to believe that the Conservationist government was somehow involved. Indeed, rumours of same eventually brought them down the next year.

They told everyone the company was simply responding to a new strain of Asian flu, but in fact "Project 42-20" was a wide-ranging experiment in forced gene-pool manipulation, its aims being to discover how to control the goblinization process. Over the past 15 years, the project had, very secretly, progressively crippled, mutilated, and generally decimated the populations of the south London housing estates. The experiment involved the wide-scale secret testing, by dispersal into a number of different transmission environments, of a huge number of experimental mutagens. Some of these caused premature abortions or produced birth-defect babies; others slowly killed many people by shrivelling internal organs or destroying their immune systems. The bastards even put one set, Generation Epsilon/Alpha 16, in the free milk they were giving to school kids, for goodness sake! It's no wonder so many people suddenly discovered they were dying. What continues to frighten me, though, is that it took nearly 15 years for this rakking gopp to come to light! All told, the investigations found that the company was responsible for the deaths of 720 people, with a further 9,500 unprovable. Since then, many hundreds more people have slowly succumbed to 42-20.

These revelations enraged the people of Brixton, Camberwell, and New Cross. The first riot, 15 days after the first and only screening of that last episode of "Medicine Bag," ended up on Tower Bridge, as the police blocked the way leading to the Adams-Hoffmann corporate headquarters in the city. During this riot, the first 19 of the Lambeth Martyrs were killed, and Tower Bridge and the nearby Thames Wharf shopping mall were badly damaged. After that night, several more serious riots broke out, but the police—closely followed by the army—were soon in control.

TINY MOTORS

ZOOOOOOOOOOOOOOOOOOOOOOOOOOOOOOOOOOOOOM!

'enough said.   ©TINY MOTORS, INC. EWING.

The Lambeth Martyrs, as everyone seemed to be calling themselves at the time, moved underground and decided to pursue more direct action. Armed with automatic weapons gladly supplied by various local criminal gangs, the first units struck at Waterloo and Victoria Stations and in the Bond Street Station Mall, killing almost a hundred innocent people. More attacks quickly followed, including the infamous raid on placid Dulwich Village, which accounted for a retired ex-prime minister among the 74 dead. The government, after trying to weather the initial storm with the standard line of refusing to give in to blatant terrorism, finally took notice. Declaring a medical emergency, they moved in the army and created the Lambeth Containment Zone. Politicians with long memories kept mentioning the words "Belfast" and "Northern Ireland," but to little effect.

In the first weeks and months after "the Squeeze" went into effect, all was calm. The Lambeth Martyrs and their many associates slipped off into hiding and lay low for a time—the Squeeze being a splendid place in which to hide! The army, meanwhile, was setting up road blocks on all major roads, stopping and searching people by the dozen, and generally eroding everything that centuries of democracy had fought to maintain. Only a House of Commons rejection of two motions to declare a state of martial law and requiring all inhabitants of the Squeeze to carry identification documents kept the situation from degenerating any further. Using techniques previously honed to perfection in Northern Ireland, the army had many successes and arrested hundreds, but there were always hundreds more to take their place.

In the last decade, the Lambeth Martyrs have regrouped as an efficient urban terrorist group, while daily life in the Squeeze has returned to an approximation of normalcy. The Martyrs have made fairly regular attacks on most of the major British institutions, some successful, others not so. The government has responded by making LM membership illegal and banning the media from carrying direct interviews with its spokespeople. All the while, the LM have been insisting on two simple demands: adequate compensation to the people of the Squeeze and the dismantling of the Squeeze itself. The government have not been forthcoming on either; their position is that the responsibility for any compensation, if indeed any is due, lies solely with Adams-Hoffmann (long dissolved, of course) and that the Squeeze will be dismantled only when the terrorism stops. Impasse.

The Squeeze today is a disturbing place. It is hard to get used to seeing army patrols on the streets of one's capital city, and harder still to understand how the residents manage to keep from freaking out! Many aspects of everyday life seem to have returned to normal, but not quite. In many ways, the area is no different to many others: the Westway, perhaps, or parts of the East End. The housing is mostly crumbling, there is no work, violent street gangs operate the black market and make crime a career, and the buses still don't run on time. But then you see the graffiti, the vast murals painted on every exposed surface, shouting defiant slogans in support of the LM's struggle. You are standing in a pub and the collection box comes round. And you can never forget your first sight of a 42-20 victim, no matter how many more you may see. Mine was a little West Indian girl, about nine or ten I'd guess; no eyes, just blank flesh; one arm withered and useless; brain-damaged, mouth drooling. I couldn't stop looking at her hair. Her mum had plaited it in Rasta dreadlocks, so neat and pretty. I ran till I threw up, but I went back, and I still go back.]<<<<<
—Pilgerman (08:19:20/17-JAN-52)

>>>>>[The day of atonement will come soon, this we vow. Our voice will be heard, and the children will weep no more. Victory!]<<<<<
—Martyr (04:52:14/3-FEB-52)

>>>>>[Additional to above. Much-criticized movement restrictions were lifted 1-MAR-44; citizens officially allowed to go wherever they please since then. But random roadblock vehicle checks still create vast traffic jams most mornings. And kids still get shot at for making too much noise while playing or for being out after dark. Administration is in the hands of the LCZ Security Committee, three creeps in suits who do exactly what the Lord Protector tells them.

On the other side, LM's weaponry has been getting more sophisticated in last few years. I suggest they are getting it from the Shidhe.]<<<<<
—Anonymous (16:41:03/14-FEB-52)

>>>>>[This one's free: Two of the scum responsible for 42-20 now work for Zeta-ImpChem (Research Division) in Tynesprawl. They are Robert Williamson, 117 Douglas Way, Bankhill, Newcastle, and Abigail Carr, Flat 4, 2 Auckland Crescent, Bardon, Newcastle. Somebody do something about it.]<<<<<
—Datagem (08:32:20/20-JUL-52)

GEOGRAPHY AND DEMOGRAPHICS

The area enclosed within the Lambeth Containment Zone is mostly flat and featureless, carved up by main roads and dotted with areas of wasteland that must look like bomb craters from the air. Only on the southern boundary does the land rise, eventually peaking past Dulwich Village, above Crystal Palace further south.

The housing is of several different types: large, crumbling Victorian terraces; mid-20th century tower blocks, also crumbling; late-20th century low-level section-built houses, mostly crumbling. The whole area is a classic example of how the urban planners got absolutely every last decision entirely wrong. In certain places, the army has deliberately demolished houses to create open ground that makes it harder to attack their outposts.

In odd corners there are more distinctive features. The BritRail mainline terminus at Waterloo is still in operation, though secure corridors are able to guide workers to the three bridges across the river. London Bridge station was closed after a devastating bomb attack in June 2047. The large National Theatre complex has been abandoned to the squatters, the companies having moved into their new premises in the West End Underplex. All but a few businesses have also abandoned the Lambeth area, once a thriving corporate and administrative centre opposite Westminster. More happily, the area around Rotherhithe is the first recipient of government redevelopment aid, and a small shopping mall and industrial park have been constructed at Surrey Quays.

Just a little further east down the river at Deptford, though, is the Metal Jungle, the local name for the immense rubbish tip now piled high on the bank of the Thames. The dumping started when vehicles were forbidden to leave the Squeeze in the early days of the emergency, and has grown prodigiously ever since. Many hundreds of squatters live on the tip, rooting through the day's new rubbish in search of a few choice items to sell.

In the southeast corner of the Squeeze, between the old cemeteries, the people have turned Peckham Rye Common into a new burial place for all those killed in the troubles. A permanent camp sits on the Common, made up of rotating groups of several hundred people who keep an unsleeping vigil over the dead.

The people of the Squeeze are all from the poor and squatter classes of society, mostly ill-educated and virtually penniless. Most are unemployed, and there are many registered disabled since the 42-20 incident. All ethnic and metahuman types are represented, though the most numerous minority are West Indians, among whom the Rastafari faith is very popular.

>>>>>[Last I heard, there were at least 2,720 troops in the Squeeze, currently from the Gloucestershire and Sussex Regiments. They operate from armoured control points, with three barracks within, and two outside, the Squeeze. If there aren't several SAS units also working undercover, I would be very surprised indeed.]<<<<<
—Slammer (22:17:36/15-FEB-52)

>>>>>[The troops are predominantly grounders, but air support is only a radio call and a few scant minutes away.]<<<<<
—Dog Soldier (18:35:57/16-FEB-52)

ECONOMY

The Squeeze is a very poor district, and has been for many years. The vast proportion of working-age residents are registered unemployed or on a government-run training scheme. The few surviving local businesses or the service industries in other parts of the Smoke offer what work is available. The only major employers close by are the New Covent Garden Market and the nearby British Industrial "Angel Towers" Arcology, both of which are officially outside the district.

In 2048 the government announced that, although the conflict with the LM had not been resolved, they would begin redevelopment grants to bring some employment and prosperity back to the district. The first project resulted in the new Surrey Quays shopping mall complex at Rotherhithe, and further developments are in the works at Bermondsey, Southwark, Kennington, and St. Johns.

>>>>>[Oh yeah, so what are we going to use to buy the contents of these lovely new shopping malls? Scotch mist? All my benefit goes on smelly skin cream to stop my body from breaking open.]<<<<<
—Sal (06:14:33/8-JAN-52)

>>>>>[The economy in the Squeeze operates almost exclusively through the black market. You really want something, you can get it from the guys at Brixton Market on Coldharbour Lane. And if they can't help you, they'll tell you someone who can. Providing, of course, you don't act like a complete chump, in which case they'll probably have you killed. Seems like a fair deal to me.]<<<<<
—Janie (20:07:47/16-JAN-52)

>>>>>[You want to talk about the gangs, let's talk about the gangs, especially the Brixton gangs and the New Cross gangs. Hard as nails, every last one of them armed and dangerous, most of them tranced to heaven and back. Ritual tattoos seem big fashion accessories with these guys, as do the removable body parts of oppos they've squared. The gangs control the market, white and black. They hire the kids for a job, pay them, then snatch it back with the other hand when it's time for the next fix. BTLs are huge with the Brixton kids, because they help them forget. Watch out for the Rush, New Cross Surfers, the Walking Wounded, the Key and the Gate, and the Eagle Star Renegades.

The street kids also have gangs, but they tend to restrict themselves to flipping each other and each other's grannies. Mind you, they do seem able to spot a stranger three streets away, and they'll take everything he's got. They call themselves names like Third World Babies, the Squeeze City Crew, and the Rabid Black Boys. What they are really useful for is as the eyes and ears of the LM. Just about all the gangs, large and small, jump when the LM demands it; those that don't end up on the Metal Jungle with the rest of the trash.]<<<<<
—Malcy (18:12:45/7-FEB-52)

>>>>>[Ain't you forgetting somebody? What about these Knights of Rage guys?]<<<<<
—Rosie Posie (18:16:21/7-FEB-52)

>>>>>[I was saving them until last, because they deserve a real big build-up. Lord knows where they came from to turn up here; perhaps they've always been here and just never shouted about it. They're prophets, the inner circle, but they call themselves Knights. There's a whole bunch of them, young and old, humans, elves, and orks, all lapsed stretches. And—get this—they all claim to be Egyptians! Well, more accurately they claim to be descendents of the Nubians, ancient black Africans who really built the pyramids and all that. They've got a bunch of predictions, too, usually the old "end of the world, we're all going to be eaten by dragons" stuff. They dress up in these pharaoh hats and robes, and carry staves with curled tops. Not that I've ever seen them, though; they stay well out of sight in the heart of the Brixton estates, under the protection of their bodyguards. I wouldn't even begin to guess how many of these guys there are, several hundred at least, but they're all young, street samurai, kill you for a smile. What the Knights are up to is anyone's guess. In the estates, they ask for a small tithe from the community in exchange for effective protection against the predations of the other gangs. I don't know what they do with their money; someone told me they don't drink or take drugs. What sort of life is that?]<<<<<
—Malcy (18:20:01/7-FEB-52)

NEIGHBOURHOODS

All of the Containment Zone's neighbourhoods are similar, though the amount of decay varies from one to another. The liveliest and most populous community is around Brixton, but this is also where the security forces are most concentrated.

>>>>>[I have included the police computer's security ratings, such as they are. The files relating to the day-to-day handling of the Squeeze are hard to get to and make desperate reading.]<<<<<
—X-Plod (01:17:13/11-FEB-52)

	Security Rating
Bermondsey: Squatter	E
The Borough: Low Class	C
Brixton: Low Class	E
Camberwell: Low Class	C
Deptford: Squatter	E
East Dulwich: Low Class	D
Herne Hill: Low Class	C
Honor Oak: Low Class	D
Kennington: Low Class	C
Lambeth: Low Class	D
New Cross: Squatter	F
Newington: Low Class	C
Nunhead: Low Class	D
Peckham: Low Class	C
Rotherhithe: Low Class	E
St. Johns: Low Class	D
South Lambeth: Low Class	C
Southwark: Low Class	C
Stockwell: Squatter	E
Vauxhall: Low Class	C
Walworth: Low Class	D

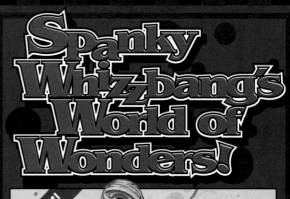

THE CAPTAIN'S GALLEY

487 GREENWOOD STREET   BTG# 715 (846-7437)

UvuLa

groove...

USEFUL ADDRESSES

>>>>>[The Squeeze is a hard place in which to do business, but it can be very rewarding. Here are some places you should know about. Just be careful out there. Note: I haven't yet checked some of these personally.]<<<<<
—Egon (22:38:36/23-FEB-51)

HOTELS

Angela Hotel (26Ba)
Cheap Hotel Archetype/1 Canterbury Crescent/Justine Dean, Manager/BTG# 718 (415-3432).

>>>>>[Well-maintained Brixton guest house, popular with the local runners. Just don't ask what the big black guys in the flak jackets are doing in the cellar.]<<<<<
—Anonymous (12:03:41/17-FEB-52)

Hole In The Wall (27Ba)
Cheap Hotel Archetype/11 Atlantic Road/Jimmy Wallis, Manager/BTG# 718 (808-5271).

>>>>>[A coffin hotel, exactly what it says. Mind you, it's a good place to hide out if you're truly desperate and the streets aren't safe anywhere. Wallis is a sneering little toad, but he knows how to keep his mouth shut and he's no friend of the baggies.]<<<<<
—Garnett Steele (22:17:34/16-FEB-52)

Hotel Palma (20Da)
Cheap Hotel Archetype/77 Walworth Road/Steve Mandrell, Owner/BTG# 718 (347-6632).

>>>>>[Or the Hotel Plasma, as it is known hereabouts. The owner has undefined connections with one of the nurses who run the drug store at New Cross Hospital. Give him your shopping list in the morning, and he'll send your order round at teatime.]<<<<<
—Slim (03:18:32/27-FEB-52)

Warburton Arms (27Aa)
Cheap Hotel Archetype/81 Acre Lane/Viv Rowlands, Owner/BTG# 718 (302-4276).

>>>>>[Bizarre hotel, popular with some of the local lowlife, modelled on a colonial-style establishment Viv used to own in Kenya. There are assegais and lion-heads mounted on the wall, cane furniture and revolving ceiling fans. Trouble is, Viv's now too old to run the place properly and it's crumbling. Still, it's an experience and a half.]<<<<<
—Tezza (22:05:35/15-FEB-52)

RESTAURANTS AND BARS

Heart Full O'Soul (20Aa)
Small Restaurant and Night Club Archetype/15 Lambeth Walk/Branford Smithson, Manager/BTG# 718 (393-1206).

>>>>>[The soul food in this place is almost enough to tempt me back to the Squeeze. Where they manage to obtain fresh crawfish in south London is beyond me, but get it they do, and cook it to perfection. If you like the taste of creole, and want to hear some of the best zydeco this side of Bourbon Street, this is the place. Weird and wonderful.]<<<<<
—Egon (23:30:05/23-FEB-51)

Rockers (27Ba)
Bar Archetype/Under 3 Railton Road/Aston Courtney, Manager/BTG# 718 (292-9541).

>>>>>[Heavy stretch drinking den, much favoured by supporters of the LM and many of the local gangsters. If you're going to drink here, you'll have to check in any weapons at the door, and be prepared to contribute to funds when the tin comes round.]<<<<<
—Tezza (23:11:53/15-FEB-52)

Stavros's (30Z)
Fast-Food Restaurant Archetype/31 Brixton Hill/Stavros Kondradis, Owner/BTG# 718 (315-5412).

>>>>>[This is cheap, very very fast, rather disgusting really. Instant doner kebabs, meat on a stick, thick yellow grease, yummy. The coffee tastes like someone squeezed a devil rat into it. Fairly desperate Greek, Turkish, some ork and troll clientele; good place to get instant muscle if your need is for speed and numbers rather than sophistication. If you can hand out any kind of heat, that's better than money. The muscle may be desperate to earn, but it's also pretty honest.]<<<<<
—Dapper D (18:53:17/1-MAR-52)

The Wolf's Head (22Da)
Small Restaurant Archetype/177 Camberwell Road/Davro, Manager/Bias Against White People/BTG# 718 (372-1996).

>>>>>[The locals call this place "Whitey's Head," because it's home to the local branch of the militant Black Ork Defence Collective. These guys are really cool, but they hate white guys with a murderous vengeance. Pity; I always found them quite tasty. JOKE!]<<<<<
—Dapper D (13:01:00/16-FEB-52)

>>>>>[Yeah, you laugh, baldrick, while you still got a head to do it with.]<<<<<
—Warthog (04:11:52/17-FEB-52)

>>>>>[Wha? I didn' say anything.]<<<<<
—Baldrick (11:26:43/5-MAR-52)

>>>>>[Oh will you shut up!]<<<<<
—Rowan (03:15:50/8-MAR-52)

OTHER

Jimmy's Hardware Store (23Ka)

Small Store Archetype/868 Old Kent Road/James Harrington, Owner/BTG# 718 (534-5155).

>>>>>[Jimmy's always been known as Jimmy the Gink, but I have no idea why. What the hell is a Gink? Anyway, this is standard stuff: ordinary tools, powerpax for the car, trivid units in the top-floor cabinets where they keep the electrical goods, all of that. But for the right money, Jimmy knows who's got the software. You need programs, IC-breakers, attack utilities, you talk to Jimmy the Gink.]<<<<<
—MesoStim (23:14:51/7-MAR-52)

Mattheson Medical (18Da)

Hospital Archetype/314 Borough High Street/Alan Towers, Administrator/BTG# 718 (486-1378).

>>>>>[This is intriguing. This small hospital is located in one of the less violent parts of the Containment Zone, and the charges here are low. Emergency care a specialty. You get offered "standard" care at a fixed rate, which is usually below the normal asking rate but unaffordable if you aren't insured—and if you're insured, you aren't coming here, right? So, the alternative is to accept an experimental treatment at a cheap rate. You have to be pretty sick to accept, but if you're here, you don't feel too good anyway, so why not agree? The really weird thing is, when they patched me up, I felt terrific. I was back on the streets a couple of days after some baldrick full of aggro filled my spleen with lead. I mean, I'm healthy, but not that healthy. And I hardly got charged a penny.]<<<<<
—Del (11:16:02/21-FEB-52)

>>>>>[As we sometimes have to point out, Del, you are a troll. Mattheson do testing for some people who specialize in specifically targeted drug actions. There are plenty of corporate people who employ your race as muscle in a country where overt firepower is strongly discouraged. Those employers would pay very, very well for drugs that accelerate body recovery and that hype the already-prodigious strength of you trolls. But be careful. These agents may burn you out or else substitute short-term accelerated recovery for long-term regrowth. You don't get something for nothing in this world. You think Zeta-ImpChem are philanthropists or miracle workers?]<<<<<
—Kendrick (18:42:17/22-FEB-52)

Washerama (23Ja)

720 Old Kent Road/Vanda Gibbons, Manager/BTG# 718 (442-1736).

>>>>>[This looks just like any other local launderette, right? So why do all these heavily muscled guys keep going in there? No one's talking, but everyone's giving me that "Don't ask me, please don' make me tell you" look.]<<<<<
—Tezza (01:35:17/16-FEB-52)

BRITAIN BEYOND LONDON

BEYOND THE SMOKE

Vast tracts of Britain are developed and overbuilt, and the boundaries that demarcate the suburbs of a city from the ghastly horizon of housing estates strung along motorways are usually only for bureaucratic convenience. In one important case, two major cities (Liverpool and Manchester) have grown right up to each other's borders. No city of Britain assumes anything like the importance of London, with its political and financial dominance, but a number of second-echelon cities are of note, not least because a sizeable number of souls live there.

BIRMINGHAM (INDUSTRIAL DISTRICT)

FACTS IN BRIEF

Population: 3,442,150
    Human: 73%
    Metahuman: 27%
Per Capita Income: £44,000 per year
Below Poverty Level: 31%
BTG Code: 21(1-9)

Home to most of Britain's remaining heavy industry, Birmingham is a hideous city where the manufacture of chemicals, plastics, and heavy industrial machine tools are the most important. British Industrial PLC and Zeta-ImpChem both have large production plants here.

Architecturally, Birmingham is a disaster: vast swaths of the city are virtually solid concrete, much of it severely corroded and discoloured. Buildings fall down regularly, often with people still inside them. Vast inner-city road networks, of a scale familiar to American visitors, lead right into (and round) the heart of Birmingham. Dominating the skyline is the central Bull Ring, a 186-storey concrete monster of shopping malls, cheap offices, coffin hotels, flop joints, down-and-out charity hostels, and other equally depressing places.

Despite the smog-filled, concrete nightmare of factories, endless roads, and filthy high-rise housing, Birmingham has another side. The city actually has more miles of canals than did Venice before it sank. Sensitive to everyone's expectations that these waterways would soon be fouled beyond imagining, the city council has kept the canals in excellent condition. The result is that many people now have their homes in, and/or run businesses from, barges and boats tethered in the canals. Some of these boats offer good cheap food, drink, and

entertainment; a little illegal, maybe, but good. Some offer just as good a way to get your throat cut. Some 44 percent of the boat-owners are metahumans, orks and dwarfs dominating, compared with a general frequency of 27 percent in the city as a whole. This floating population is one of the reasons Birmingham ("Brum" to most Brits) has only a vestigial undercity.

Gang warfare is vicious, but strictly confined to southern inner-city areas. Racial violence between orks and trolls and human supremacists is a fact of life but unusual for a British city. The orks and trolls have allied with the poorer Asian community, which is numerous (16 percent of the city population), to form vigilante squads that usually pack improvised weapons and the odd crude (and unreliable) hand firearm or two. They only bring out their precious rifles and heavier weapons in the event of a major disturbance. There are well-defined Asian/ork/troll neighbourhoods, while dwarfs and elves tend to be more generally dispersed.

Lastly, Birmingham is home to the prestigious International Business Associates group, which has a small habitat in the northern Perry Barr District. This organization specializes in business forecasts and commodity brokering, and its financial analysts have an excellent reputation. The IBA is widely believed to be controlled by the GA and HKB megacorporations, or at least to give them preferential treatment so far as expert analyses and staff transfers are concerned.

MERSEYSPRAWL (LIVERPOOL/MANCHESTER)

FACTS IN BRIEF

Population: 6,485,350
    Human: 71%
    Metahuman: 29%
Per Capita Income: £48,000 per year
Below Poverty Level: 24% (Manchester)/32% (Liverpool)
BTG Code: 61(1-9)

Two rather different cities have fused into one vast metropolis, which is today known as Merseysprawl (to the anger of Mancunians, because the name comes from the Liverpudlian River Mersey). Liverpool is a port city that now receives very little incoming or outgoing trade. Some light industry remains, but with almost 30 percent of the population unemployed, the city's future prospects are grim. The government has pumped in aid, subjecting areas of inner Liverpool to "reclamation" exercises. Now the unemployed can look at banks of flowers on grassy knolls as they struggle to survive in the pervasive atmosphere of torpor and decay. Unfortunately, this cosmetic exercise has not successfully obscured the fact that Liverpool's Victorian sewer network is just about at the stage of terminal collapse. The 2050 outbreak of cholera and typhoid fever resulted in the appointment of a Royal Commission to investigate the causes, and a report of their findings is expected soon.

>>>>>[Soon! Ha! You mean in five years. Why bother? I mean, a monkey could see why the sewers fall in. Jeez, a politician could see why they fall in. Royal Commission? What a joke!]<<<<<
—Scouser (16:46:37/5-APR-52)

>>>>>[Yes, but the judge leading the commission is the second cousin of the Junior Minister for the Environment and he's being paid £95,000 a year to spend one day a week on the commission. You have to find jobs for the boys.]<<<<<
—Tzara (19:12:12/5-APR-52)

Goblinization occurred with an extraordinary twist in Liverpool. In the black community of dock workers, seafarers, and labourers that has existed here for over 250 years, 44 percent underwent goblinization, the highest rate recorded anywhere in the world. The Black Orks are, however, a proud cultural group in Liverpool, and the only vibrant cultural minority in the city. Painting, sculpture, crafts, and poetry (including recitals) are their mainstream work, and they do very well at them. The group has an average per capita income 12 percent higher than other employed Liverpudlians, an amazing statistic that reflects their skills and hard work. The Black Orks have their major enclave, with homes, workshops, open-air permanent exhibition centres, and more, in the northern Bootle area of Liverpool, and they have done much to clear up the filthy River Mersey along this stretch.

Manchester is a more relaxed and urbane city. It has prestigious higher-education institutions and a good share of research laboratories, which have been integrated with the fine Victorian architecture of the city (the best example is the Town Hall, where the council meet). Its art galleries and Museum of Transport are popular tourist sights, and have been expanded into meeting places with all facilities: malls, libraries, coffee shops, vidscreen auditoria, children's play centres, and more. Manchester is also the leading light of much popular British culture—the major hit bands of recent months, Sharper than Light and Identity Zero, both come from the burgeoning Manchester club scene. Both elf and dwarf couture are fashionable here. Dwarf wannabees may seem a strange idea to some, but Manchester has got plenty of them. The dwarfs live mostly in the southwestern Stretford area, home of the

famous Manchester United football team, while elves have no distinct enclave.

The one blot on the Manchester skyline is the growing influence of Chinese Tongs, who have amassed considerable fortunes through the operation of protection rackets for many years. They use this economic power to buy up enough businesses of one type to corner the market and drive out competitors (through price-cutting, negotiating with suppliers not to supply their competitors, or if all else fails, just plain violence). So far, the Tongs have gone a long way toward monopolizing the home trideo-disk retail market, ethnic food distribution, and the specialty-food trade. They also run more traditional Tong businesses (notably drugs).

NEWCASTLE AND TYNESPRAWL

FACTS IN BRIEF

Population: 1,445,765 (Newcastle only)
   Human: 64%
   Metahuman: 36%
Per Capita Income: £41,000 per year
Below Poverty Level: 33%
BTG Code: 544

Newcastle is the home of "the Geordies." Their reputation, richly deserved, is as people who are none too smart, drink vast quantities of beer, talk at length about regurgitating it, have appalling dress sense (and worse regional accents), are intensely sexist, prone to fisticuffs—and yet are also fairly affable, honest, and humorous. Their home city manages to sustain Geordie cheerfulness in spite of exceptional pollution. Tynesprawl is not far from the fringes of the Northern Toxic Zone and "bleeds" (eruptions of toxic effluent into the sprawl's water supplies or ground subsidence from chemical corrosion) are commonplace. Because Tynesprawl also suffers chemical smogs and outbreaks of serious viral diseases, the general health of the population is very poor.

>>>>>[Hardly surprising is it? Tynesprawl gets 21 percent less government regional support than it should, given its socio-economic and deprivation profiles. This may have something to do with the fact that we didn't vote for swine like the Conservationists when they were in power and we aren't taken in by hippy-dippy flower-waving mellows now. We want money, social services, a decent place for our kids to live, and JOBS.]<<<<<
—Carol K. (17:22:56/6-APR-52)

>>>>>[And to see the porcines spiralling slowly around in the sky.]<<<<<
—Flat Cap (17:23:41/6-APR-52)

>>>>>[No, the politicians can stay where they are right now.]<<<<<
—Carol K. (17:24:00/6-APR-52)

Newcastle has a notably large population of dwarfs (11 percent) and orks (18 percent), and both groups play a major role in politics here, forming the backbone of the Socialist Workers Party, whose national headquarters is in Newcastle. With the SWP running the city council in collaboration with a tiny rump of Democrats, social services and education get major priority. Children whose parents lack money get a better education in Newcastle than anywhere else in the U.K., although they still end up with a thick Geordie accent. This is beginning to bear fruit. Geordies are gradually working up through universities, then returning to Tynesprawl to put their energies into the city's life and businesses. Geordie metahumans in particular have a fierce loyalty to the city, their families, and their races. Tynesprawl is now home to as high a number of small, innovative businesses as anywhere in the country. It is projected that the per-capita income of the city will increase by 50 percent within three years, an astounding forecast.

The Geordies are still angry at the government's response to the paraVITAS epidemic that hit Newcastle in 2047, killing more than 100,000. Not only was emergency aid from the national government slow in arriving, but the Geordies believe that precautions against a further outbreak have been inadequate.

NOTTINGHAM

FACTS IN BRIEF

Population: 622,945
  Human: 62%
  Metahuman: 38%
Per Capita Income: £52,000 per year
Below Poverty Level: 26%
BTG Code: 602

Nottingham is the self-styled "Queen of the Midlands," a city that has managed to avoid being ruined by skyscrapers and heavy industrial developments. The major industry is armaments, led by Integrated Weapon Systems, whose national HQ is in the Eastwood suburb, and their elite subdivision Bond & Carrington, manufacturer of customized weapons, usually for top corporate customers. But Nottingham also has a swarm of small industries in communications, entertainments, and baroque industries such as lace-making (still a tradition). It also has the Sherwood Theme Park, a bewildering combination of Robin Hood nostalgia and paranimal zoo.

Nottingham has a significant (32 percent of total human) population of Asian, Chinese, and Afro-Caribbean origins. The minorities get along well, but the Chinese have a growing bad reputation because of Tong activity. The Nottingham Tong groups certainly organise and coordinate with their Manchester counterparts. In June 2048, Tong-Chinese agents slaughtered 32 members of a major Indian crime family in what is now known as the Hirwani massacre.

Metahumans are drawn to Nottingham because of its reputation for tolerance toward minorities. This arises partly from the human population's heavy percentages of racial minorities and partly because business, culture (notably theatre and music), and communications with the rest of the U.K. and abroad are strong and burgeoning. A well-established elven enclave has grown up in the suburbs of Mapperley and Gedling to the north of the city, while a large group of extended dwarf families has bought up and occupied extensive property in the central Sneinton District.

Lastly, the Queen's Medical Centre is a leading centre for combining tissue-cloning with the new recombinant-transform technology pioneered at Cambridge. Much work remains to be done, but this research holds out the possibility for creating at least some body organs that age at a much slower rate than the biological norm. The Centre's wetware research is integrated with work being done at Cambridge University, and is also making significant advances.

CAMBRIDGE

FACTS IN BRIEF

Population: 237,500
  Human: 68%
  Metahuman: 32%
Per Capita Income: £87,000 per year
Below Poverty Level: 28%
BTG Code: 223

Cambridge is a major centre of research and development in the U.K. The university is wealthy, has a reputation second to none in Europe for life sciences research, cyberscience, and electronics, and takes many public school products and turns them into politicians and civil servants (top science needs brains, so these come from elsewhere). Around the university are many research institutes where professors and dons have second jobs as consultants. Fuchi Industrial Electronics has its European HQ in Cambridge, and its habitat 3 miles north of the city centre is an amazing feat of modern architecture. It is also unusual, being 44 stories high. Cambridge city planners have not allowed the construction of buildings taller than 16 stories, so the city maintains some of the charm of a skyline, including the legendary dreaming spires.

Cambridge is on the edge of the dangerous Stinkfens, and so the River Cam must undergo major depollution and filtration at a series of locks along its length entering the city. Expeditions in search of paranormal creatures and further Awakenings within the Stinkfens are sometimes mounted using integrated air- and river-vehicle access. Such expeditions claim the lives of a few students each year, so higher education at Cambridge usually requires a disclaimer form for life science graduation.

Some 12 miles south of Cambridge, but within its zone of research facilities, is Royston, where a major stone circle with a central standing stone erupted during the Year of Chaos. This is a major druidic site on the May ley. Many druids live in and around Cambridge and Royston, which explains the university's excellent, hermetically orientated occult studies program. The university is a major recruiting point for druids.

>>>>>[Just like it was for Russian spies a century ago.]<<<<<
— Mole Man (17:32:54/16-APR-52)

CARDIFF/CAERDYDD

FACTS IN BRIEF

Population: 552,800
    Human: 63%
    Metahuman: 37%
Per Capita Income: £47,000 per year
Below Poverty Level: 28%
BTG Code: 222

The centre of Welsh local government, the regional Parliament has its meeting place in Cardiff. It also has many other Welsh national centres; the National Sports Centre, the Welsh Royal Infirmary (where researchers eagerly experiment with shamanic and "alternative" therapies and where the standard of care is good due to private research and treatment funding), and Cardiff Arms Park, home of the Welsh national game of rugby football (not so different from American football but without all the body protection). Cardiff Castle is an excellent medieval walled castle that has become a druidic meeting place since a stone circle erupted within its stone cellars in 2011. The National Museum of Wales, housing exhibits from pre-Roman times, is also in Cardiff. Its dracoform section, presenting the history of the Welsh dragon from mythic times to the present day, is especially strong.

Cardiff docklands long ago lost their original function, but are now home to a warren of research and business groups specializing in a weird diversity of interests: alternative energy sources, paramedicine, folklore and druidic/bardic culture, publishing (MetaCymru Press, specializing in the works of Welsh metahumans, is a house that has won prestigious prizes in recent years), and ethnic cookery. The restaurants here are unusual by British standards, mixing traditions with reckless abandon.

>>>>>[Friends, countrymen, hell even Romans, listen to some good advice. These Welsh guys have this stuff called lava bread. It's not actually from a volcano, it's made from seaweed. I had a plate of the stuff at a half-Rawalpindi half-Welsh elf restaurant, which served it marinated in a creamy almond and curry sauce with lime pickle and some things called leeks. The leeks are like onions, but whiter and softer and kind of cylindrical, and they were stuffed with cloves, coriander, turmeric, and fennel puree. I guarantee, these people have discovered the best cure for constipation the world has ever known. The thing with Brits is that they're conservative guys, but when they work themselves up to an experiment, it's just total abandon. Be careful out there.]<<<<<
—Racker ZZ (22:13:42/6-APR-52)

Elves are the dominant metahumans in Cardiff, and racial relations are generally good. One point of note is the famous Griffiths family of trolls who live in a row of houses in Castle Street. This charming extended family (now of 48 souls) has its own theatre in Cardiff, where they produce versions of classical plays (Shakespeare, Sheridan, Restoration comedies, and G.B. Shaw are their favourites) that are truly unique interpretations. Their travelling troupe includes two sasquatch immigrants from Phoenix, who tend to sound and special effects, and a short-tempered female elf mage who acts as road manager.

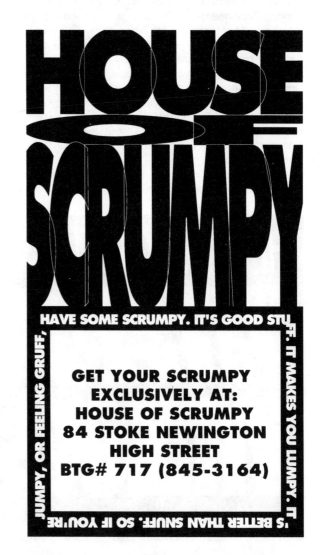

EDINBURGH

FACTS IN BRIEF

Population: 1,044,000
    Human: 72%
    Metahuman: 28%
Per Capita Income: £58,000 per year
Below Poverty Level: 24%
BTG Code: 311

Edinburgh is the regional capital of Scotland, and its regional Parliament meets in the castle on the hill known as Arthur's Seat. Edinburgh has a tradition for culture, literature, theatre, the performing arts—and parochial snobbery. All are deserved. The city is also home to the university, whose huge Royal Infirmary hospital has a fine reputation as the best all-round medical centre in Europe. Advanced skillsoft-implantation research is conducted in the university's neuro-ergonomic systems analysis labs, and the courses in occult studies offered by the Parapsychology Department are of the highest quality. Edinburgh is also the site of New Tolbooth Prison, the second-most-important high-security prison in the U.K. (after the huge Parkhurst complex on the isolated Isle of Wight).

Edinburgh also boasts the National Museum of Scotland, the National Portraits Gallery, the (Walter) Scott Memorial, the Royal Botanic Gardens (overseen by druids), the Edinburgh Paranormal Zoo, the Scottish Museum of Metahuman Arts and Crafts, and the Palace of Holyroodhouse, the official residence of the king in Scotland.

Transys Neuronet has its national headquarters in Edinburgh, with a network of research facilities built on the old Meadows parklands around the Royal Infirmary, and down toward Princes Street, the huge arterial roadway that is the central commercial pulse of Edinburgh. These laboratories employ more than 25,000 research and auxiliary personnel. Their research concentrates on medical applications of skillsoft- and neural-enhancement technologies, and has generated many lucrative new patents for Transys in recent years. This may be the leading edge of applied medical wetware research in the U.K.

OTHER CITIES

Of the other larger cities of the U.K., Glasgow is the second city of Scotsprawl. Though its gang warfare is infamous, the activity is confined to well-defined areas of the city and is an almost exclusively human preserve. Bristol is an affluent city where service industries dominate the economy, and large areas of the city have been rebuilt in a peculiarly repellent mock-Tudor style. It has a reputation for pretentiousness and parochial smugness. Southampton is a major South Coast port for vessels incoming from the Mediterranean and North Africa as well as the luxury liner trade from New York. It has a major naval installation (as does Portsmouth westward along the coast), which has given the dock district a violent character. Smuggling is strong here, which also contributes to a high body count. Southampton is a grey, depressing city with grey, depressing (and downtrodden) people. Leeds is an industrial city, rather like Birmingham on a smaller scale, but not quite so vile to look at (or live in). Oddly enough, it is the centre of the entertainment industry in the Midlands area, and its huge studio complexes specialize in the production of trideo soap operas and mediocre dramas.

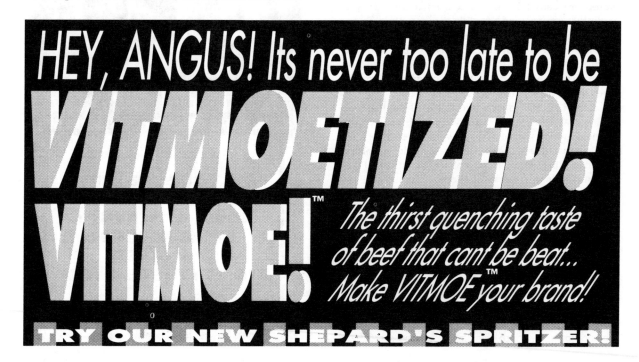

Beyond the central U.K. sprawl and the choked connurbation of Scotsprawl lie a number of distinct zones. Some are habitable, some not, few of them bear much resemblance to Britain's cosy image as a green and pleasant land. Exact borders are never easy to locate. Toxic zones change as druids cleanse the land or as corporate dumping extends them. Wild lands contract and grow as free nature spirits, active druidic convocations, and allied forces compete with sprawl growth, deforestation, acid rain, and other land-destroying agents. Habitable zones beyond the sprawl are often the most stable areas: the country estates and preserves of nobles or the country retreats of the most favoured corporate executives and hangers-on.

TOXIC ZONES

These barren lands vary in exact form, but all share certain characteristics. None can sustain plant life beyond simple scrub, grass, and a handful of tenacious weeds. They cannot provide potable water, either from surface water or from water tables deep under the ground. Many areas are barely habitable at all, with radiation or toxic effluent levels so high that survival beyond a few months is not possible. Some toxic zone areas are habitable, but only if the dwellers are willing to give birth to high percentages of deformed children, to suffer rates of cancer 10 to 30 times higher than the general population, and to suffer the ravages of a wide range of respiratory disorders and myriad other diseases. Or, of course, if they don't have much choice.

>>>>>[Well, rakkie, there are reasons for not having choices. We are old. I suppose we're lucky to have seen 60 years of life apiece, and we'd rather be here in the Yorkshire Dales than in a place like Leeds. We could be living in some rat-infested trap in the sprawl, but we wouldn't live long. The racist abuse didn't take long to get scrawled on the wall when my wife was going through the agony of transformation. Don't believe what they say about British tolerance. Orks are OK, but you wouldn't want one living next door, right? Especially if she's married to a human.]<<<<<
—Flat Cap (13:25:02/28-FEB-52)

>>>>>[Hmmm. Maybe there is some electricity supply to the toxic after all. Do British Power know about this? Are they levying charges?]<<<<<
—Striper (19:14:52/28-FEB-52)

Toxic zones have no facilities: no water pipes, no electricity pylons or mains, no gas pipes, no medical services, or other social amenities. The roads are in a bad state of repair, although corporations occasionally maintain those leading to their (often illegal) toxic dump sites. There are strict government regulations pertaining to toxic dumping even in the toxic zones, but the government spends next to nothing on any form of enforcement so dumping is largely uncontrolled—except by Deep Green vigilantes and the more radical druids in Scotland.

EAST ANGLIAN STINKFENS

Polluted by vast nitrate deposits from over-farming, these miasmatic farmlands are also sodden from coastal erosion, the choking of the old Norfolk Broads waterway systems, the collapse of drainage systems, and chemical dumping from the light industries around Cambridge, Royston, and environs. The air is damp and dank, and pockets of methane and more dangerous gases frequently bubble to the surface of the marshlands. Isolated hilly areas can support permanent habitations, although these are usually just shanty towns, but the usual dwellers live in canal boats and barges semi-permanently anchored along the region's waterways. Some of these boats and barges are quite large-scale affairs, home to up to 30 or 40 people, and with oil-fired electricity generators and similar luxuries. At the other end of the scale, the most desperate have nothing more than a rotting wooden punt. These flat boats are propelled by a man standing on a flat surface at the back of the punt (imagine a very, very flat gondola without the charm), using a simple punt pole. The dwellers make a living (of sorts) from fishing, reed-harvesting, government-funded land reclamation (a fairly hopeless and perennial battle), working on the coastal defence systems of the east coast, beachcombing, blasting away at the few remnants of water fowl in the area, and generally scavenging. The Stinkfens are the one place in Britain where the paranormal corpselights are a hazard that cannot be dismissed as a freakishly low risk.

YORKSHIRE FRINGE ZONE

This enclave was part of the U.K. sprawl until 2037 when the government ordered the area evacuated. The hills in the area remain undeveloped, but there are major stretches of decaying buildings, especially along the coastal strip. Pollution and radiation hazard were the official reasons given for evacuation of the built-up areas, an operation that took nearly five years. However, the fringe zone is protected by armed coastal patrol vessels of the Royal Navy, and the fully guarded border is protected by razor-wire barricades, explosive and neurochemical mines, and savage trained dogs. Why the government needs to take such pains to cordon off the area is subject to much speculation.

>>>>>[It certainly isn't pollution. OK, Scarborough was a real dump and the Teeside and Cleveland filth they used to dump off out there wasn't pretty. But they didn't have to spin it like it happened. My understanding is that, for some reason, a lot of late-wave Awakening was going on round there. Evacuated people give all kinds of stories, obviously. They're usually confused. After all, the Templars put DKR-177 in the water, which would make anyone get a bit confused and forgetful, right? Something the government didn't want anyone to know about was waking up around the place. Must have been a slow Awakening. Must have been BIG. Must have been indestructible, too. Makes you wonder.]<<<<<
—Phantom (04:14:27/1-MAR-52)

>>>>>[Paranoid.]<<<<<
—Skin-2 (04:15:00/1-MAR-52)

NORTHERN TOXIC ZONE

This is easily the largest of the British toxic zones. For decades this area served as the dumping ground for the great central England industries in and around the Birmingham industrial district and Merseysprawl. As government restrictions gradually prevented them from dumping in south England, the corporations were forced to begin dumping all their effluents, corrosives, and other joyous by-products of technological advancement into these lands. And with the corporate heads and executives living in the south, they appreciated the benefits of this policy.

The Northern Toxic Zone is a shifting patchwork quilt of different torments. A central-northern radioactive zone resulting from a 2035 meltdown of the Yarrow reactor complex is a major hotspot that does not move much. The chemical toxic zones are more labile, however. Permeation of chemical effluents into the deep water tables has been progressively more marked in the last 15 years, resulting in minor landslides, some earth tremors, and in 2048, a major gas spout in the area just north of Merseysprawl, where a 500-foot plume of flaming toxic gases went searing into the sky for a week. The combustion products just happened to be mildly neurotoxic, and

while they dispersed out to the Irish Sea that time, no one is too confident about what might happen next time around. The public only heard about this occurrence because it was within the range of trivid cameras. The everyday toxic shocks of the deep zones usually go unnoticed by sprawlfolk and government alike.

One problem that can only get bigger for the government is the export of pollution from this zone into the Irish Sea. The government can usually lie about pollution that creeps down the coast to Merseysprawl, usually managing to pull a successful cover-up, and/or to plead that it is doing something about it. The latter generally consists of appointing a Royal Commission to report on it. (Royal Commissions, comprised of civil servants and "experts," are most often corporate poodles who work on geological time scales.) The Shidhe of Tir Nan Og have, however, made clear their extreme distaste for being the recipients of British toxic chemicals and radioactivity, and they have done it in ways the British government does not want publicly known. The Shidhe have a fairly traditionalist taste for direct expression.

The Cumbrian Lake District, a less-polluted area in the Northern Toxic Zone, is the centre of a little-known but furious power struggle. Corporate interests are attempting to resettle the areas along the coastal strip, with major construction work going on for research laboratories, productive capacity, and residential units. Merseysprawl is too anarchic and too expensive to attract major new developments, but the cost of sea transport from here to Merseysprawl would be low. So, the corporates—led by British Industrial and IWS—are trying to move back in. Since IWS uses the Lake District for low-level flying tests of its advanced planes, they already have a foothold with their heavily guarded research installation and airstrip on the coast. They are being resisted by the indigenous population of drifters, old folks who refuse to move out from their beloved lakes, valleys, and hills, back-to-nature types trying to do what they can to clean up the area, and other raggle-taggle groups. These people would not be able to hold off corporates with mercenaries, of course, but they have allies in two other interested groups of settlers.

One group is the Cumbrian Orks. Having fled the pollution and poverty of Tynesprawl and the grime and squalor of Merseysprawl, some 80,000 orks live in the Lake District. They are by no means an underclass in terms of skills and resources, however. The longing for an ork tribal identity has attracted many with important skills, and small ork villages in the area have good amenities (including power generators). Other orks who have become successful in British society are known to be supplying the Cumbrian Orks with money, resources, and supplies.

The other group is more dangerous by far. A cell of some 20 or so toxic shamans is known to operate along the borders of the Lake District, the Toxic Zone, and Merseysprawl. This group uses human sacrifice to replenish the land and strengthen their servant spirits, and attacks the sprawl itself with toxic spirits in their role as avenger shamans.

SCOTTISH FRINGE TOXIC ZONE

This narrow coastal strip has a bizarre history. In 2016, a terrorist action created a huge oil spillage from a North Sea oilfield. In a matter of days, the spill covered the entire coastal area of this zone, despite gale-force winds that should have driven the slick back out to sea and broken it up. The slick actually advanced inland, along the largely uninhabited strip zone, generating and carrying with it a choking cloud of highly acidic and lethal gas. The slick penetrated more than 20 miles inland, settled into the ground, and simply burned away all semblance of life. This area is now totally uninhabitable. The reasons for this unique and terrible phenomenon are wholly unknown.

SCOTTISH NUKE ZONE

More officially known as the Scottish Irradiated Zone, this area was formed by the explosion at the old Dounreay nuclear power station in 2011. Wholly uninhabited, the zone is known to be home to some toxic spirits and also to some distinctly unpleasant Awakened creatures of vengeful nature. These creatures are often allied with the more radical and violent Scottish druids of the Wild Lands.

HABITABLE ZONES

These areas are outside of the major sprawl developments. They are a mix of forest and agricultural lands, country estates, luxury corporate landholdings, and other areas. Because of lower population density, much lower building density, and other similar factors, these zones are defined as distinct from the sprawl areas. In the tourist areas of the Western Habitable Zone, for example, the significant factor is the apparent low technological level. Indeed, the Brits of this zone still serve warm beer and ale with hand-pulled beer pumps in their little country pubs! Of course, the owner of the place also runs his accounting, temperature control, gravity-assisted pumping (the hand pull is a feint), and just about everything else in Ye Olde Pubbe with chips and computers. It's the appearance that counts, not the reality.

Law enforcement here follows similar principles. The genial British bobby on his bicycle survives as an attractive photo-opportunity for camera-toting tourists in scenic villages. He packs heat in an underarm holster, however, and a radio alarm will have the place swarming with gun-wielding armoured police within a couple of minutes, arriving via APC or 'copter.

WESTERN HABITABLE ZONE

The Western Habitable Zone includes most of southwest England, and is the exclusive reserve of the rich and privileged. Any form of building and development is almost impossible here; getting planning permission is hopeless. It is an area of rolling gentle hills, country seats and mansions, corporate rolling acres, gentle leafy glades, the occasional scenic village (where a strictly regulated number of people are allowed to live to service the tourist trade), and some 85 percent of the still viable British agricultural land (although over-farming is bringing alarmingly decreasing yields). There are occasional areas of isolated pollution and larger population centers, but government regulations are tight and permits are needed for permanent residence here.

>>>>>[You don't need to head far from Bristol to get out into the country here. If you've got a permit, stay at one of the little country Scrumpy Houses. Scrumpy's the drink they used to make from fermented apples—when there used to be apples, that is. With the failure of the Kent apple harvests, the drink is mostly chemical now, but it's still strong stuff. You can still find cheddar cheese as it used to be at some farms. Eat it with fresh bread and you'll never be able to stomach that processed rakk again. Try to get a pass for the Dartmoor Fringes; they're wild and are still home to red deer and those magnificent stags. The country churches and chapels are also worth visiting. They're often tiny and easily missed, but some are nearly a thousand years old. A thousand years old. I mean, can you imagine living with stones that old around you?]<<<<<
—Renton Rambler (19:25:51/2-MAR-52)

KENTISH HABITABLE ZONE

This is partly a luxury settlement for the most important corporate executives shipped in and out from Kentish mansions by underground bullet train, partly a secluded site for secret government research installations disguised in many acres of forest, and partly a quarantine zone for anyone arriving from France who is deemed worthy of interrogation. Building density is low, which distinguishes this area from sprawl development. Several government ministers also have their official residences here, large mansions surrounded by hunting grounds and large acreages of fields and forests. They can entertain major corporate and foreign government figures at these comfortable retreats. The area also includes at least three druidic lodges, although these are not of major importance. Folkestone, a pleasant coastal town just down the coastline from Dover, is the site of the fine new educational facilities founded by the Universal Brotherhood, a philanthropic organization recently established with UCAS financial backing.

Within the Kentish Habitable Zone is a small area of irradiated land around the coastal site of Dungeness, which suffered a partial meltdown in 2004 and distributed severe fallout over the local beaches of New Romney and Camber Sands, resulting in the deaths of more than 6,000 people (including about a third of a group of 800 attending a gaming convention). This area shrinks every year as the government expends more money cleaning up the site; even after half a century, there's plenty of radioactive soil and sand to shift.

WELSH HABITABLE ZONE

Part of this area, again, exists as a country retreat for Welsh nobles and important corporate figures who work in the the Midlands and Merseysprawl. Because the rail network is poor here, executives usually use personal air transport; sales of the Commuter and Airstar, and IWS's

new Blackmoth, are burgeoning. There are some towns of moderate size, but once again, the resident population is limited in number (a permit is needed for residence). The Welsh countryside is picturesque. Except for Snowdonia in the Wild Lands, the mountains and hills are not particularly impressive. Wales lives from cultural tourism. Museums of Welsh industrial history are depressing sights (fully restored coal pits lose their charm after repeated viewing), but the country's long association with bards, druids, King Arthur and the Round Table, Merddyn (Merlin), and the like ensures a good income. And Wales has always had the dragon as its national symbol, which takes on a new significance in the Sixth World.

With the increasing pressure from the expanding Midlands of central England, the Welsh Habitable Zone is the most rapidly shrinking in the country. Welsh nationalists use rear-guard terrorist actions to attack new settlers and settlements in Wales. The New Sons of Glendower are the leading exponents, attracting some public sympathy because they try to attack only property instead of people.

>>>>>[Yes, but they're so feeble. I mean, they actually use explosives! No cement-eating slow corrosives, anti-synthetic quasi-viruses, structural smart agents. What's wrong with these guys? Don't they know what terrorism MEANS?]<<<<<
—Zoe Flash (23:15:13/4-MAR-52)

>>>>>[Would you buy a second-hand slow corrosive from this person?]<<<<<
—PRN (23:15:44/4-MAR-52)

>>>>>[Yes.]<<<<<
—Deep Green (23:16:00/4-MAR-52)

>>>>>[Me too. Hey girl, where are you? Want to meet for dinner and talk dirty weaponry sometime?]<<<<<
—PRN (23:16:19/4-MAR-52)

SCOTTISH HABITABLE ZONE

This narrow strip lies between Scotsprawl and the Wild Lands beyond; there are no definite boundaries because the Wild Lands are slowly advancing year by year. The Scottish Habitable Zone, a mix of top-quality dormitory settlements, tourist ski chalets and walking hostels, nature walks and rambles, and even a couple of bird and wildlife sanctuaries, lies in the shadow of the great Grampian Mountains. For a huge fee (at least £450 per day), it is still possible to wade out into a Scottish river and attempt to reel in one of the rare salmon that have managed to get across the Atlantic, gasped their way through the oxygen-deficient, polluted waters of the Irish Sea, and evaded the monoline nets of the poachers who plague every river in the country at frequent intervals. The Scottish Habitable Zone also includes a number of country mansions and Scottish castles that are important tourist attractions and provide a welcome additional source of income for the Scottish clan chiefs and nobles who own them.

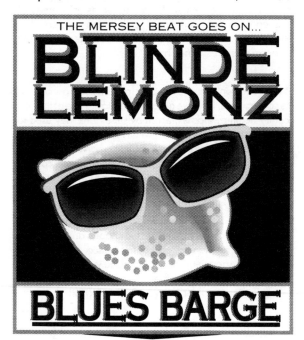

THE WILD LANDS

The three areas known as the British Wild Lands differ greatly from one another. Just about the only thing they have in common is a strong focus for metahumanity, the Awakened creatures of Britain, and/or powerful magic.

LAW IN THE WILD LANDS

The rule of British law does hold sway here, but only nominally. That is, some form of policing usually exists, but it may be 50 miles away from a lonely road in the Caithness Highlands. They raise taxes in the area, but it may be a Scots clan chief who collects them on behalf of the government—and how much gets to the regional Parliament in Edinburgh is unpredictable. The relationship between the people of the Wild Lands and the government is typically British; the locals do not offend the law in too flagrant or spectacular a manner and the agents of the law do not maintain too obvious a presence.

CORNISH WILD LANDS

The Cornish Wild Lands, probably the least important of the three, fall within the estates of two nobles—the youthful Duke of Tintagel and Marazion, and the Earl of Dartmoor. These two are on excellent terms, cooperating fully in policing these territories. They have erected security to keep intruders out, and they work with druidic interests because of the many important magical sites in these lands.

The bulk of the Cornish Wild Lands are the almost wholly unpopulated moorlands of Bodmin Moor and Dartmoor. The ruling nobles have reforested areas around the moorlands, but the low soil fertility of the moors themselves prevent woodland advancing onto them. This is one reason why very few souls want to live here. The other reason is the increasing presence of hostile Awakened creatures. Best known among these are the Cornish hell hounds, but they are by no means the major threat.

Away from the moors, there are village settlements along the coastal strips. The nobles will not permit development of these, major population growth from an influx of ex-sprawl dwellers, and the like. For one thing, both nobles want their holdings to remain attractive to tourists, which means maintaining a convincing semblance of traditional Cornish quaintness. Second, both nobles are anti-modernists wealthy enough to forego the extra revenue from developments. Third, the druids and the Green

Party both exert strong pressure on them; the Green Party in particular has made much of maintaining Cornwall as unpolluted, natural, pristine terrain. It vaunts Cornwall as an example of the success of Green policies.

>>>>>[Ha! There's a nice geological reason for that. It takes a long time for the billions of gallons of low-level toxic waste dumped down the old tin mines to seep into the water table, and in many cases, it just disperses out to sea. It might look OK, but there are enough hot spots around. Cornwall was just lucky that it didn't get dumped with the really nasty toxic stuff.]<<<<<
—Phantom (19:44:32/27-FEB-52)

>>>>>[No one's arguing that.]<<<<<
—MesoStim (19:44:41/27-FEB-52)

Areas on the fringes of the Cornish Wild Lands are important for alternative energy supplies. A series of barrages for tapping wave power operate along the Severn River and Bristol Channel, leading down along the north coast of the Cornish lands. On the edges of both Dartmoor and Bodmin Moor, there are unsightly windmill estates, where hundreds of these noisy generators produce electricity for local homes and light industry.

>>>>>[Local homes full of poor sods who can't sleep a wink for all the blasted whirring!]<<<<<
—Insomniac (03:22:55/3-MAR-52)

THE CORNISH BARDS

There are a few shamanic druids in the Cornish Wild Lands. It is they who term themselves druids, and they do share some characteristics with their Celtic brethren. They are rural dwellers, they have suitable totems (Eagle, [Wild] Cat, and Owl being the most common), they meet at stone circles and related sacred sites, and their ways of magic are certainly shamanic. They don't, however, have magical groups or grades of initiation, and they are generally simple souls with a fairly primitive attitude toward alliance with nature. Many are simply shamanic adepts. One factor that marks them out as distinctly unusual is their bardic emphasis. Cornish druids learn the

Cornish tongue and the recitation of epic poems and lays in that (very obscure) language. Lastly, at least some of the Cornish druids are believed to have links with the Breton druids of Broceliande Forest and its environs. A number of Cornish bard-druids from Tintagel are known to have visited their French cousins at the Broceliande site, where Vivien allegedly imprisoned Merlin within a tree.

>>>>>[Sure, they're doddery old sandals who do their sing-song poems in a language nobody can understand, making like trancers, yeah? Well, that's what they want you to think. I say, if these guys use metamagic, as reputed, then they know what power is about. Maybe they choose not to use it some ways, or not to explore some avenues of their power too deeply, I don't know. But just because they don't make much noise doesn't mean they're empty.]<<<<<
—Phantom (22:17:17/1-MAR-51)

WELSH WILD LANDS

These comprise two settled territories (and one other): Gwynedd in North Wales, Snowdonia in northwest Wales, and the Dragon Land. Although the two settled regions are very different, the effective powers-that-be are strongly sympathetic to one another and so there is no fixed border between Gwynedd and Snowdonia. While British rule technically operates here, a delicate balance exists between government law enforcement and the effective

rulers of these lands. The rulers do not oppose the government in any dramatic or ostentatious manner, and the government takes a modestly relaxed attitude to law enforcement. Thus, the local police in Snowdonia are technically responsible to the Home Office, but the chief constable is quite friendly with the Countess of Snowdon and sees her social secretary on a regular basis. There's no formal ratification of all this, merely an all-round understanding about the balance of law and rulership. The largely unsettled territory is known as the Dragon Land, and is home to one of the three known and named Welsh great dragons.

LANGUAGE

Some 85 percent of the people of the Wild Lands speak the Welsh language, and 25 percent of them (40 percent in Gwynedd) speak only Welsh and no English. All road signs and other official proclamations are bilingual Welsh/English. It can be quite a culture shock for a visitor to encounter an elven shepherd blocking the road with his sheep, loudly cursing the driver of an automobile in fluent Welsh!

METAHUMANITY

Wales has a significant (22 percent) population of elves. A majority of them are "back-to-nature" types. They have no real affinity with their English cousins, and the powerful Welsh elves—the Countess of Snowdon and her advisers—have no love of English aristocratic elves either. Dwarfs (7 percent) have a natural enclave in the Welsh mines, whether they're looking for coal, shale, silver, gold, or orichalcum. Orks and trolls (total 7 percent) are usually found only in the South Wales sprawl.

GWYNEDD

Besides a few scattered towns, Gywnedd is true wildland. It boasts few services or amenities, and road networks are poor and of unpredictable quality. The local population is composed of native Welsh speakers, who glean a living from the land any way they can (sheep and goats are major livestock animals), and the Gwynedd elves. Gwynedd is a major centre for back-to-nature elves of Britain, who have initiated reforestation and detoxification programs over the last 15 years. A licensed elven militia patrol the borderlands between Gwynedd and the most distant areas of Merseysprawl, making careful enquiries about government permits for travel to and residence in Gwynedd. Most elven communities are in the coastal towns of Colwyn Bay and Rhyl, and in New Denbigh inland.

The majority of the elves simply want to establish an enclave where both nature and their own culture can flourish. Even if the elf and Welsh-speaking communities do not mix much, they share a mutual respect and some fellow feeling. The Welsh folk also appreciate the elven love of their land, their efforts to return it to nature, and their use of sustainable agriculture. Without doubt, however, some among the elves take other paths. A small minority are fiercely partisan, taking Tir Tairngire as their social role-model, and advocating anything from a general referendum to win independence for Gwynedd to full-scale terrorist action to force the government to establish and mandate an elven homeland. These elves certainly have their respective links with their cousins across the sea and with terrorist groups. But most elves are content to let their representatives take their seats in the Welsh Parliament in Cardiff and express their views there. They feel their understanding with the government in London works well enough.

Another two minority groups among the Gwynedd elves are more intriguing. Though anti-industrial feeling is strong among the elves, it is also undeniably true that New Denbigh is not short of advanced cyberdecks. Likewise, the elves who use them take some pains to make sure that no one can find out what they are doing with them.

>>>>>[No joke. Why do these nice, peaceable, mellow pixies have IC that thick? You don't need it for keeping data on whether the bracken's spoiling the soil on the Brecon Beacons. Get past it and they seem to be storing agricultural data, which is reasonable, with all that green stuff there. But buried away is something rather more interesting. They disguise other data underneath. Bundles of it on underground caves, caverns, water tables, filtration systems, seismic data, ore deposits, the works. I thought they liked clean air, blue skies, trees, and green stuff. What do they want to know about down there?]<<<<<
—Mole Man (03:33:36/02-MAR-52)

The other minority group is intriguing, though hard evidence is still scarce. There are persistent rumours of animus and anima free spirits living among the Gwynedd elves. They are said to be rare, relatively recent arrivals among the elves. Still young, they are naive and curious spirits, given to wandering, passionate love affairs with the elves, and a thirst for knowledge. How true these tales are and what are the longer-term aims of these free spirits is uncertain.

SNOWDONIA

Snowdonia is ruled by Rhiannon Glendower, the Countess of Snowdon, from her home at Harlech Castle. Rhiannon is of elven blood, young and unmarried, and a forceful and charismatic politician in the House of Nobles. At Harlech, she maintains a phalanx of 80 Knights of Glendower (also known as Knights of Harlech). Her personal guardians, the unsmiling Knights are admired for their prowess and personal chivalry. They are also deeply feared. Attacking one would be a quick way to commit suicide. Though some are always on duty in the castle, others travel throughout the Countess' lands and into Gwynedd.

>>>>>[These shriekers are truly monsters. They're a mix of human and elven warriors who have access to the very best personal weaponry, personal cyberware, and exceptional cerametal plate armour. This armour has extensive chipping programmed to facilitate heat dispersion, responsiveness to neuromuscular signalling (the armour moves at exactly the same time as the wearer because it's wired to his efferent nerves and motor/intentional neural systems), carapace-mounted personal weaponry, and other functions. Those who do not favour personal-enhancement cyberware are known to be expert physical adepts.]<<<<<
—Wilder (03:22:16/17-MAR-52)

>>>>>[It's not all tech, though. Some of it's magic boosted and some of it's just pure ability. The armor's a masterpiece of design and construction, and I know for a fact that Fuchi's offering a one-million nuyen "finders fee" to anyone who can bring them a suit, with or without wearer. To the best of my knowledge, 27 have tried, but none has even come close. I *saw* one of the Knights, one of the lesser ranks in red and silver, take a point-blank assault cannon round without flinching. Sure, it knocked him on his rump, but only for a split second. The armor was barely even dented.]<<<<<
—Falcon (23:53:13/21-MAR-52)

>>>>>[Obviously, you went for the bounty and failed.]<<<<<
—Weaponsmyth (06:38:40/22-MAR-52)

>>>>>[*Obviously.* I personally rocketed after burning everything I had in a power bolt that would have shredded an APC. Guess what? It didn't even scratch it. I took that as a sign from God.]<<<<<
—Falcon (12:32:50/22-MAR-52)

>>>>>[Then you are wiser than I had thought. "The Captain of the Guard" sends his thanks for the field testing and his regrets about your woman.]<<<<<
—Weaponsmyth (22:06:08/22-MAR-52)

Within her ancestral holdings, the Countess encourages traditional Welsh life: farming and a little mining. The most important locations, beyond question, are the orichalcum mines of Blaenau Ffestiniog and the mountains and hills of central Snowdonia itself.

Orichalcum, an "impossible" substance normally only created through the magical processes of alchemy, is reputedly actually found in the mines, preserved within unusual quartz formations. Globes of orichalcum weighing 5 to 30 grams are found sealed within long (up to 3 feet), pendulous stalactites of translucent quartz in the shape of an elongated pear. Veins of this freak combination are rare, but a series of caverns holding thousands of these stalactites has been painstakingly uncovered over the last 25 years in Blaenau (and possible elsewhere in Snowdonia).

>>>>>[Yes, and don't think Rhiannon doesn't know how to call in the power this represents. I know of two greedy corporates who sent in serious street force to hijack or acquire this material. I also know the past histories of the people who planned and carried out the raids. They were heavy, right? They sure weren't snakeboys. And they never got into the first cavern, never opened the first sealed casket. Everyone knows about the Knights, but she has magicians, she has technology, she has surveillance and drones, she has watchers and guardians and free spirits. The people who get the orichalcum pay for it in kind. That means hermetics out of the top drawer, the Welsh druids, guys whose time is worth 10,000 nuyen an hour and who'll fly halfway round the world to pick up a few crystals of the top grade from her. What do you think they pay with? It isn't money, so you tell me.]<<<<<
—Rimbaud-SW (20:16:42/30-MAR-52)

>>>>>[I hear Blaenau isn't the real place. Sure there's some there, but it's mostly buried below Mount Snowdon.]<<<<<
—Snake-smoke (22:00:05/30-MAR-52)

>>>>>[Like you'll be if you don't keep quiet, you stupid gator.]<<<<<
—Rimbaud-SW (00:08:13/31-MAR-52)

>>>>>[I insist that she is not pulling the orichalcum out of the ground. She can't be, the material *cannot* occur naturally. It just can't. It has to be made.]<<<<<
—Magister (21:00:36/5-APR-52)

>>>>>[Who says it wasn't? Oh, don't look so confused.]<<<<<
—Minstrel (00:01:52/14-APR-52)

DRAGON LAND

Southwest Wales, at the southern end of the Cambrian Mountains, is sparsely populated. Only a few sheep farmers, fishermen along the coasts, slate quarrymen, and determined back-to-the-land people eke out a living in this non-resourced territory. This terrain is the home of the Welsh great dragon who has taken the name of Rhonabwy. His lair is in the general vicinity of the deserted village of Llandovery, though for obvious reasons, it is not known exactly where he lairs. Rhonabwy is fiercely territorial and uses all his resources to keep any mass settlement or corporate interest in his land firmly at bay. The dragon brought with him, from his centuries of slumber, a mass of gold that he has carefully invested to amass a considerable personal fortune. Almost all of this is dispersed in a portfolio of investments and what appear to be speculative stock holdings spread over a broad range of countries, industries, and services. Maybe the dragon is conservative. Maybe he's very, very clever. One thing he certainly isn't is penniless.

>>>>>[I heard a story about Rhonabwy from a magician who seemed to know one end of a focus from the other. There's the second dragon in Cardigan Bay, of course—the one whose name isn't known, so they just call it the Sea Dragon. Has a lair in an underwater cave somewhere along the coast in the Dragon Land. Story is that Rhonabwy and the Sea Dragon were imprisoned in an endless struggle with each other before the Awakening. The magician told me that the Arthurian legends refer to them when Merlin speaks of their struggle below the stone that seals them in. They've been struggling for so long that they're not sure what to do now they're awake. They'll take decades yet to figure out how to renew their struggle, given that they're freed.]<<<<<
—Streamer (16:43:05/2-APR-52)

>>>>>[Garbage. You want to talk Arthurian, look east along the coastline.]<<<<<
—MesoStim (16:43:23/2-APR-52)

>>>>>[The name Dragon Land also owes something to the existence of a few wyverns about the place, especially out by the western coastline. Voracious feeders and pretty aggressive. Firedrakes, too, the whole zoo!]<<<<<
—Griffith (17:35:55/2-APR-52)

Lastly, though not strictly in the wild lands, the settlement in Caerleon is truly a part of the Welsh Dragon Land. In addition to there being a major ley nexus with a major stone circle used by druids, the third Welsh great dragon, Celedyr, has his lair here. This is far underground below an ancient Roman amphitheatre, and Caerleon has as good a claim as any other similar place to have been the site of Camelot. Celedyr's history is exceptionally secret, even for a dragon. He has been seen only three times since his Awakening, but the developments above his lair have been startling. Over the years, Transys Neuronet has constructed a fine research installation around the amphitheatre. The company's own accountants estimate that in the last four years £362 million has been spent on advanced cyberware, cyberdecks, and software for this installation. It is also known to have an entirely self-contained Matrix, with no connections to the outside world.

Just why this corporation is stacking up vast amounts of highly sophisticated cyberware around a very, very quiet great dragon is anyone's guess. There is also the extraordinary mystery of the bodyguards and settlers in and around the site, who are known to have the specific favour of the dragon. A group of Knights of Rage and their entourage, some 120 strong, guard the installation. The presence of watcher spirits and other magical surveillance testifies to the presence of shamans among these colourful people. The Knights wear full African regalia, declaim their apocalyptic messages, and say nothing of their purpose here.

DEATHCORE 51

DEATHCORE 51

Britain's Laser

Entertainment Source!

For today data on all that is

nd matters from nuevo-thrash

to the rudest grindcore, don't

miss a single issue of

Deathcore.

Feature hypermedia on the

hottest bits and doers and all

the underground nasties.

MUSIC

And now, a seperate

VID

macrofashion section. What's

SIMSENSE

t, what's not, who's wearing it

AND EVERYTHING

and how's it taste?

IN BETWEEN

When just news isn't enough,

catch what matters

TOUR,

for people who matter.

VID,

DEATHCORE 51

AND SIMCHIP

RELEASE DATE

SERENA'S

The largest selection of Hermetical supplies in London

NEWSNETT

NEWSNETT™,
Britian's premier news
channel, bringing the
important information
to the important people.
24-hour-a-day field
teams on the scene,
bringing the news to
you, where it happens,
when it happens.

>>>>>[Such an alliance shows something very deep at work. It goes way back to Celtic roots far in the past, when Celts and North Africans came into extensive contact. Ireland is the best place for finding Egyptian ruins, but the Welsh coast has produced plenty, too. And Celedyr's known to be a great traveller through the insides of earth and rock. Word is that he has unearthed and brought up sacred stones from the ancestors of the Knights, and that they bear messages and inscriptions that are to the Knights what scriptures are to others. Besides that, the dragon has some need for the Knights, and as for the company, well, I didn't say I could explain everything.]<<<<<
—Carol K. (02:15:52/3-APR-52)

THE WELSH DRUIDS

Like their Scottish brethren, the Welsh druids are almost entirely shamanic in magical orientation. They are rural dwellers, living in the Habitable Zone, Gwynedd, Snowdonia, and even in the Dragon Land.

Welsh druids are on at least fair terms with all the diverse races and creatures who dwell in their land. They are warmly appreciated by the Welsh folk of the north lands because of their use of health magic, and by the elves because of their clear sympathy with the idea of an elven homeland in Wales and because of their genuine modesty and kindness to the elves. Rhiannon Glendower has always been impressed by the honesty and impeccable manners of the Grand Druid of Wales, old Griffith Meredioc. Why the druids are able to live in the Dragon Land and maintain their sacred circles there is less clear. Rhonabwy has let it be known that they have his blessing, if not actually his favour, to go about their business. Somehow, the druids always manage to find their niche and get by.

Druidic circles are only fairly loosely associated, although all are subject to the edicts of the Grand Druid, as elucidated at the Grand Eisteddford convocation following Beltane. The aims of the Welsh druids, as a collection of loose groupings, are, however, straightforward. They seek an independent homeland for Wales, the full restoration of Welsh language and culture, and the regeneration of the lands of Wales. Because Wales is one of the least polluted areas of the U.K., the regenerative goal is not one tinged with the desperation or anger that has perverted other British druids into the realms of the toxic shamans elsewhere. Welsh druids are also keenly aware of their role as guardians of druidic oral culture, despite the claims of their Cornish brethren, and the great poetry competitions at the Eisteddford are only the most obvious manifestation of this.

>>>>>[The Welsh druids have an image of being good guys, getting along with everyone, reciting poems, and loving Welsh culture and the land. Let's all read the Mabinogion and Geoffrey of Monmouth, right? Don't be fooled. They're just as political as the English, only they're less obvious about it. Word is, the old gold mines in central Wales still have some mileage left in 'em and Rhonabwy isn't the only one to have grabbed some of the goodies. The doddery old Grand Druid and his circle have their fingers on enough pounds sterling and corporate stock to have real influence. They definitely oppose the Lord Protector and the English druids at their own game—somehow.]<<<<<
—Mole Man (01:11:16/4-APR-52)

>>>>>[It's also intriguing how they manage to keep on the right side of everyone. Rhiannon Glendower's no fool and she receives them with genuine warmth. Don't forget the dragon also lets them move unchallenged across his lands. The pixies in Gwynedd split their veggie burgers with them and their influence in the Welsh Parliament is usually said to be conciliatory and wise. Which means there's only one question worth asking: what the hell are these people really up to?]<<<<<
—Phantom (02:05:13/4-APR-51)

Major Welsh Druidic Sites

Along the Stalker ley lie several of the Grand Lodges of the Welsh druids, where settlements more permanent than simple stone circles can be found: Beaumaris Castle, Blaenau Ffestiniog, Llandrindod Wells (home of the Grand Druid), and Caerleon. Important stone circles and other sacred sites of larger druidic circles include the Dan Yr Ogof caves in the Dragon Land, the Lydham Ring a few miles west of the old village of Lydham in mid-Wales, and the stone circles outside the towns of Fishguard, Lampeter, Ruthin, and Aberdaron. The centre of the town of Brecon was dramatically altered in 2011 when a huge stone circle broke through the ground, flattening the town centre. The druids have built a ring of stone archways around the circle, which is one of their rare semi-urban sacred sites.

In the case of these larger circles, at least a handful of druids share a communal existence in simple living quarters within a mile or two. These may be stone huts, thatched cottages, or any similar "primitive" dwelling. Such communities often are the centre of druidic magical operations such as enchanting, talismongering, alchemy, and the like. But a Welsh druidic shaman may just as easily be a simple hill farmer so far as immediately obvious appearances go. The only castle site they possess is Beaumaris Castle, leased from the Countess of Snowdon, where the circle of the Grand Druid usually resides. Here the druids maintain museums and libraries of Welsh cultural artifacts and live a semi-monastic life in cloister-like cells.

SCOTTISH WILD LANDS

These lands are partly owned by absentee (usually noble) landowners, and partly true wildlands abandoned to the spirits, Awakened creatures, and wild druids who roam them freely. Human habitations are few and far between, although a few hardy types still live as crofters, fishermen, and shepherds. Roads are treacherous away from the main arterial roads, the roads from Scotsprawl to Oban, Fort William, and the Kyle of Lochalsh (from where ferry services operate to the Isle of Skye and the Hebrides) along the west coast, and the central/eastern roadway to Inverness, Nairn, Elgin, and Fraserburgh. These roads are joined by a third leading from Inverness to Fort William. As this passes within a mile of the length of Loch Ness, prominent road signs warn drivers of the existence of freshwater serpents.

Travelling within the central Grampian region and into the mountains of Moray and Caithness in the far north can be hazardous for several reasons. Not least of these is the weather. If a sea mist sweeps in or a carpet of cloud and mist begins to descend from the mountains of the region, visibility can fall from a couple of miles to 20 yards within 15 minutes. In winter (and winter means late September to April), snow and even blizzards are a very real hazard almost anywhere in the Wild Lands.

A second major hazard are the Awakened and paranormal animals in Scotland. Though usually shy and reclusive, some of these creatures have become increasingly curious (at best) or aggressive (at worst) in recent years. This may be related to the influence of the wilder druids of these lands. The activities of free spirits are also increasingly unpredictable here.

Third, the rule of law hardly extends outside of inhabited areas in Scotland. Travel five miles out of a town or village and you won't be seeing any agents of law enforcement. PANICBUTTON for medical assistance and it won't arrive (except along the arterial roads). You're on your own out here.

SAFE TRAILS

The Scottish Wild Lands are not totally out of bounds, however. A strong tourist route runs west to the Kyle of Lochalsh and on to Skye, the sacred Isle of Iona (now a druidic site), Lewis, Mull, and the other western islands. The ferry journeys (about £10 per person, or £40 for an automobile with up to five passengers) are excellent if the weather is good. The sea is relatively unpolluted here. Accommodation is good, but very expensive, reflecting the costs of finding (and keeping) service help, importing fresh produce, and the like (add 25 percent to London costs).

DRUIDIC SITES

Scotland's one line of magical force connecting druidic sites has the shape of a scythe or sickle, with the handle being a straight line connecting the magnificent stone circles of Callanish in Lewis to the north, through Dunvegan Castle and circles and the magnetic hill and stone circles (which erupted through the rock in 2011) of Canna, and down to Iona to the south. The "blade" then sweeps up through Lochdonhead, the castle on Mull, through Castle Stalker at Portnacroish, and ends at the foot of Ben Nevis, where another stone circle erupted into prominence in 2012. All these sites are sacred circles to Scots druids, and a small community of these shamans is always nearby. Druids from individual groups wander across the lands, so the composition of any group is never the same from week to week, but watcher spirits are always in attendance at these sites.

Other druidic sites are not located on great leys, although they are all located on minor local ley lines. The most important are the Midmar Stone Circles, on the edge of the Wild Lands west of Aberdeen, the sinister and exceptionally tall (24 feet) Black Stones outside Elgin, the Witch (Standing) Stone of Dornoch, the Camster Grey Cairns (burial sites) close by the Scottish Irradiated Zone, and the Smoo Cave on the far north coast of Scotland. Last but not least is the ruined castle and circle at Drumnadrochit on the banks of Loch Ness itself.

SCOTS CLANS

The old Scottish clans (from the old Gaelic *clann*, meaning "children") are more dourly adhered to among the hardy, almost atavistic settlers of the Wild Lands than elsewhere in Scotland. The major clans are the Gordons, Stewarts (a divided clan), Campbells, Macphersons, Mackenzies, and Macdonalds, and the antipathy between the Campbells and Macdonalds is legendary. The clans are distinguished, most typically, by the colour tartan they wear in their kilts. The clans actually control the operation of law in many areas and have their own individual interpretations of justice.

The clan differences are exacerbated by their attitudes to metahumanity. The Campbells reject UGE and goblinization, and have expunged from their heirs and descendants any clan members "contaminated" in this way. The Macdonalds, on the other hand, have accepted their metahuman clan members with pride and a true delight in the strength this diversity adds to the clan's racial identity. Other clans have views in between.

The clans have a difficult relationship with the druids. The Scottish druids reject the clan system as irrelevant; a druid belongs to the land, and if a totem calls an individual to the shamanic life, he sheds his clan allegiance and his old way of life as a snake sheds its skin. The clans grudgingly accept that they have no influence over the druidic path, but they resent the occasional loss of their best scions to the druidic way. The occasional clan chieftain may be paranoid enough to believe that a loss from his clan that he feels especially keenly is a sign that the druids actually oppose him. There have been no druid/clan conflicts to date, but the possibility exists that one may appear over the horizon at any time.

SCOTS DRUIDS

These are the wildest of all the druids of Britain. Their dress is ragged and careless, and they really do live in caves and the most primitive stone cottages. Many are so poorly educated that they cannot write or even scrawl their own names. Their organization is fairly anarchic. There is no accepted Grand Druid (or other leader), and when they meet at one of their sacred sites on the Scythe ley at the druidic festivals (and every druid attends at least two of these each year), the druids decide matters by democratic vote if confronted by the need for any major decision. Even the training of initiates is a fairly haphazard business, and an aspirant must often wander for weeks before finding a suitable teacher. Somehow, though, his totem always guides him to the right place at the right time. Most of the Scots druids speak Old Gallic, an arcane language.

The Scots druids have certain concerns in common with their Welsh cousins, including the regeneration of the land, combatting development, and the like. But each group usually emphasizes certain activities, or gives it a particular unique twist.

Regenerating the land has important twists in Scotland. The extensive programs of coniferous reforestation of 1980–2035 on the estates of landowners were simply tax dodges and wholly unsuited to the natural ecology of Scotland. The dead-floored pine forests blotted out beautiful vistas and local wildlife alike. It is generally agreed that the transformation of the forests of the Monadhliath

Mountains in the spring of 2036 was the first revelation of the unique powers of the Scottish druids. Practically overnight, nearly 20 square miles of pine forest was transformed into deciduous woodland. Many of the new trees did not survive the bitter winter that followed, but waves of change gradually began to spread through the Scottish forests as pine changed to beech, ash, elm, even oak in some districts. And the forests themselves began to grow and spread over the lands.

Creatures that had long been absent from the lands of Britain likewise were seen again. Bears and wolves were the most dramatic examples, with the first timber wolf sighted in 2037 and a pair of bears seen fishing hopefully for salmon in a river at the foot of the Cairngorm Mountains the following spring.

Second, the Scots druids have begun the work of extending the network of ley lines. They have yet to bring a new great ley into existence, but this is surely only a matter of time. A large group of Scots druids are occasionally seen walking in single file along an unseen track, following a single leader who carries a pair of ankh-tipped staffs, one of ash, one of oak. The lead druid is known by the ceremonial title of dodman. As he walks, he traces a line with his staves, which can be seen as an emergent ley by astral assensing.

>>>>>[Expect more. Along Loch Ness these sandals are up to more, working down to Ben Nevis. They're going to be trying to extend the great Scythe ley along Loch Ness. Anyone want to guess what Nessie's going to get up to if she has a great ley to stroll along?]<<<<<
—Sarathea (11:42:52/3-MAR-52)

>>>>>[Depends on whether or not Nessie's only a freshwater serpent, doesn't it?]<<<<<
—Wilder (05:19:40/12-MAR-52)

Third, the Scots druids have a marked affinity with all paranormal animals found in their lands, and with another paranormal agency that is unusually active in the Scottish Wild Lands. These are the free nature spirits of Scotland. They are known to be relatively common, to be more powerful than most, and to be strongly allied with the druids.

Thus, Scottish druids are amassing enormous magical power and alliances with magical creatures and forces. The uses to which they will put these do not seem centrally directed, yet appear to have a purposiveness that reflects a collective unconscious at work. The boundaries of the Scottish Wild Lands roll further down the mountainsides and hillsides of Scotland month by month. Even the Irradiated Zone and the filthy Fringe Toxic Zone are slowly shrinking. As yet, the Scottish druids mostly avoid intruders or keep them at bay with mist and mountain spirits that confuse, obfuscate, and prevent travel. But when their power comes up against the habitable and sprawl zones, real struggle could surely commence.

The land of Ireland, although not part of the U.K., is a potentially vital player in British politics. Though unified in 2014 after a series of magically enhanced terrorist strikes, Ireland is still a land divided in many ways, and one both very magical and very dangerous.

One can enter Ireland by air, through Shannon Airport (the only international airport now open in Ireland), and by sea to Larne, Dublin, and Galway. The land does not exactly welcome foreign visitors, who are registered and often quarantined by customs and immigrations officials. Foreigners need a *very* good reason for entering Ireland. They will also be struck on arrival by one simple but startling fact: everyone in authority in Tir Nan Og is metahuman (metahumans always use the name Tir Nan Og; humans will often use the older name). The Shidhe have risen to rule the Emerald Isle, and they have a firm grip on power in most of the land. Only their own divisions might be their undoing, but there are plenty of these.

THE SEELIE COURT

Under the authority of their Queen, Lady Brane Deigh, the Shidhe of the Seelie Court (located in Galway some four miles inland from the huge sea rocks known as the Giant's Causeway) rule the land. The Shidhe are a mixture of Awakened creatures. Most are elves, having matured from the wave of UGE that produced more elven children (a staggering 41 percent of all births from 2010 to 2020) than anywhere else in Europe. Leshy, wearing cloaks of leaves and ferns, simper and snicker at the Court's edges. The small, shy, good-natured furry Gruagach attend upon the elves, and playful munchkins wander around the Shidhe's halls causing minor havoc wherever they go.

The Shidhe elves are the undisputed rulers, however. Powerfully magical, they are known to favour illusion spells, and also are known to bicker and disagree among themselves fairly continuously. Despite their apparent favouring of nature and rejection of technology, they possess and use high-tech instrumentation and computer systems. They deny it, keeping their equipment concealed and cloaked in illusion, away from prying eyes.

THE EMERALD ISLE

Tir Nan Og never suffered the pollution ravages of the mainland U.K. Since their bloodless coup of 2034, the Shidhe have systematically run down Irish industry, allowing old industrial plants to fade into oblivion, becoming overgrown and decayed. British spy planes have observed that the natural collapse of such buildings and the wild flora and fauna regeneration on industrial sites progresses some 10 to 15 times faster than normal processes would operate. Magical forces must be involved. The English druids are intensely interested in this, and Britain has made repeated attempts to discover the Shidhe secrets, but so far unsuccessfully. The Shidhe have also allowed infrastructure (roads, rail links) to run down, though they maintain water travel and telecommunications systems.

As indicated, travel to Tir Nan Og is difficult. Only those who have previously arranged entry may arrive by air at Shannon Airport. Anyone lacking this permission is denied landing rights. Many aircraft have failed to return from unscheduled flights to the Emerald Isle.

Entry by other means is difficult, if not impossible. As Tir Nan Og is an island, the only other possible method of entry is via water. There are legal points of entry, as mentioned above, but with the same restrictions as Shannon Airport. The only other alternative is illicit entry.

To counter this, the Shidhe have raised what is known as either the Veil or the Curtain, depending on who is speaking of it. As near as can be determined, the Veil is a powerful illusion/confusion spell that blocks travellers from approaching the island. All appears well until the traveller suddenly finds himself completely turned about or heading in the wrong direction. The Veil extends several hundred feet into the air, not high enough to interfere with air travel.

>>>>>[There's actually an easy way to get around that—autopilot. Drug yourself silly so you won't touch the controls, or else hardwire them so you can't (but then you'd better tie yourself down so you don't jump out and try to swim back!). Let the boat take you where you want to go because the Veil doesn't affect electronics, only the sentient mind.]<<<<<
—Voyager (06:33:20/13-JUN-52)

>>>>>[But be careful anyway. The Shidhe do patrol the waters (and air) and have been known to deal harshly with intruders they find. Boats have sometimes drifted back to the English coast to display their horrid contents.]<<<<<
—Tadhg Uisgean (23:20:51/14-JUN-52)

The Shidhe have removed major corporate concerns from Tir Nan Og. Only small-scale, virtual cottage-industry concerns remain in the land. Due to telecommunications, trideo, and datafaxing, it is possible for the Irish economy to retain some viability. And Tir Nan Og has two major resources—art and magic.

Irish poets, musicians, and writers have played a leading role in European art for some 150 years, and the export of their works (and the influx of money through royalty payments) earns Tir Nan Og significant sums of foreign exchange. The second major export is magic. Specialist enchanters and alchemists produce orichalcum that is exported in carefully regulated quantities; magical foci and other items are also exported. There are persistent rumours of the Shidhe collaborating covertly with Rhiannon Glendower to create a European cartel on orichalcum exports, but the truth of this has never been established.

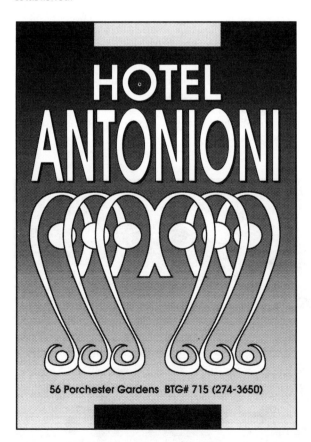

HOTEL ANTONIONI

56 Porchester Gardens BTG# 715 (274-3650)

POLITICS OF TIR NAN OG

This is a land riddled with divisions, unstable and dangerous. The major oppositions are described below.

IRELAND-BRITAIN

The druids of Britain deeply resent their exclusion by the Shidhe, who have systematically eliminated druidism in Ireland. The Scottish druids, simpler men and closer to the forces of nature, are less opposed to the Shidhe than the English, but they too resent the Shidhe's treatment of druids (said even to include their ritual murder). The Shidhe, in return, have a perfectly rational suspicion toward an imperialist country that enslaved their homeland for hundreds of years, treating the population exploitatively and often brutally. The Shidhe are also angry at the radioactive pollution that drifts down the coast from nuclear installations, the wastes seeping into the Northern Toxic Zone for decades, then accumulating in the estuaries and rivers of eastern Ireland. This has so provoked the Shidhe that they have made magical threats against Britain.

HUMAN-METAHUMAN

A significant number of the remaining human population of Ireland is now actively engaged in a struggle for an independent human Irish homeland in the north of Tir Nan Og, which they call New Ulster. They use terrorist actions, including biological and chemical weapon strikes against the Shidhe, when they can get the appropriate dirty weapons. The Shidhe use magical strikes in reply. For example, they often send spirits to track humans to discover terrorist bases or supply lines.

>>>>>[The Ulster humans won't last much longer. Pressure from the Unseelie Court will force Lady Brane to take action within the next few months. It will not be pretty. My guess is she call up a Wild Hunt. By the blood, the young nobles have been hungry for one in any matter.]<<<<<
—Caitrín (17:29:34/2-JUN-52)

METAHUMAN-METAHUMAN

Other metahuman races, orks and trolls, have not fared well under the Shidhe, who treat them virtually as lower forms of life. The Shidhe exclude these races from any form of decision-making. The processes of UGE and goblinization gave rise to fewer of these other races than elsewhere; only 7 percent of adults in Tir Nan Og are orks, trolls, or dwarfs. Stories are rife of semi-systematic infanticide by elves, leshy, and others of the Shidhe.

SHAMANIC-CHURCH

Ireland always had a powerful Catholic influence, and now the shamanic interests of the Sixth World struggle against the old Catholic faith. This overlaps with the Shidhe-human conflict, but is not identical. Some humans prefer shamanic paths, a handful of elves have become born-again fundamentalists, and some enlightened Catholics have even embraced shamanic insights as valuable additions to the ways of faith. The Sylvestrines, members of the Order of St. Sylvester, are the best-known case in point. Relations between Tir Nan Og and the Vatican (the Papal State) are permanently strained.

>>>>>[That's not the most important schism by any means. I hear too many tales of an Unseelie Court in the west of Tir Nan Og, where darker and twisted cousins of the Awakened folk plot to overthrow their bickering cousins and establish a pure metahuman state. That means a policy of genocide toward the humans of the country. Somehow, I don't think the Orangemen of New Ulster are going to buy this.]<<<<<
—Phantom (16:12:16/11-MAR-52)

>>>>>[That's just rumour. No one's actually seen this alleged Unseelie Court. It's just a sick human fantasy about what might happen if radical metahumans get to rule a country.]<<<<<
—Coinneach Laochilain (16:46:44/11-MAR-52)

>>>>>[There are also rumours that Brane Deigh is opposed by a more powerful force—the Daoine Shidhe, the most highly Awakened of all races. She fears their presence; they are spirits, come to benignly possess the Shidhe in a symbiotic relationship. "Queen" Deigh bends all her magic to protect herself against this.]<<<<<
—Maebhdh Raghallach (01:15:32/12-MAR-52)

>>>>>[I don't know about any of this, but Lord, don't these people have difficult names?]<<<<<
—Hal (04:14:42/12-MAR-52)

>>>>>[And that's not the half of it. Everything here are rough translations from the original Celt/Gaelic and mixes down from different regions and time periods, presumably. For example, Tir Nan Og itself has been written as Tir na n'Og, or Tir Na Nog. If the Shidhe say it's Tir Nan Og, which means Land of the Young, by the by, so be it. The word Shidhe itself (pronounced SHEE) can be written without the "h," as Sidhe, and then again without the "e." In fact, I hear the wonderful sprites of the Unseelie Court prefer it that way, without the "h" but with the "e," that is. The ruling Shidhe (sorry sprites) are all of the Tuatha De Danann (TOOTHA DAY DANAN).

Good old Maebhdh says back a couple of messages that the Tuatha De Danann are opposed by the Daoine Shidhe (THEENA SHEE), who are spirits come to possess the Tuatha. The way I understand, the Daoine Shidhe are actually another group of Shidhe, either directly or loosely affiliated with those that founded Tir Tairngire.]<<<<<
—Tadhg Uisgean (23:23:41/14-JUN-52)

FOREIGN RELATIONS

The Shidhe of Tir Nan Og are exceptionally xenophobic and isolationist. They have only the most formal diplomatic relations with any foreign power. Relations with the Salish-Shidhe Council, despite what the name might imply, are no different. If anything, they are more strained because the Shidhe resent the Native Americans' adoption of the term "shidhe."

The Shidhe's relations with Tir Tairngire are also said to be poor.

GAMEMASTER'S SECTION

STREET SLANG

Visitors to these shores regard as quaint and charming the multitude of accents employed by Britons, but in everyday life these accents serve to deliberately divide and exclude different parts of society. Every group of people, whether separated by area, age, wealth, or class, has its own highly developed style of speaking, often so exaggerated that two people could speak exactly the same words and not understand one another. Fueled by soap operas, pop stars, vj catch phrases, sports heroes, and the merging of a dozen different races and nationalities, the jargon of U.K. shadowrunners and street kids picks up and discards words on an almost daily basis. Heavy corporate types, meanwhile, tend to converse in strings of initials and acronyms, while those involved in government and the nobility have slipped back into a formal, neo-Victorian manner of speech, suffused with ritual courtesies and long-lost words that reveal the status of the speaker by the number of syllables they employ.

Traditional elements of rhyming slang are a commonplace; one notable case is "sep" for an American (sep = septic = septic tank = Yank = American).

Note that many slang terms on the following list mean different things to different people. For example, a suburbanite uses the word rakkie to describe himself, but when used by a street kid, the term is scornful. Besides the words and phrases given here, see also **Shadowrun**, p. 161. Some younger members of society (and some older ones who should know better!) think it extra-slick to use modern North American slang.

Note that the symbol Δ beside a word in the following list means street-use only.

Ace, acing adj. Rubbish. Δ
Aggro n. Trouble.
Bagger, baggie n. Policeman. Δ
Baldrick n. Ork (derogatory).
Banging adj. Superb. Δ
Barefoot adj. Unarmed, innocent. Δ
Blood n. Ambulance, doctor. Δ
Box v. To kill. Δ
(The) box n. Trideo screen, computer.
Boxed adj. Dead, broken, useless. Δ
Brum n. Birmingham.
C-net n. Major part of U.K. Matrix.
Demi-tech n. Cannibalised technology.
Dino n. Unarmed policeman. Δ
Dodgy adj. Risky, unsafe, borderline illegal.
Downtime n. Night.
DX n. Area far away. Δ
Elvis adj. Dead (e.g. "He was Elvis").

Flip v. Mug, rob, cheat.
Fluff n. Pollution, bad weather.
FRO v. (vul) Go away. Δ
Gator n. Big-mouth. Δ
Gonk (out) v. Sleep.
Gopi n. Young Asian girl.
Gopping adj. Dirty, polluted.
(Go) whiteline v. To kill, stop.
Haircut n. Corporate employee. Δ
Hilda n. Female troll (derogatory).
Home n. (archaic) Friend; also adj.
Jam hole n. Hiding place. Δ
Jammie n. Vehicle. Δ
Ken n. Corporate worker (derogatory). Δ
Kylie n. Young British girl (derogatory).
Mellow n. Stupid, air-headed person (derogatory).
Mop out v. To hide. Δ
On adj. Fashionable. Δ
Open adj. Crawling with police, generally unsafe. Δ
Orbital n. Outer London.
Oppos n. Enemies.
Overground n. Central London (street level).
Pitch n. Corporate-administered area.
Pixie n. elf (derogatory).
Plazzy n. Useless (derogatory). Δ
Proff v. To steal. Δ
Rags n. Cigarettes. Also drugs (Δ).
Rak, rakkie n. Jerk, suburbanite (derogatory).
Rak off v. Go away (derogatory); also **Rakking** (adj.) useless.
Roller n. Rich person.
Rub v. To have sex relations; also **Rubbing** (adj.) and **Rub off/ out** (v.).
Safe adj. (archaic) Cool, OK, I agree.
Sate n. Friend. Δ
Sandal n. Druid (derogatory). Δ
Scoob n. Drinks.
Sensi n. The Matrix. Also drugs (archaic).
Sep, septic n. American.
Shazzy adj. Cheap (esp. a person); also n. Δ
Sherbet n. Drinks.
Slabside n. Busy city or sprawl centre. Δ
Slamming adj. Fast, good. Δ
Slim adj. Weak. Δ
Slint, slinty n. Major creep (derogatory); also adj.
The Smoke n. London.
Snag v. To arrest. Δ
Snakeboy (-girl) n. Street kid. Δ

Sov n. Pound (sterling)
Spammed v. Made to look a fool. Δ
Spin it v. (vul) Get out of here. Δ
Spit n. Rain. Δ
Spitside n. Street-level (seen from below). Δ
Splash v. To blow up, hit, strike. Δ
Square v. To kill, stop. Δ
The Squeeze n. Lambeth Containment Zone (SE London).
Squid n. Troll (derogatory).
Stan n. Male troll (derogatory).
Steam v. To mug, steal.
Steaming adj. Drunk.
Stiff v. To cheat, swindle.

Stretch n. Rastafarian. Δ
Strip n. Built-up area.
Swiss adj. Expensive.
SX n. Essex (area east of London).
Templar n. Officer for Lord Protector.
Term n. Friend, trusted person. Δ
Terminal adj. Good, great. Δ
Trancer n. Substance addict. Δ
Trid n. Trideo
Ulu n. Middle of nowhere.
Wilma n. Suburban housewife.
Wraith v. To kill.
Zoo n. Shopping mall. Δ

PARANIMALS OF BRITAIN

Before the Awakening, Britain was a country with a much narrower range of wildlife than North America. Consequently, paranormal animals are not as diverse in scope or distribution within the ravaged lands of the country as they are elsewhere. The following brief descriptions are for species documented in **Shadowrun** and in **Paranormal Animals of North America**. Sentient species are not included here.

As noted previously, the Northern Toxic Zone may well be home to many deformed or toxified versions of paranormal creatures. Nothing can be said with absolute certainty because expeditions into these lands are not exactly common. It would certainly be possible that someone in a northern area of the U.K. sprawl might one day see a flock of gargoyles flying down from the poisoned hills to the north with added powers—perhaps venom and petrification. Gamemasters are free to take any creatures from **Paranormal Animals of North America**, add some suitable powers such as noxious breath, venom, petrification, or even a newly designed one (spitting acid would be highly suitable) and then introduce it into a U.K. toxic zone. From there, the creature can go anywhere the gamemaster wants.

In the Cornish Wild Lands, two types of paranormal animals in particular are unusually common, compared even with other Wild Lands in the U.K.; these are great canines. Sightings of Cornish hell hounds are frequent, in packs of up to nearly 20. The Cornish black dogs are a separate, larger, but equally dangerous predator. Use the profile for the Bogie (**Paranormal Animals**, pp. 34-35), but 50 percent of those on Dartmoor also have the power of confusion, while 33 percent of those on Bodmin Moor have the additional power of cold aura. The black dogs are not shapeshifters.

The free nature spirits of the Scottish Wild Lands are believed to be more powerful than most (with 1D6 + 1 spirit powers, which almost always include sorcery), and to be strongly allied with the druids. They thus count as guardians (**Grimoire**, p. 91) and are believed to be allies conjured by druidic shamans and then deliberately freed to follow their own paths in the world.

AWAKENED CREATURES

BANSHEE

The Banshee is found in the Cornish and Welsh Wild Lands and on the borders of the Habitable Zones (Welsh, Western). The Gwynedd elves are known to keep an especial watch over banshees, doing as much to protect them as they do to keep potential victims away.

BIRDMAN

These creatures are rare, but small numbers of them live in what is left of the Kentish orchards, where apples still grow.

BLACK ANNIS

A small community of black annis exists on the edge of Dartmoor, sheltering in small caves they have excavated and in the fringe woodland. The black annis is believed to be an Awakened form of the mandrill or some other ape that escaped from Exeter Zoo in 2010.

BLOOD KITE

The blood kite is widespread in the U.K., even in urban areas. In Wales, a darker red version (the red kite) is particularly common.

BOGIE

The bogie's main U.K. habitats are in the Cornish and Scottish Wild Lands, and it also ventures into the Western Habitable Zone.

BOMBARDIER

A red/brown furred version of the bombardier lives in the forested areas of the Scottish Wild Lands.

BOOBRIE

A relative of the standard form of the boobrie inhabits the west coast of Scotland and down into Cumbria.

COCKATRICE

At least two flocks of cockatrice have been reported in the East Anglian Stinkfens, and they must be unusually pollution-resistant to live here. No reliable reports place them elsewhere in the U.K.

CORPSELIGHT

The corpselight is a dangerous hazard in the East Anglian Stinkfens. It is also reputed to be common in the Northern Toxic Zone, where a toxified version may exist. No systematic studies are planned, however.

DEVIL RAT

The devil rat is a widespread scavenger in the U.K. In urban centres (e.g., Liverpool) where sanitation networks are beginning to collapse, large colonies of these creatures are becoming a major hazard as disease vectors. Unpleasantly stronger (Body 3) and more aggressive versions of these creatures swarm in some areas of the Northern Toxic Zone.

DZOO-NOO-QUA

A small number of dzoo-noo-qua apparently exist in the Brecon Beacons (mid-Welsh mountains) and in the Grampian Mountains of Scotland. The creatures are extremely reclusive, and present no threat to human or metahuman life.

FIREDRAKE

A single family group of firedrakes has been reported in the western coastal Dragon Land in Wales.

GABRIEL HOUND

The gabriel hound is widespread in the U.K., although not common anywhere. It is usually found on the edge of sprawl areas and lairing in deserted underground and undercity locations within sprawls.

GARGOYLE

Gargoyles are common throughout Britain, especially in urban areas and places where old structures are still present. British gargoyles seem also to violate known taxonomy in that both winged and wingless specimens have been observed, along with the rarer six-limbed type, whose form has no bearing on the sex of the creature.

GHOSTS

Britain has a high frequency of ghosts in many haunted locations, so they are predominantly apparitions.

GHOULS

The British government has a bounty of £10,000 payable on elimination of any certified ghoul. Ghouls are a menace in the Western Habitable Zone, in particular, with the ghouls of Taunton now a legendary menace. At least two are believed to be magically active and to use powers of illusion to protect a pack of almost 25 of their own kind.

GLOAMING OWL

The gloaming owl is widespread in forested areas. Owl shamans insist that the creature's ability to instil fear is only willfully used to drive away those whose thoughts and feelings are not in accord with the spirit and sensitivities of the woodlands and the creatures that live there.

HELL HOUND

A creature very similar to the standard hell hound lives among the Cornish black dogs that run on the moorland. It has also been reported in Cumbria, the edges of the northern U.K. sprawl, and in Wales.

HOOP SNAKE

An Awakened version of the common adder, the only native British poisonous snake, exists. Use the Hoop Snake profile from **Paranormal Animals of North America** for this creature. The adder is found in many grassland and lightly wooded areas, and is not aggressive unless threatened or startled.

INCUBUS

These are rarely reported, but have become active on the outer fringes of London and in the eastern section of the central U.K. sprawl. They have also been reported in the Stinkfens and the Kent Habitable Zone. The incubi in the Stinkfens are reputed to have psychokinetic power.

LESHY

In the forests bordering Bodmin Moor and Dartmoor are forest spirits similar to leshy. Leshy are also reputed to live on the Shetland and Orkney isles to the far north of Scotland, although this has not been established with certainty.

LESSER ROC

A few of these nest on the west Welsh coast and at the extreme tip of Cornwall, around Land's End.

SABRE-TOOTH CAT

These are occasionally reported in the Western Habitable Zone and Cornish Wild Lands. Awakened versions of great cats that escaped from Exeter Zoo in 2010, they tend to avoid humans and metahumans, but will attack isolated individuals.

MIKE.N 91'

SALAMANDER

Salamanders have an affinity with certain isolated standing stones, where they are known to remain motionless for hours, as though awaiting some signal or presence. Druids are studying which stones and which times are involved to discover any possible pattern or meaning to this behaviour. As yet, no pattern has emerged.

>>>>>[Only because they haven't been fitting the right regression equations. They just haven't been feeding in the right data, the old fools. The salamanders are waiting for the new leys to become activated. If anyone's going to harness their powers, it'll be the Scots. Keep your eyes on Drumnadrochit.]<<<<<
—Carraig (01:15:32/22-APR-52)

>>>>>[I'm not so sure. The salamanders' presence is often followed by the appearance of a watcher spirit. I don't know who places the spirit on the site, but I don't think it's the druids or the salamanders themselves. Anyone out there like the idea of free watcher spirits?]<<<<<
—Phantom (11:15:46/22-APR-52)

>>>>>[Evidently not.]<<<<<
—Phantom (15:15:44/26-APR-52)

SEA DRAKE

Sea drakes have been reported in the Irish Sea off the Dragon Land. A pair of them have also been sighted in Tremadoc Bay, close by Harlech Castle.

SERPENT, FRESHWATER

Many Scottish lochs have freshwater serpents. Loch Ness has at least one, probably two, and many Scottish lochs have associated stories of magical water horses, which are now believed to have been prematurely Awakened freshwater serpents with the illusion power.

SERPENT, SALTWATER

Many Scottish lochs are seawater lochs (Loch Duish being a notable case), and have these serpents as estuarine dwellers.

SHAPESHIFTER

It is alleged that some bear and wolf shapeshifters live among the Scottish druids, but this is uncertain. It is a common smear tactic for one Scottish clan head to claim that another is a shapeshifter, and so this rumour about druids may be just a spin-off from this tactic.

TOXIC SPIRIT

Toxic spirits inhabit all the toxic zones of the U.K.

UNICORN

A sizeable group of unicorns dwells around Castle Harlech, in the estates of the Countess of Snowdon. Others are known to live in the Cornish Wild Lands.

WYVERN

Several sightings of wyverns have been made in the Dragon Land.

ARMS AND EQUIPMENT

Because it is so difficult to smuggle weaponry into Britain, foreign-based runners may have to try to purchase equipment after they arrive in the country. This will be expensive because it is almost impossible for a foreigner to get a permit for possession of anything more dangerous than a hatpin in the U.K. And even if he does, he's not guaranteed to find a fully functional, top-quality weapon. Below, prices are given for items from the basic **Shadowrun** (abbreviated to **SR**) rules and also from **Street Samurai Catalog** (abbreviated **SSC**).

Also, certain items from the **SSC** will not be available simply because Ares Macrotechnology is not a major supplier of arms within the U.K. The police, agents of the Lord Protector, and the military pack a few Ares products and some other foreign imports, but are mostly equipped with IWS products. Because many arms and items that come onto the black market are from local sources, IWS is the usual manufacturer, not Ares. Other black-market equipment comes from a variety of sources, when available. For example, an equivalent of the Ares Manhunter can be had as the IWS Bountyman, the Seco LD-125 from Israel, or the Pakistani KhanTech A15 pistol.

GENERAL RULES

Assume that the Ares and Ingram weapons listed in **SSC** and **SR** are available as IWS equivalents. They are usually given generic equivalent names; thus, the Ingram medium and heavy MG become simply the IWS medium and heavy MG. For more specific models, IWS usually uses simple serial numbers: their equivalents of the Ares pistols in **SSC** would simply have codes of IWS-P20, IWS-P25, and so on. The highest-quality IWS weapons are the Bond & Carrington specialist weaponry, usually handguns for corporate executive self-protection. These are almost always made to specification for individuals and individual corporate concerns, and runners will not be able to purchase them (except second-hand, from someone who knew the someone who terminated the original owner).

The cost for any firearm will be higher than prices given in previous sourcebooks. Work from the following multipliers:

Purchase of a hand weapon (non-firearm)	150%
Purchase of a hand weapon (firearm)	200%
Purchase of an automatic weapon	250%
Purchase of a heavy weapon	400%
Purchase of accessories	As for the weapon type
Purchase of explosives	400%

The availability of heavy weapons and explosives is very low, indeed. Actually finding a contact able (and willing) to supply such material within the U.K. would be a run in itself.

NON-OFFENSIVE ITEMS

Non-offensive equipment, such as vision-enhancers, communications systems, surveillance measures, and the like are legally available, but shops that sell them are difficult to find. Such items cost 150 percent of listed **SR** and **SSC** prices.

Highly unusual items (such as survival gear) are not available except from specialist industrial suppliers. Chemsuits, for example, simply are not commercially available in U.K. shops of any kind. Industrial suppliers also keep records of their customers, which the Administrative Bureau of the Lord Protector's Office can get around to checking anytime.

CYBERWARE

All cyberware in the U.K. must be licensed from the Lord Protector's Administrative Bureau. Shops supplying cyberware must register the licenses of all their customers for the goods they purchase. It is almost impossible for anyone who is not an important corporate employee to get a license for offensive personal cyberware such as a smartgun link, and regular cybershops do not routinely stock such ware. For a suitable fee, however, they may be able to advise the customer privately where to go to find a black market source.

All non-offensive cyberware costs 200 percent of the prices given in **SR** and **SSC**. All offensive cyberware costs 300 percent of those book costs.

Elective surgery rules (**SR**, p. 144) apply as normal, but medical costs (**SR**, p. 145) are actually 10 percent lower in the U.K. (only private treatment; cyberware implantation is not available on the National Health Service).

Shadow clinics (**SSC**, pp. 98–99) exist in the U.K., but they are ultra-hard to find (add 2 to all target numbers listed) and virtually the exclusive province of only the highest corporate elite, druids, and their ilk. It is virtually certain that these clinics would not treat foreigners (save for corporation heads!). Or maybe a player character with a million-nuyen credstick. Standard rules apply for cheap cyberware (**SSC**, p. 100), except that this is almost always street goods. Shops will not bother with it, because any customer who has gone to the bother of obtaining a license will not want cheap demi-tech. Cheap cyberware may be implanted by back-street cyberdocs at a 25 percent discount, but conditions for recovery from wounds will be Bad, Intensive Care unavailable, and any form of transplant out of the question. On the up side, however, the medical costs are 25 percent lower during recovery time.

CYBERDECKS AND PROGRAMS

Cyberdecks must also be licensed by the Lord Protector's Administrative Bureau in the U.K. For private individuals, a license for anything up-market from the Allegiance Alpha is almost impossible to obtain (and hence only specialist shops keep anything better). Only corporate interests can get licenses for anything more powerful. This means that runners who want anything better will have to (1) smuggle it in from abroad, (2) steal it within the U.K., (3) buy it on the U.K. black market (usually a home-made equivalent; see **SR** p. 117 and **Virtual Realities**, p. 24), or (4) get custom improvements to existing models from illegal operators. On the latter two options, the black market price for a cyberdeck is (14 + 2D6) x 100 percent of the listed book price (**SR**, p. 105 and **Virtual Realities**, p. 32). A successful Opposed Negotiation Test can reduce this by 10 percent. Managing to find and purchase a top-of-the-range model such as the Fuchi Cyber-7 or the Fairlight Excalibur is a run in itself. Indeed, someone might hire the runners for precisely this reason. One side-effect of all this, of course, is that there are a few people running around naked in the Matrix out there.

Combat software is illegal in the U.K. Masking programs are rarely licensed for personal use (possibly for a university research scientist, for example). Defence and sensor utilities require licenses, but these are usually granted fairly readily. Lastly, white and grey IC are licensed for some private and all corporate use. Officially, black IC is illegal, but it is known to exist (despite official denials) in certain governmental databases. Persistent rumours say that the Administrative Bureau turns a blind eye to its use by certain corporations also.

>>>>>[It's a lot more vicious than that. The bureau actually supplied some black IC—top experimental stuff from their own boys planned for their own machines—to HKB. Then some rumour hit InfoNet that HKB has a fast-turnaround extrapolation of financial analyses in the Far East. There were deckers onto it so fast the Matrix was crawling with them. I think about a third got out without being completely boxed or brain-wiped. The government got excellent information on the efficacy of its new protection and money for the Treasury coffers. HKB got some very effective software at an attractive price. Very cost-effective. That's what this country needs, financially responsible government.]<<<<<
—Mole Man (03:58:14/30-APR-52)

DRUIDS

The following game rules apply to the Celtic shamanic druids. Where these rules relate to **The Grimoire**, page references are included. Rules and guidelines that are not mentioned here stand unaltered from the **Shadowrun** and **Grimoire** rules.

TOTEMS

Druids revere the Sun and the Moon as primal forces of life, but they also have animal totems that reflect the focusing of life force in life forms. Celtic druids use the following totems: Eagle (especially Scottish), Wolf (Scottish only), Bear, Cat (Wild Cat), Owl, Wyrm (Welsh only). The last three require explanation.

Owl is described in **The Grimoire**, p. 108. There is an Urban Cat totem on p. 107 of the same book, but this is not suitable for druids, who have a Wildcat totem.

WILDCAT

Characteristics: Wildcat is not strong in body, but is possessed of great stamina and capable of enormous speed over short distances. Wildcat is aggressive, quick to anger, and vicious when cornered. She is reclusive, secretive, and a nocturnal creature with superb night vision. Wildcat is not too intelligent, however, being readily deceived by appearances, despite her keen senses. Nor is she anywhere near as cunning as her urban counterpart, but she is powerful and not to be provoked!
Environment: Anywhere in the British Wild Lands (except Cornwall).
Advantages: +2 dice for combat and health spells, +2 dice for conjuring any nature spirit during hours of darkness.
Disadvantages: A Wildcat shaman cannot ever allow his home stone circle to be damaged or destroyed; he must attack any creature attempting this, fighting to the death if necessary (no tests of any kind to evade this responsibility!). Wildcat shamans also subtract 1 dice from Resistance Tests made against illusion spells. Wildcat is aggressive only when cornered or directly threatened; Wildcat shamans are not kamikaze killers.

WYRM

Characteristics: Wyrm is a great lizard, slow and ponderous, a nonmagical cousin to dragons or, some say, a stunted form akin to the axolotl. Wyrm is the totem proudly flourished by the Welsh Dragon shamans or Dragon druids (improperly self-named, it should be pointed out), who understand the affinity of their totem with the great national symbol of their land. Wyrm is not intelligent, nor is he swift. He is slow to act and unable to

seize the initiative when events transpire rapidly. But he has strength, great recuperative powers, and is merciless once he has the upper hand over an enemy. He is peaceable, but unforgiving if provoked. Lastly, Wyrm has a singular power of will, and can dominate others simply by force of this will.
Environment: Mountains.
Advantages: +2 dice for health and manipulation spells, +2 dice for conjuring mountain spirits.
Disadvantages: Wyrm often does not know when to let go: if engaged in a combat or other ongoing opposed activity (like playing out a session of the Druidic Stone Game), Wyrm must make a Willpower Test with a Target Number 6 to quit and do something else instead. Wyrm is also slow and lazy, and sleeps for lengthy periods. Wyrm shamans must sleep an average of at least 70 hours per week.

>>>>>[Didn't I hear something about some druids using different, non-animal totems like Sun, Oak, Zephyre, and Stream?]<<<<<
—Wonderer (06:32:45/12-FEB-52)

>>>>>[Aye, they're out there all right. Don't know much about them, not even rumours. Couldn't tell ya.]<<<<<
—Wynde (21:05:09/24-FEB-52)

FETISHES

Druids use one and only one reusable fetish: the golden sickle. They use one and only one expendable fetish: mistletoe. Druidic fetishes may not be bought from a talismonger. The druid must pick his own mistletoe using a golden sickle, and for use as a fetish, the sickle must first be consecrated by an initiate of first grade or higher at his home sacred circle. This is accomplished at the ritual accepting him as a Grade 0 initiate, and the aspirant druid must expend 1 point of Karma to bond his sickle to him. Otherwise, neither the sickle nor any mistletoe he gathers are usable as fetishes.

SACRED CIRCLES

Druids do not have a medicine lodge as such. They have sacred circles, which are stone circles that serve as their meeting places. In some rare instances, a singular standing stone, sacred cave (such as the Dan Yr Ogof caves in the Dragon Land), or holy loch (for Scottish druids) can serve as their meeting place. Because all druids have only rural totems, and because the druidic faith emphasizes the unity of all nature, the circle need not be in the same environment as the druidic totem. However, every druid has a home circle, which is in the same environment as that suitable for his totem, and special rules apply to aspects of his dealings with spirits at his home circle.

SPIRIT CONJURING

The following rules make fairly extensive reference to **The Grimoire**, an invaluable tome. If the book is not available, ignore the references to **The Grimoire**'s expanded rules for spirits.

A druidic shaman may conjure only certain nature spirits from among the many listed in **The Grimoire** (p. 78; see also **SR** pp. 185–186). Note that druids may never conjure Spirits of Man. Following are the nature spirits a druidic shaman can conjure.

Spirits of the Land: forest and mountain spirits
Spirits of the Sky: mist and storm spirits
Spirits of the Waters: lake, river, and sea spirits

Druids can more easily conjure the above-named spirits than can most shamans because of their profound identification with nature and the innate magic of the places where they built their sacred circles (which often reemerged and regenerated during the Awakening). The following rule modifiers apply:

• Any druid automatically adds 1 to his Conjuring Skill if he is within a number of miles of a stone circle equal to his own Essence Rating.

• Any druid automatically adds 3 to his Conjuring Skill if within the same distance (miles x Essence) of his home sacred circle for conjuring a spirit of the appropriate domain (this will almost always be mountain or forest).

• Any druid of Grade 5 (or higher) initiation adds a further 1 point to his Conjuring Skill under all circumstances.

• Any druid successfully conjuring a nature spirit can gain a number of uses of the spirit's power equal to his successes at Conjuring, plus 1, or plus 2 if at his own Home Circle.

For example, Arisaig, a Grade 7 druidic initiate, is trying to fend off an attack by thugs trying to raid his druidic circle for magic; they got wind of the alchemical work he had been doing. He decides to teach them a lesson by conjuring a mountain spirit to attack them. He has a Conjuring Skill of 7, but gets to roll no fewer than 13 dice. That is, he gets a bonus of 3 because this is his home sacred circle, a further 1 because he is a sufficiently high grade of initiate, and a further 2 because he is a Wildcat shaman and the goons made the mistake of attacking at night. He calls for a spirit of Force Rating 6, and rolls the dice. His player rolls 4 sixes. Because he is at his home sacred circle, he adds 2 to the number of services (uses of spirit power) he can call upon, for a total of 6. The vengeful Wildcat shaman begins to will the series of accidents that the spirit will cause to befall his enemies.

DEPARTING, BANISHING, AND UNCONTROLLED SPIRITS

Nature spirits will remain to serve a druid for longer than usual; they remain for up to 24 hours, until the first dawn *following* their conjuring. Uncontrolled nature spirits are unlikely ever to attack a druidic shaman. The usual rules (**SR**, p. 87) DO NOT apply; an uncontrolled spirit will only attack the druid on a successful roll of 2D6. Otherwise, the spirit simply vanishes.

Druids have superior skills at banishing nature spirits if they so choose (**SR**, p. 88). The same bonuses apply to Conjuring Skill for the purposes of banishment (depending on location and initiate grade) as they do for conjuring itself, except in the rare case of one druid trying to banish a spirit conjured by another.

ENCHANTING

Enchanting is covered in depth in **The Grimoire**, pp. 40–49. Following are a handful of special rule modifiers that apply to druids.

ENCHANTING GEAR

Enchanting gear works very differently with druids. Druids do not need anything like 100,000 nuyen for alchemy or a 10,000-nuyen enchanting kit for talismongering. Their restrictions are quite different. They must always initiate enchanting operations at dawn at one of the great druidic festivals (Imbolc, Beltane, Lugnasad, Samhain). For talismongering or alchemy, all that is then needed is a druidic cauldron and a supply of suitable raw materials (always plant material or minerals from sacred or exceptional sites such as Merlin's Cave or Fingal's Cave in the Hebridean Islands, or water from a holy loch). These cauldrons are passed on from druid to druid, and cannot be purchased. Every druid usually has two or three such, and only druidic initiates of Grade 5 or higher actually know how to make

Their sacred ritual nearly complete,
the druids begin to command the elements.

Trouble afoot in the Squeeze. Hope you brought friends.

In the wrong place at the wrong time. What will he do?

Guardians of Castle Harlech; Rhiannon Glendower's CyberKnights

them (this takes some 20 days). A senior druid will always ask a junior for some definite service (such as trawling for a very obscure plant in a dangerous Wild Lands area packed with murderously nasty paranormal critters) before handing down a prized and precious cauldron. The cauldron must always use absolutely pure spring, lake, or loch water; if in doubt, the druid can undertake a seven-dawn ritual purifying the water at a stone circle (no tests required; it just slows the druid up).

The Gathering Test (**Grimoire**, p. 41) is easier for druids in the case of plant materials, where the Target Number for them is 3. If a nature spirit is assisting, the standard Spirit Force Rating bonus (**Grimoire**, p. 42) applies.

Making alchemical radicals (**Grimoire**, p. 43) is easier with plant materials for druids. To determine the success of this operation, they add a bonus 2 dice to their Enchanting Skill.

FOCUSES

Druidic enchanting is almost entirely limited to spirit focuses and power focuses (although druids with more aggressive totems such as Wildcat have been known to be fairly enthusiastic about weapon focuses). So far as exotic materials go (**Grimoire**, p. 46), these are almost invariably (roll of 2–10 on 2D6) herbal and available within the homeland of the druid (11–12 means the component is mineral, but still within the homeland). The material basis for the focus must always be a virgin telesma (**Grimoire**, p. 47). The target number for success in the case of a (nature) spirit focus is 5 for a druid, rather than the usual 6. Lastly, druids only rarely bond magical items other than those of their own making. If one ever chooses to do so, the Karma cost is 50 percent higher than the values listed in the **Grimoire** (p. 49).

HUMAN SACRIFICE

The information on blood magic is given to assist the gamemaster ONLY for purposes of plot device. No player character will EVER learn the rituals needed to perform this magic. NOT EVER. It is exclusively the province of non-player character druids, who will not reveal the ritual to anyone for whom they do not have utter and complete knowledge. See page 29 of **The Grimoire** for a related game rule.

The ritualistic basis of getting something important out of human sacrifice is known to only the highest-level druidic initiates. With a ritual sacrifice undertaken at the first light of dawn at the great druidic festivals, a druidic initiate of this level can effect a human sacrifice at his home sacred circle, given the presence of at least six other druids of any initiate grade(s). Using a human sacrifice, he can strengthen an ally or free spirit or use the blood of the sacrificed victim to purify the land. See Chapter 14 of **Choose Your Enemies Carefully** for ideas on how to set this ritual in a story. Sacrifices must be completely willing. Anything else results in a toxic effect.

BACKGROUND COUNT AND DRUIDIC MAGIC

The magical effects that operate as a result of the Background Count of ley lines are fairly straightforward in game terms: the level of Background Count is applied as a negative modifier to the target number for all magical tests performed by druids that are not actively in opposition to the nature of the site. Spells,

(researches, and so on) that would damage the site do not count (and the Background Count would add the modifier, tripled, as a penalty to the target number for the magical operation, if appropriate). Use of polluting spells, bringing a toxic spirit conjured elsewhere into the area and maintaining control of it, and displays of area-effect gross damage magic will similarly be hindered rather than aided. Some gamemaster discretion is needed here. Try thinking like a stone circle many thousands of years old: Does Stonehenge like this spell? Does it feel right here? The druid tends to get the benefit of the doubt. For enemies of druids who attack them here, the Background Count always applies as a penalty modifier to the target number for magical tests.

Background Count value for Grand Lodges on minor leys is 1; for those on great leys, it is 3, with the following exceptions: Stonehenge, the Sunken Island, Warwick Castle, and Caerleon have a Background Count of 4. Some special isolated sites on minor leys have a Background Count of 2; examples include the vast quartz-lined Carnglaze Caverns of Cornwall, the stalagmite-encrusted limestone cave complex at Cheddar in Somerset, and Fingal's Cave in the Scottish Hebrides Islands.

Certain sites may have special effects in game terms. The gamemaster can design these individually, but it is known that salamanders (**Paranormal Animals**, pp. 136–137) and both watcher and guardian spirits (**Grimoire**, pp. 90–99) seem to arrive unannounced at certain sites, be they stone circles or standing stones. Special effects on spirit conjuring may well exist at different sites if the gamemaster desires.

CORNISH BARDS

A few shamanic druids inhabit the Cornish Wild Lands. They term themselves druids, and they do have some characteristics allying them with their Celtic brethren. They are rural dwellers, have suitable totems (Eagle, [Wild] Cat, and Owl being the most common), they meet at stone circles and related sacred sites, and in game terms and for rules purposes, they are certainly shamanic. They do not, however, have magical groups or grades of initiation and they are generally simple souls with a fairly primitive attitude toward alliance with nature. Many are simply shamanic adepts. One factor that marks them out as distinctly unusual is their bardic emphasis. Cornish druids learn the Cornish tongue and the recitation of epic poems and lays in that (very obscure) language. They are an exception to the normal game rule that only initiates can use metamagic (**Grimoire**, pp. 22–23); they appear able to use Centering against Drain (at least), using poetic recitation as their centering skill. Lastly, at least some of the Cornish druids are believed to have links with the Breton druids of Broceliande Forest and its environs. A number of Cornish bard-druids from Tintagel are known to have visited their French cousins at the Broceliande site where Vivien allegedly imprisoned Merlin within a tree.

ENGLISH HERMETIC DRUIDS

As stated earlier, the English druids practice a form of magic that is hermetic in nature. There are no game system differences between the hermetic tradition described in the **Shadowrun** rules and the magic practised by the English druids, with the exception of those differences noted in the **Druids** section of **Government and Power**, page 33 of this book.

U.K. TIMELINE IN BRIEF

2000-2010

2004

First nuclear meltdown at Dungeness in Kent creates localized irradiated zone.

2005

Conservative government established regional parliaments in Scotland and Wales.

2009

King Charles III is crowned in Westminster Abbey.

2010

VITAS (Virally Induced Toxic Allergy Syndrome) pandemic results in death of 26 percent of U.K. population and extends into the coming winter.

2011-2020

2011

Year of Chaos. Sizewell B nuclear power station suffers critical meltdown, resulting in total death count of 17,000 from cancers in the next three decades; in Scotland, Dounreay suffers the same fate, creating the Scottish Irradiated Zone. Floods hit central and southern England, destroying much property. Toxic leaks from landfill sites erupt into an epidemic of pollution. First magical attacks are made on military targets in Northern Ireland. Celedyr, a Welsh great dragon, is sighted on 26 December in Caerleon. First elven and dwarf children born as UGE (Unexplained Genetic Expression) begins to make itself felt. Stone circles and standing stones erupt through the earth as great leys are activated.

2012

King Charles III abdicates in favour of his son, George VII.

2012

Formation of Hildebrandt-Kleinwort-Bernal (HBK) megacorporation, an increasingly major power in world financial affairs in coming decades.

2014

Following magically enhanced terrorist activity, the governments of the U.K. and Eire sign the Treaty of Galway establishing the United Free Republic of Ireland.

2015

Hong Kong breaks free from mainland China and proclaims independence. The British government uses its influence to protect Hong Kong, but is duped by megacorporations and loses face over the incident.

2016

PM Lena Rodale assassinated, as are the leaders of other world powers. Major oilspill in the North Sea creates the Scottish Fringe Toxic Zone.

2021-2030

2021

George VII announced dead. Rival bloodlines compete for the throne. The Windsor-Hanover claimant, supported by megacorporations, becomes George VIII. Office of Lord Protector established; first Lord Protector is Lord Marchment, a leading light of the New Druidic Movement. First wave of goblinization hits the U.K.

2025

Conservative Party renamed the Conservationist Party, wins general election under new PM Kenneth Redmond. U.K. Constitution Act formalizes roles of Parliament, royalty, and the Lord Protector. All U.K. police are now routinely armed.

2026

Oxford and Edinburgh universities establish B.Sc degrees in occult studies; Cambridge follows suit in 2028.

2027

The Lord Protector's office drafts the Magical Practitioners Registration Bill, which Parliament passes into law.

2028

Conservationist government takes Britain out of the EEC.

2029

Great Computer Crash of '29. Birth of the Matrix. Druidic schism over technology foreshadows Celtic/English druidic schism.

2030

UCAS (United Canadian and American States) established by the Act of Union. The U.K. establishes strong political relations with UCAS through its old Canadian commercial, educational, and political ties.

2031-2040

2031

Euro Wars begin in Europe. The U.K. is not an active participant in military terms, but many rumours exist concerning covert and technical actions.

2033

Nightwraith bombers strike both sides in the Euro Wars, effectively ending Western and Central European involvement. Swedish surveillance states the aircraft were of U.K. origin; this is denied by the government, and the truth is never established.

2036

First anti-metahuman atrocities follow as copycat versions of Alamos 20,000 actions occur in UCAS. These activities are limited to isolated pockets of overt violence in the U.K., where systematic institutional racism is more the British style.

2036

In Scotland, regeneration and transformation of native forests begins. In the following year, species formerly extinct in the U.K. begin to return to the Wild Lands (wolves and bears).

2037

In North America, elves establish Tir Tairngire. Very early on, links are established with young elven British aristocrats.

2038-9

Discovery of Adams-Hoffmann gene-pool manipulation in London leads to terrorist missile strikes on political targets. The Lambeth Containment Zone is established to minimize future terrorist actions.

2039

Massive chemical spillage on Teeside Industrial District kills over 70,000 from nerve gas effects. Outcry over ecological (and secret military) implications of this event leads to schism in the Conservationist Party, resulting in its election defeat of 2041. Pan-Europa strike introduces a wood- and biofabric-destroying virus that wreaks havoc on many London sprawl buildings.

2040

Discovery of the Conservationist government's active encouragement of the Adams-Hoffmann study foreshadows the downfall of the government early the following year.

2041-2050

2041

Policlubs become organized in Europe. British policlubs are generally Green-oriented, but a typically British eccentric fringe also exists. The first Green government is elected, and rules to the present time (2052), with Democrat support from 2045 to 2047.

2043

Rhiannon Glendower becomes Countess of Snowdon; Gwynedd elves make major advances in Welsh regional Parliament. Knights of Rage group at Caerleon to serve the dragon Celedyr.

2047

Para-VITAS outbreak kills 120,000 in Tynesprawl; believed to be the work of eco-terrorists of unknown identity.

2048

Toxic eruption of gas north of Merseysprawl generates vast gas plume; fallout products drift to Ireland (Tir Nan Og).

2050

Outbreak of cholera and typhoid in Merseysprawl from collapsing sanitation systems.

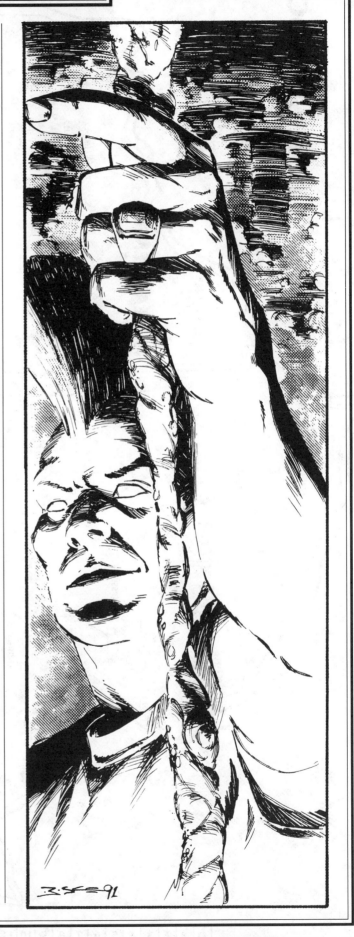

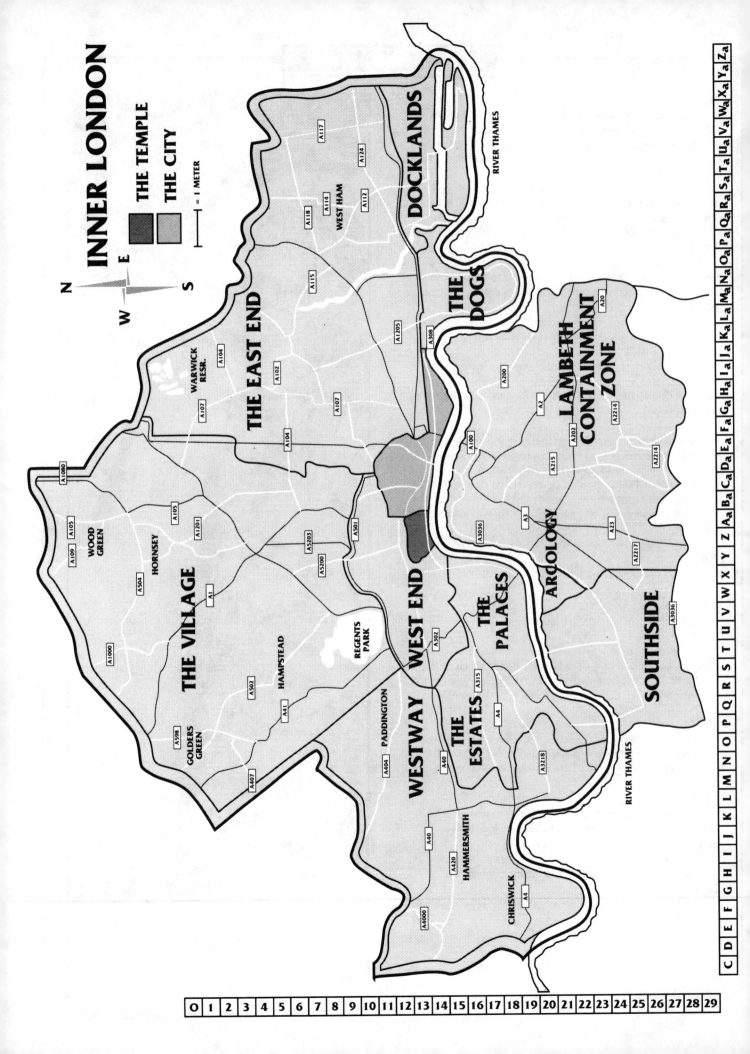

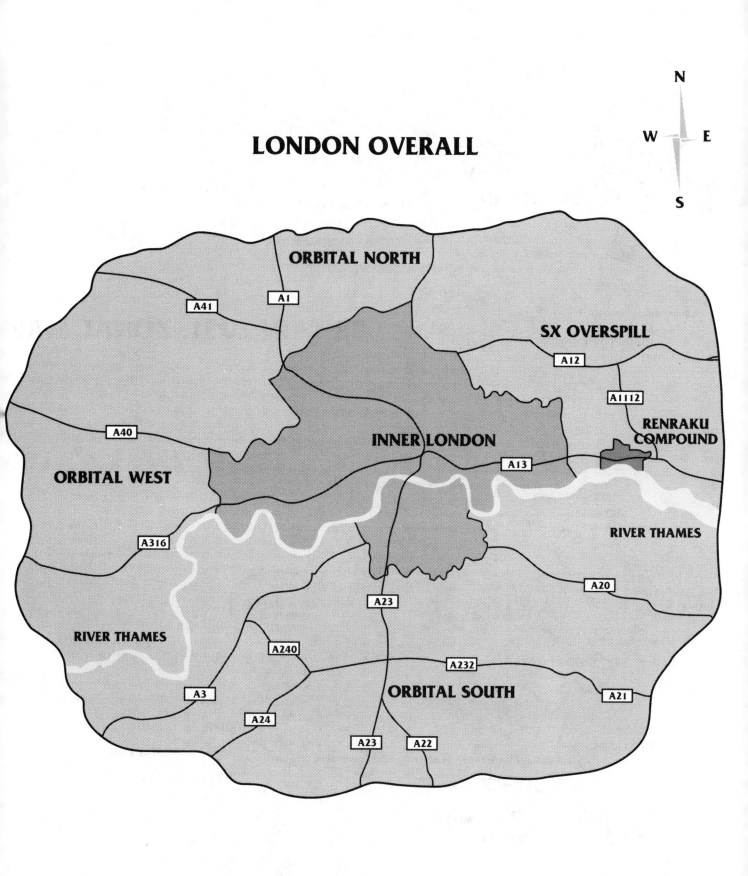

LONDON OVERALL

SCOTTISH IRRADIATED ZONE

CAITHNESS

SCOTTISH WILD LANDS

MORAY

SCOTLAND

SCOTTISH FRINGE TOXIC ZONE

SCOTTISH HABITABLE ZONE

SCOTSPRAWL

EDINBURGH

GLASGOW

BRITAIN 2051: ZONAL MAP

NEWCASTLE

TYNESPRAWL

MERSEYSPRAWL

TEESPRAWL

GWYNEDD

SNOWDONIA

LIVERPOOL

LEEDS

MANCHESTER

WELSH WILD LANDS

CASTLE HARLECH

NOTTINGHAM

WALES

EAST ANGLIAN STINKFENS (TOXIC)

BIRMINGHAM

WELSH HABITABLE ZONE

DRAGON LAND

BRISTOL

LONDON

CARDIFF

DOVER

CORNISH WILD LANDS

KENT HABITABLE ZONE

WESTERN HABITABLE ZONE

SOUTHAMPTON

KENT TOXIC ZONE

DARTMOOR

BOCHIN MOOR